MANSFIELD COLLEGE
OXFORD

Presented   by

The Publisher

1998

RESEARCH ON BRITISH HISTORY IN THE FEDERAL REPUBLIC OF GERMANY 1995-1997

An Annotated Bibliography

edited by
Andreas Fahrmeir

GERMAN HISTORICAL INSTITUTE LONDON

London 1998

Published by
German Historical Institute London
17 Bloomsbury Square
LONDON WC1A 2LP

Tel: 0171 404 5486
Fax: 0171 404 5573

e-mail: ghil@ghil.prestel.co.uk
Homepage: http://www.homeusers.prestel.co.uk/ghil/

ISBN 0 9533570 0 7

PREFACE

The present volume is the fourth in a series of annotated bibliographies of research on British history in the Federal Republic of Germany which the German Historical Institute London (GHIL) has published since 1983. It is the intention of this series to provide a convenient survey of research on British history which has appeared in Germany, not least for scholars who do not usually use German-language materials. The abstracts were written by Research Fellows of the GHIL.

Some features of this *bibliographie raisonné* have, however, been adapted to changing circumstances. It will now be published at shorter intervals, to keep pace with the increasing number of publications. It is anticipated that the bibliography will be published at intervals of two to three years in future.

While every care has been taken to make this bibliography as complete as possible, the shorter interval between the publication of works and the publication of the bibliography has made it more rather than less dependent on the co-operation of authors and publishers, and it is inevitable that items which should have been listed have been overlooked. All we can do to explain shortcomings is to show how it was compiled. The books included here have been selected from publishers' catalogues, the *Historische Bibliographie*, and the official list of books in print compiled by the Deutsche Bibliothek. As in the previous volumes, the sole qualification for inclusion remains the place of publication. In this respect, the bibliography testifies to the increasing use of English in the lists of German publishers. However, the apparently straightforward criterion of the place of publications has sometimes been modified in favour of common sense. For instance, while most series published by the Berne-based company Peter Lang, which has an office in Frankfurt and publishes numerous dissertations submitted to German universities have been included, the series American University Studies has not.

The list of articles is mainly based on the *Historische Bibliographie*, published annually with about one year's delay, and the journals held by the GHIL's library. For 1997, we have been obliged to rely heavily on responses to requests for information published in the GHIL's *Bulletin*, and announced at the general meetings of professional organizations concerned with the study of British history in Germany, the

Arbeitskreis Deutsche Englandforschung and the Prinz Albert Gesellschaft.

The compilation of this bibliography would not have been possible without the review copies generously supplied by the publishers. In fairness to those firms which were so helpful, we have made no effort to trace and include books of which no review copies were sent; they are merely listed. Special thanks go the authors who have responded to our request for information, Angela Davies and Jane Rafferty, who have edited and in part translated the text, and Jacqueline Gamperl, who undertook part of the bibliographical research. The main credit, of course, is due to Andreas Fahrmeir, who took upon himself the considerable task of editing this volume.

London, June 1998   Peter Wende

CONTENTS

HOW TO USE THIS BIBLIOGRAPHY

Both the articles and books sections of this bibliography are divided into five categories: 'general studies', 'sixth to fifteenth centuries', 'sixteenth to eighteenth centuries', 'nineteenth century', 'twentieth century', and 'Imperial and Commonwealth History'. Within these categories, articles are arranged alphabetically by the name of the first author; books are arranged chronologically or, where a chronological ordering was not possible, from more general to more specific works. Works falling into two of our subdivisions are listed in the earlier one. All references to books or articles, either in the index or in individual entries (for example, to a book of collected essays in the listing of an article) are to the number of the entry, not to page numbers.

BOOK REVIEWS

BRITISH HISTORY
General Studies

[1] MICHAEL MAURER, *Kleine Geschichte Englands* (Stuttgart: Reclam, 1997), 526 pp. DM 20.00

'Short' histories of countries can be organized in all sorts of different ways, with very different types of readers in mind. This one, the third volume in a series of histories of European countries, is primarily designed as a handy reference book, and as such it serves very well. It is divided into six major periods, all of which are introduced by a brief 'sketch of the era'. The chapters which follow these introductions are short summaries of major events and concepts, covering politics and social history, as well as developments in the arts. The list of section headings for the chapter on 1815 to 1837 gives an impression: 'Romanticism', 'Waterloo to Peterloo', 'Foreign Policy: Castlereagh to Canning', 'The Reform Crisis', 'The 1832 Reform Act', 'Social Reforms', and 'Religion and the Churches in an Era of Change'. A number of chronologies and maps accompany the text, which is concluded by a concise bibliography.

Andreas Fahrmeir

[2] HANS C. SCHRÖDER, *Englische Geschichte* (Munich: Beck, 1995), 136 pp. DM 14.80

This slim paperback reference book compresses within its one hundred pages some fifteen hundred years of eventful English history – from the Anglo-Saxon kingdoms to the Conservative government of John Major. The author sees the length restrictions of this series as a blessing. It helps him to focus on main themes and general questions which are then illustrated by significant details. Such a work can hardly ever claim originality, but can have essential usefulness as a beginner's guide and as a source for quick reference. This is exactly what Schröder achieves. The brief bibliographies are well selected.

Bärbel Brodt

[3] *Großbritannien – London*, Brockhaus: Die Bibliothek. Länder und Städte (Leipzig: F. A. Brockhaus, 1997), 544 pp. DM 185.00

This Brockhaus series on 'Länder und Städte' consists of several volumes by specialists who present European countries and cities to the general reader. This one on Great Britain/London could well be compared with the following one on Ireland/Dublin, as both volumes follow the same methodological pattern. The books are magnificently produced with a high bibliophile profile, and are provided with many quality pictures, maps, statistics, and some chronological tables which easily introduce the reader to the country and its capital. Besides chapters on geography, architecture, traffic, economics, the character of the people, plants and animals, interesting places to visit, etc., the history of the country and its capital is presented in detail, from the beginning to the recent past: from Stonehenge to New Labour. In keeping with the rest of the series, the book narrates the broad lines of history, giving many dates and biographical information rather than analysing crucial historical questions. The historical parts are organized in a clear chronological manner, there are no historiographical experiments, but the reader is furnished with reliable facts. The refreshing character of this text-book means that it can leave out one or the other event which some readers may have expected and concentrate instead on other points. Naturally the post-1714 period receives most attention, but the time of the Anglo-Normans and the Elizabethan age, for example, are also well covered. The series' aim is to inform, not to make a scholarly contribution to a recent historical debate, and its primary task of providing comprehensive historical information is well fulfilled. The main streams of British political history are linked together with economic, social, cultural, intellectual, military, religious, and other aspects of the country's past.

Benedikt Stuchtey

[4] *Irland – Dublin*, Brockhaus: Die Bibliothek. Länder und Städte (Leipzig: F. A. Brockhaus, 1997), 544 pp. DM 185.00

This magnificently produced volume in the Brockhaus series 'Länder und Städte' covers a kaleidoscope of Irish themes, ranging from a survey of landscapes throughout time, the economy, and population to the cultural history of the island. Whereas both the Republic of Ireland and Northern Ireland are described, the South predominates. The editors' aim was to deliver a broad guide to the history and culture of the island which spans the entire history and includes the present-day image of Ireland. Although this ambition necessarily means a selection of themes, the backbone of relevant historical, cultural, and general information is guaranteed throughout. This is most obvious in the in-depth coverage of Dublin. In this instance, an art historian's point of view adds considerably to the appreciation of the city's more hidden treasures and mentalities. However, in keeping with the general character of the series, the highly volatile political situation in Ireland is not the primary focus of this book. In the light of recent developments in the Northern Ireland peace talks, abstaining from an outline of sectional interests is probably a wise decision. Aimed at the interested general reader, this volume is splendidly illustrated and produced.

Ulrike Jordan

[5] THOMAS KIELINGER, *Die Kreuzung und der Kreisverkehr. Deutsche und Briten im Zentrum der europäischen Geschichte* (Bonn: Bouvier, 1996), ix + 268 pp. DM 39.80. Also available in English as *Crossroads and Roundabouts: Junctions in German-British Relations* (Bonn: Bouvier, 1996), ix + 268 pp.

This book was written with the encouragement of the German and British governments. In a highly entertaining way, it paints an informative and colourful picture of German-British relations over the centuries. Individual chapters concentrate on mutual perceptions, cultural comparison, close economic co-operation (often underestimated), Britain's influence on the reconstruction and democratization of Germany after the Second World War, and finally, on Britain's role in the process of integrating Germany into the Western Alliance on the one hand, and Germany's role in integrating Britain into the European Union on the other. Facts, collected in separate 'Spotlights', are presented in the form of extracts from newspapers, television documentaries, interviews, and literature. This book was written to debunk caricature and cliché on both sides of the Channel. It therefore often investigates the historical and cultural background of the context in which various stereotypes came into being. Yet among the things worth knowing about the often mutually enriching relationship between Britons and

Germans is what makes them different. The last chapter is devoted to these differences: German *Geist* as opposed to British common sense, German faith in the state compared with British scepticism towards it, red traffic lights as a legal demand in Germany and merely a well-intentioned request in Britain, and finally, the German cross-road as the most reliable form of traffic regulation versus the British roundabout as an expression of voluntary restraint and the desire for flowing, flexible regulation. This book is well and originally illustrated, and has a bibliography and name index.

Sabine Freitag

[6] ALEXANDER GAULAND, *Das Haus Windsor* (Berlin: Siedler, 1996), 254 pp. DM 68.00

This highly impressionistic account of the English and British monarchy from the Middle Ages to the present is written for a popular market. It is enriched with numerous illustrations and interspersed with reflections on themes as diverse as English traditions, English eccentrics, the gentleman ideal, and the non-conformist Oscar Wilde. Full of quotations but without references and abounding in bold statements about British history and society, the book raises the question of whether it is of any value even for a wider public.

Dagmar Freist

[7] ANDREAS THIELE (ed.), *Erzählende genealogische Stammtafeln zur europäischen Geschichte*, vol. 4: *Die Britische Peerage, ein Auszug* (Frankfurt/M.: R. G. Fischer, 1996), vi + 321 pp. DM 120.00

This book contains genealogical tables of some seventy-five British noble families. The author says that he has selected these in relation to their importance and connections with the royal family. The work does not merit more than a very brief account; all the information in it is obtainable elsewhere and the inclusion of passages reminiscent of a gossip column in a tabloid newspaper do not enhance its scholarly value.

Bärbel Brodt

[8] HERMANN SCHREIBER, *Irland. Seine Geschichte – Seine Menschen* (Gernsbach: Casimir Katz, 1997), 358 pp. DM 38.00

This is not a scholarly account of Irish history, but an essayistic overview that concentrates on Ireland and its people in the Middle Ages without giving much attention to the nineteenth and twentieth centuries. Schreiber is fond of Irish fairy tales, and thus his text is pervaded with anecdotes which form colourful stories. We learn of pirates and saints, about the destinies of a people on an island with its druids and missionaries and cultural-religious rituals. Once modernized, a romantic and remote country loses much of its attraction, so the reader is much less informed about the Ireland that emerged from the seventeenth century, characterized by the tensions between a Protestant and a Catholic definition of past and present. The author tends to favour the Catholic perspective on Irish history. Daniel O'Connell, famously called 'The Liberator', is compared with Napoleon because both were born under the sign of Leo. The book follows a strict chronological narrative and paints the picture in terms of political and military events.

Benedikt Stuchtey

[9] DIETRICH SCHULZE-MARMELING (ed.), *Nordirland. Geschichte, Landschaft, Kultur und Touren* (Göttingen: Verlag die Werkstatt, 1996), 479 pp. DM 49.90

It may come as a surprise that the six provinces of Northern Ireland, ravaged by almost thirty years of civil war, could be a suitable destination for tourists. However, a beautiful landscape and a fascinating cultural heritage are enticing. This book, which is far more than simply a travel guide, seeks to lead the reader through this historic place and to show that many of the present problems exist as the result of unexplained secrets of the past. The authors describe in detail the history and causes of the Northern Irish 'troubles' which dominate perceptions of this part of the British Isles and which need to be understood: whether by the visitor (who is also given a good deal of practical information such as addresses of hotels, restaurants, museums etc.) or by the inhabitants, in their cities, football clubs, and pubs. No public holiday, hardly any place of work, can be rightly appreciated if not seen in the context of Protestant-Unionist versus Catholic-Nationalist standpoints. Although more recently a growing understanding seems to be developing between the different political and religious groups, the day-to-day reality is one of an unresolved conflict whose roots go back centuries. The book opens provocatively by comparing the situation in Ireland to South African apartheid, with full sympathies, in the Irish case, on the side of the Catholics, the alleged 'losers' in Northern Irish history. The historical part starts at the time of the 'Ulster plantation' in the early seventeenth century, and gives due weight to the significance of the Volunteers and United Irishmen, the famine, and the problem of Protestant separatism, leading to the vital: 'Quo vadis, Northern Ireland?' The last section contains an informative glossary listing some central terms such as 'discrimination', 'emigration', 'human rights', and 'sectarianism'. There is also a detailed chronology of Irish/Northern Irish history.

Benedikt Stuchtey

[10] HILDEGARD L. C. TRISTRAM (ed.), *The Celtic Englishes*, Anglistische Forschungen, 247 (Heidelberg: C. Winter, 1997), xii + 441 pp. DM 88.00

This book contains papers read at a conference organized by the University of Potsdam in September 1995, and devoted to the variations of English spoken in the 'Celtic' countries of Wales, Scotland, Ireland, and Newfoundland and Labrador. Many of the papers are detailed linguistic analyses of the local versions of the English language spoken there, which – to the eye of the layman, at least – seem to bear out Manfred Görlach's opening remarks that there is no such thing as a single Celtic English, but which will be of little interest to historians, except for those who take the 'linguistic turn' very seriously indeed. However, a number of papers – Gwenllian Awbery on Wales, Philip Payton on Cornwall, C. I Macafee and Colm Ó Baoill on Scotland, and Graham Shorrocks on Newfoundland and Labrador – relate the evolution of language and the rise of English in their areas to social, political, and economic developments, and thus throw a different, if not always new, light on the history of the Celtic Fringe.

Andreas Fahrmeir

[11] *Hannover zwischen den Mächten Europas 1633-1918: Eine Dokumentation zur Geschichte Niedersachsens auf CD-ROM* (Göttingen: Heinrich Prinz von Hannover, Hannover Media Produktion, 1996). 1 CD-ROM for IBM PCs (Windows 3.x or higher, double-speed CD-ROM drive, 8 MB RAM, sound card, mouse). DM 49.90

This enjoyable CD-ROM on the history of Hanover was produced by four museums located in the former kingdom: the Historisches Museum in Hanover, the Bomann-Museum in Celle, Schloß Marienburg bei Nordstemmen, and Fürstenhaus Herrenhausen. It includes texts, voice-overs, pictures and film clips, and even a (very select) bibliography on this electorate, kingdom, and Prussian province, organized by chronology and by rulers, and places considerable emphasis on the personal union of Hanover and Great Britain.

Andreas Fahrmeir

[12] PETER KRÜGER (ed.), *Das europäische Staatensystem im Wandel. Strukturelle Bedingungen und bewegende Kräfte seit der Frühen Neuzeit*, Schriften des Historischen Kollegs, Kolloquien, 35 (Munich: Oldenbourg, 1996), xv + 272 pp. DM 98.00

The publications of the internationally famous and prestigious *Historisches Kolleg* in Munich reflect the high profile of the conferences it holds annually. Each year an eminent historian is invited to bring colleagues together to discuss themes of mutual interest. Peter Krüger's book, which contains seventeen essays ranging from the seventeenth to the twentieth century, deals with the question of how the European 'system of states' has changed since the early modern period, and how its constitution and structures survived to some extent, but also had to adapt to modern developments. According to the idea of this book, an ideal system is a multitude of political organisms which are culturally, economically, and politically intertwined and which aim at interaction in the long run, rather than at the destruction of their mutual relations. The essays cover many aspects of West, Central, and East European history. The only one which addresses British history is by Anselm Doering-Manteuffel **[384]** who discusses the role Britain played in the process of transforming the European system of states between 1850 and 1871. The revolutions after 1815 challenged established relations between the states and reflected the crisis into which the system had plunged. Therefore the system of 1815 became not only increasingly anachronistic but also dysfunctional, and from then on few members of the European concert were as interested in the destruction of the results of the congress of Vienna as Britain. The events of 1871 finally brought to an end what 1815 had begun. This interesting volume, which leads to contemporary history, unfortunately leaves out the period between the wars. Here Britain played a decisive role in the European political system of states and it influenced developments that became apparent only after 1945.

Benedikt Stuchtey

[13] HANS SCHAUER, *Europäische Identität und demokratische Tradition. Zum Staatsverständnis in Deutschland, Frankreich und Großbritannien* (Munich: Olzog, 1996), 158 pp. DM 49.00

As the title and the European flag on the cover make clear, this is a guide for European citizens to the peculiarities of the political systems in what the author regards as the three major European countries. There can be little doubt that it serves its purpose well, even though it is vulnerable to the charge that a very brief exposition of the social and political histories of Britain, France, and Germany cannot but turn out to be very schematic. Three chapters briefly trace the political history of France and Germany since the French Revolution, and of Britain since Magna Carta. Two concluding chapters discuss the question of why parliamentary democracy developed comparatively late in Germany, and what the major differences between the three political systems under scrutiny are.

Andreas Fahrmeir

[14] HANS SÜSSMUTH (ed.), *Deutschlandbilder in Dänemark und England, in Frankreich und den Niederlanden. Dokumentation der Tagung Deutschlandbilder in Dänemark und England, in Frankreich und den Niederlanden, 15.-18. Dezember 1993, Leutherheider Forum* (Baden-Baden: Nomos, 1996), 461 pp. DM 78.00

West Germans, always anxious about their image abroad, have been wondering non-stop since unification how they are perceived by their neighbours. This collection of essays edited by Hans Süssmuth is the result of yet another conference on this never-ending puzzle. After two introductory chapters on Germany and Europe, and on '*Länder* Images' in general, there are five chapters with up to half a dozen essays on the Danes, the Dutch, the French and 'die Engländer', and their diverse relationships with the Germans. Apparently Poles and Czechs do not matter as much as west Europeans. There are five contributions on Anglo-German perceptions, three of a more historical and scholarly nature, and two on public opinion since German unification. Wolfgang J. Mommsen [**182**] looks at the changing and, above all, ambivalent image of 'England' – the favourite notion – as conceived and developed by Germany's intellectual and political élite from the late eighteenth century, with only occasional glimpses of British ideas about Germany. His analysis makes it abundantly clear that Britain's example, both as a model to follow and to reject, had a much greater influence in Germany than vice versa. Mommsen speaks of the love-hate relationship, and examines in particular the positive role-model of the British constitution for the moderates among early Liberals in Germany and the anti-British propaganda of German academics during the First World War. The stereotypes were clearly cast before the Great War. What was to come was the popularization, if not vulgarization of pre-conceived ideas about the commercial and utilitarian mind-set of the English. Peter Pulzer from Oxford focuses on Germany's changing image in Britain between 1815 and 1914 [**448**]. The title says it all: 'Model, Rival, and Barbarian.' Throughout the nineteenth century Germany was admired for its scholarship both in science and the humanities. With the perception of Germany as a commercial rival and the naval race, attitudes changed, only to degenerate into outright hostility during the First World War which, in retrospect, was more decisive than the Second. Pulzer also traces the thesis of the 'Two Germanies' or the 'Other Germany' (that is, the good one), which is a distinctive and recurrent feature of Anglo-German relations. Günther Blaicher [**161**] approaches his subject as a literary historian. His contribution on anti-German stereotypes in English literature is no doubt the most amusing in this section. He thinks that there are five different Anglo-Saxon attitudes in the perception of Germany, which he then sets out to examine in detail: a Protestant, an empirical-pragmatic, an aesthetic, a liberal-democratic and a rationalist disposition – it being understood that Germany always constituted the opposite. As a professor at the Catholic university of Eichstädt, he takes great delight in the detection of anti-Catholic, or more pointedly anti-

Baroque sentiments amongst English travellers. The last two articles are of purely contemporary relevance. Surveying British media coverage of the unification process, Hans Süssmuth and his collaborator Christoph Peters [592] come to quite different conclusions from those reached by David Gow [509], Bonn correspondent of the *Guardian*. While Süssmuth paints a picture of overall friendliness and fairness with regard to the British quality press, Gow states categorically and to my mind correctly: 'It remains a fact that the image of Germany in the British press is predominantly negative' (p. 282)

Lothar Kettenacker

[15] DIETRICH SCHWANITZ, *Englische Kulturgeschichte von 1500 bis 1914* (Frankfurt/M.: Eichborn, 1996), 500 pp. DM 78.00

This cultural history, which covers the period from the early sixteenth to the early twentieth century, aims to encompass a multitude of cultural aspects of English history. Based on the conventional premise of the dawn of modernism around 1750, this massive survey does not hold many surprises for historians or literary critics. Its major shortcomings, however, are an over-emphasis on literary history at the expense of the visual arts and architecture, built on an underlying structure of textbook history. This belies the author's acknowledged debt to scholarly inspirations as unconventional and thought-provoking as the works of Michel Foucault, Niklas Luhmann, Philippe Ariès, and Norbert Elias. Unfortunately, the flow of the text is all too often hampered by cumbersome syntax and abstractions. The book benefits from a selection of excellent illustrations.

Ulrike Jordan

[16] INA SCHABERT, *Englische Literaturgeschichte: Eine neue Darstellung aus der Sicht der Geschlechterforschung*, Kröners Taschenbuchausgabe, 387 (Stuttgart: Kröner 1997), xiv + 682 pp. DM 48.00

This comprehensive survey of English literature from the early modern to the late Victorian age presents a welcome addition to the many textbooks on literary and cultural history already in existence. The main emphasis is on the concrete discussion of works, which is preceded by a lengthy theoretical section. The author follows an evidence-based approach to gender-focused analysis of English literature. Her findings are noteworthy and often document an informed choice of exemplary works and themes, such as, for instance, the complex changes in Victorian narratives. While she adopts the traditional chronological divisions like Enlightenment and Romanticism, she introduces recurrent themes such as 'equality and compatibility of the feminine and masuline' or 'the role of desire in literature', and analyses them with close reference to chosen works. This is a book for readers already familiar with English literature of the sixteenth to nineteenth centuries, who will find new insights into old problems like the Romantic phenomenon of writing couples (the Shelleys, the Wordsworths, the Lambs etc.). This is true even if readers disagree with the author's fundamental presupposition that the gender principle is one of the driving forces of content and style in literature, and thus of the society and culture it mirrors and criticizes.

Ulrike Jordan

[17] HEINZ ANTOR, *Der englische Universitätsroman: Bildungskonzepte und Erziehungsziele*, Anglistische Forschungen, 238 (Heidelberg: C. Winter, 1996), xiv + 750 pp. DM 148.00

This 750-page *Habilitation* presents the history of the English university novel from its origins in the mid-eighteenth century to the present. The emphasis is on the hitherto neglected period before 1945. It includes numerous non-literary texts such as pieces on educational theory and socio-cultural documents, to shed particular light on the whole issue of education. The author, who works closely with sources, approaches all aspects of the university novel chronologically. Beyond an examination of how the genre changed, he also deals with the discussion on liberal education and the role of the disciplines, lecturers and students, curricula and examination systems, reform of higher education, and the role of women. The book makes it clear that the university novel is particularly characterized by dialogue which critically juxtaposes the various positions in the educational discussions of the last 250 years.

Marita Baumgarten

[18] RAIMUND SCHÄFFNER, *Anarchismus und Literatur in England. Von der Französischen Revolution bis zum Ersten Weltkrieg*, Anglistische Forschungen, 248 (Heidelberg: C. Winter, 1996), 578 pp. DM 128.00

Anarchism has not played a central role in British political life, but as a cultural factor anarchic social theory can certainly not be marginalized. In contrast to other socio-political ideas, anarchism does not represent a continuous development. Rather it has flourished at times of social, cultural, and political change and has often been disseminated in literary works. This is the starting point for the present impressive study which looks at the connection between anarchism and literature in England between the French Revolution and the First World War. Schäffner discusses, for example, the pre-history and history of anarchism up to 1914, presents anarchic works as symbols of social, cultural, and moral decline, analyses anarchism in the works of socialist intellectuals such as G. B. Shaw, and looks at the socio-cultural milieu of anarchism, mainly in the twentieth century. The great social and political upheavals serve as the historical background, alongside industrialization, for investigating how English literature incorporated anarchic ideas. William Morris, Edward Carpenter, and Oscar Wilde, for example, stood at the intellectual crossroads of art and anarchism, originally 'invented' by the late English Enlightenment and Romanticism (William Godwin, Thomas Holcroft, William Blake, P. B. Shelley). Subjectivism and radical individualism were counterweights to traditional poetic positions, but were also a protest against state norms and social restrictions, against centralization and bureaucracy, against modernization and technical rationalization. The task of the poet was not only to find new modes of expression; he also had a political role whereby the autonomy of art became a mirror of social and political liberty. This does not necessarily indicate an instrumentalization of literature for political means, but it shows the close and important connection between literature and politics, between criticism and the call for social change. Anyone who has read James Joyce's *The Dubliners* will appreciate the plea for unlimited freedom of the individual against church, state, and social conventions. According to anarchist principles, neither aristocratic-feudal nor bourgeois ideas, neither industrialism nor capitalism could withstand a criticism which itself, though anti-traditionalist, constitutes a new tradition right up to the present: that of peaceful education, the balance between the sexes, the relation between élites and the masses, etc. In the author's view, this anarchic literature, and its key figure Godwin, demonstrate that the late Victorian idea that no British branch of anarchism existed is wrong, and as such a reflection of a specific and problematic way of adopting art with the politics left out. This very informative and solid book is a *tour d'horizon* of Victorian literature and teaches the historian how profitable interdisciplinary studies can be.

Benedikt Stuchtey

[19] GÜNTHER LOTTES (ed.), *Der Eigentumsbegriff im englischen politischen Denken*, Veröffentlichungen Arbeitskreis Deutsche England-Forschung, 16 (Bochum: Brockmeyer, 1995), xiv + 247 pp. DM 49.80

This volume is a collection of articles by some of the most eminent German scholars of British history on the idea of property in English political thought *c.* 1600 to 1900. The authors trace the history of the idea of property from its origins in the breakdown of the English feudal system to its new social significance in the nineteenth century. During the process of its formation the idea of property developed three distinctive features which the editor sums up in the introduction to this book: first, property in English political thought is expressly an individual right and incompatible with common or public property; second, property does not entail personal privileges or direct access to power; and third, the English idea of property has a universal component which becomes evident when the seventeenth-century discourse on property and power gives way to eighteenth-century social and economic theory and its reflections on property. Property and labour (which according to Locke is one aspect of property) define the individual's relationship to society and the world. Only towards the end of the nineteenth century is the tradition of individual ownership modified by the concept of the 'collective' which adds a social dimension to the idea of property. In contrast to continental Europe where the importation of the English idea of property provoked social upheaval, it was a positive factor in the English context, forming the basis of social consensus until the nineteenth century.

In loose chronological and thematic sequence the eleven contributors to this volume take up individual aspects of Lottes' broad outline of the history of the idea of property. Only a few can be mentioned here. The editor analyses the emergence of the idea of property when feudal rights broke down [218]. Hans-Dieter Metzger [299] looks at Locke's theory of property from the perspective of politics and state theory rather than economics against the background of actual historical developments and the history of ideas. Ronald G. Asch [251] gives a detailed analysis of the dispute surrounding the crown's right to levy taxes and the individual right to property which eventually culminated in a conflict over the King's sovereignty. Helgard Fröhlich [269] looks at the role of parliament and property in early seventeenth-century constitutional ideas. Andreas Wirsching [343] deals with the emergence of a new discourse on property under the influence of radical traditions of the eighteenth century, the emancipation of labour, and education. Willibald Steinmetz [321] bases his diachronic study of the semantics of the term 'property' on parliamentary debates about voting rights and political representation. Other contributors include Ian Hampsher-Monk [276] writing on John Locke's theory of property, Gerd Stratmann [324] on property in eighteenth and nineteenth-century English literature, Michael Weinzierl [336] on liberty and property in the eighteenth century, and Karl H. Metz [425] on social aspects of the theory of property at the turn of the twentieth century. This volume's diachronic approach to a central theme of English history as well as the overall high quality of the articles make this book an invaluable contribution to the study of the history of ideas in the early modern and modern periods.

Dagmar Freist

[20] KEVIN CARPENTER (ed.), *Robin Hood: Die vielen Gesichter des edlen Räubers/The Many Faces of that Celebrated Outlaw* (Oldenburg: Bis. Bibliotheks- und Informationssystem der Universität Oldenburg, 1995), 303 pp. DM 40.00

Robin Hood, hardly in need of an introduction, is now also the subject of a joint project of the Oldenburg University Library and the Faculty of Literary Studies and Linguistics there, which also organized a touring exhibition of the man and the myth. The bilingual work under consideration here is the resulting catalogue which is supplemented by fourteen fairly specific essays. Amongst the authors are Barrie Dobson and John Taylor [202], Sir James Holt [209], and Stephen Knight [176], all of them leading experts in the search for 'the real Robin Hood'. The interest of the studies pursued at Oldenburg and of the present catalogue is by no means confined to the Middle Ages. We are presented with a wealth of material, illustrating the myth (one might almost say the cult) of Robin Hood in all centuries from the fifteenth to our own and over a geographical space which extends as far as Japan. It seems that the legend of Robin Hood is indeed a universal phenomenon, designed and developed to enable one to mirror oneself in this determined and compassionate champion of the cause of the people, struggling to secure liberty and justice for all – if he ever existed.

Bärbel Brodt

[21] DAVID L. CAREY MILLER and REINHARD ZIMMERMANN (eds), *The Civilian Tradition and Scots Law: Aberdeen Quincentenary Essay*, Schriften zur Europäischen Rechts- und Verfassungsgeschichte, 20 (Berlin: Duncker & Humblot, 1997), 394 pp. DM 136.00

This book contains papers delivered at a conference marking the quincentenary of the University of Aberdeen held on 4 and 5 September 1995. Its topic is the influence of the 'civilian tradition' – the civil law, the Canon law, and the subsequent *ius commune* on the Scottish legal system. More comprehensive than some *Festschriften* for institutions, it is divided into three main sections, which deal with the past, present and future of the topic. They are preceded by an introduction and an essay describing the foundation of law teaching at the University of Aberdeen by Hector L. MacQueen [222]. Part 1 covers the influence of Roman law and Roman legal thinking in Europe. Part 2, entitled 'Taking Stock', deals with the present state of Scottish law, while part 3 contains three essays on the probable influence of civil law on the ever more important field of European Community Law.

Andreas Fahrmeir

[22] FRANZ BOSBACH and HANS POHL (eds), *Das Kreditwesen in der Neuzeit/Banking System in Modern History: Ein deutsch-britischer Vergleich*, Prince Albert Studies, 14 (Munich: Saur, 1997), 183 pp. DM 78.00

This conference represents the Prince Albert Society's first venture into the field of economic history. That this is no break with its tradition of placing topical problems in a historical context will be obvious: the debate about financial systems has, if anything, reached new intensities with the controversy over the introduction of a single European currency and British responses to this plan. The editors have approached the history of financial systems through the different forms of banks which were most characteristic of different stages in economic history: merchant banks, private banks, joint stock banks, and central banks. Separate essays deal with each of these types in both Britain and Germany. British banking history is of course complicated by differences between England and Scotland. While this aspect is not one of the volume's major topics, it does contain a contribution on the Bank of Scotland [262]. The final section of the book documents the conference's final panel discussion, which dealt with the present and future roles of the City of London and of Frankfurt as banking centres.

Andreas Fahrmeir

[23] BARBARA KORTE, *Der englische Reisebericht: Von der Pilgerfahrt bis zur Postmoderne* (Darmstadt: Wissenschaftliche Buchgesellschaft, 1996), 236 pp. DM 48.00

The English-speaking world has proved to be fruitful ground for travel writing, perhaps because British culture invites or challenges people to travel. From the eighteenth to the early twentieth century, travel reports were among the most widely read forms of writing. Travel accounts can be read as documents of cultural history, and are valuable sources for anthropologists as well as historians.

The study by the scholar of English literature Barbara Korte under review here makes clear that travel reports do not only convey history, but possess their own history and genesis as a textual form which has always been subject to historical change. The volume is divided into two parts. The introduction presents the features unique to the genre of British travel writing. Different forms of text evolved in response to journeys with different purposes and goals. As autobiographical texts, travel reports always reveal something about the travelling 'I' as well as about the world that it travels through. They provide insights into the ways of thinking and modes of perception of the travelling author. Some forms of travel writing – including reports of voyages of discovery and scientific exploration, of trading and colonizing, as well as of pilgrimages and missionary journeys – relate more strongly to the objective world, and try to convey the impressions received as objectively as possible. And there is travel writing that relates more strongly to the subject. In this form of the genre perception as an aesthetic pleasure becomes a purpose in itself, as in accounts of the Grand Tour or tourist travels.

The second part of this study presents the historical varieties of English travel writing in the form of detailed extracts. It includes samples of writing by medieval pilgrims, early modern explorers' reports, accounts of the Grand Tour, tourists' journeys, and women's travels, as well as of post-modern travel literature. An extensive bibliography invites the interested reader to delve further.

Sabine Freitag

[24] RAINER SÖCKNICK-SCHOLZ, *Reisen in Irland im Spiegel älterer Reisebeschreibungen: Katalog zur Ausstellung in der Universitätsbibliothek Oldenburg vom 7. 10. – 19. 10. 1996* (Oldenburg: Bis. Bibliotheks- und Informationssystem der Universität Oldenburg, 1996), 121 pp. DM 15.00

Prince Pückler-Muskau's journey to Ireland in 1826 produced one of the most famous German nineteenth-century travel accounts of this country. Its author, who wanted to visit the parks and find a wealthy woman to remedy his poor financial situation, complained about the bad travelling conditions, though he himself was certainly no good judge of Irish hospitality. In the fifteenth chapter of the *Pickwick Papers* Charles Dickens portrays a 'Count Smorltolk', obviously a literary caricature of Pückler-Muskau, showing how he behaved in a foreign country and how different his descriptions of Ireland were from the perceptions of his contemporaries. The present small catalogue, printed for a special exhibition in the university library of Oldenburg, provides a brief introduction to the development of travelling in Ireland, the experience of the mail-coach, the beginnings of the railway, and travelling on rivers and canals. Numerous quotes from original travel-reports, maps, and pictures make it an entertaining small booklet. However, the reader who wants to be informed academically should turn to the volume by Andreas Oehlke, *Irland und die Iren in deutschen Reisebeschreibungen des 18. und 19. Jahrhunderts* (1992).

Benedikt Stuchtey

[25] WOLFGANG MACKIEWICZ and DIETER WOLFF (eds), *British Studies in Germany: Essays in Honor of Frank Frankel* (Trier: WVT – Wissenschaftlicher Verlag Trier, 1997), x + 162 pp. DM 49.50

The essays assembled in the *Festschrift* for the British Council's language officer and deputy director cover a very broad range of topics. Only two of them actually deal with British studies, one with the 'Challenge of the New Eastern Europe for British Studies and German Universities' (Christopher Harvie **[173]**) and another with 'British Studies and Teachability' (Gerd Stratmann **[192]**). Most of the contributions are specialized pieces on such matters as novel maps of London, Lord Halifax and Mary Woolstonecraft **[291]**, or 'Mrs. Thatcher and the Playwrights' **[568]**.

Andreas Fahrmeir

[26] JENS-ULRICH DAVIDS and RICHARD STINSHOFF (eds), *The Past in the Present: Proceedings of the 5th Annual British and Cultural Studies Conference, Oldenburg 1994*, Studien zur Germanistik und Anglistik, 10 (Frankfurt/M.: Lang, 1996), 160 pp. £22.00

The editors of this collection of ten essays, nine of which originated as papers delivered at the Oldenburg British and Cultural Studies Conference, argue that the mechanisms through which history 'has always been used in a very conscious and deliberate manner to provide interpretations of what is happening in the present' have become better known today than in previous centuries (p. 7), particularly since the inclusion of hitherto neglected groups in national historical discourses is changing them at an unprecedented rate. The brief individual papers examine the function of historical discourse in a number of media, for example, on screen (Peter Bennet **[487]**), in German textbooks (Friederike Klippel **[175]**), and in museums (Eddie Cass **[495]**), and with reference to various topics such as suffragettes and suffragists (Jutta Schwarzkopf **[587]**), the Northern Ireland conflict (Martin Richter **[571]**), and the 'nation' (Susanne Scholz **[316]**).

Andreas Fahrmeir

Sixth to Fifteenth Centuries

[27] MICHAEL RICHTER, *Irland im Mittelalter: Kultur und Geschichte* (revised edn, Munich: Beck, 1996), 216 pp. DM 48.00

This is the second, somewhat revised edition of Richter's outstanding and ambitious attempt to cover one thousand years of Irish history (cf. review by Peter Alter in Frank Rexroth, ed., *Research on British History in the Federal Republic of Germany 1983-1988*, London, 1990, no. 21), and the author has very wisely made only a few changes. Richter has added further titles (up to 1993) to his bibliography, updated and enlarged his footnotes, and included some very fine illustrations. This book is very well written and should be compulsory reading for those interested in Ireland in general, and its medieval history in particular.

Bärbel Brodt

[28] IAN BRADLEY, *Der keltische Weg. Keltisches Christentum auf den britischen Inseln, damals und heute* (Frankfurt/M.: Knecht, 1996), 205 pp. DM 48.00

This book offers an account of the development of Celtic Christianity, written more with those in search of spiritual development than with historians in mind. It is a nicely produced, very readable work, which can also be used as a guide to Celtic monuments in Britain.

Andreas Fahrmeir

[29] GABRIELE KNAPPE, *Traditionen der klassischen Rhetorik im angelsächsichen England*, Anglistische Forschungen, 236 (Heidelberg: C. Winter, 1996), xx + 573 pp. DM 128.00

Knappe provides a comprehensive and learned account of the study and influence of classical rhetoric, in the technical sense, in Anglo-Saxon England. Her extensive and carefully organized work includes a long survey of the study of rhetoric in the classical world, and an appropriate account of the relevance of rhetorical studies to Carolingian learning. She divides the Anglo-Saxon period into three; firstly the centuries before the ninth, secondly the ninth century before Alfred, thirdly, from the time of Alfred to the Norman Conquest. In important respects the evidence is fullest for the first period. For example, she points out that in Alcuin's poem on *The Bishops, Kings and Saints of York* he says that his teacher Ælbert had taught rhetoric in the school there. It would appear that knowledge of classical rhetoric was to some extent acquired through such general works as Isidor's *Etymologies*. Rhetorical knowledge chiefly appears in the fairly numerous works from Anglo-Saxon England in this period concerned with grammar. The evidence for the last two centuries of Anglo-Saxon England is generally of a different order, because most of the surviving texts are in the vernacular. Knappe interestingly considers the possible relationships between the classical rhetorical tradition and Anglo-Saxon poetry, and the *Homiles* of Aelfric. This book is an important contribution to the study of the pre-Conquest literature and culture of England.

Bärbel Brodt

[30] SUSANNE SCHÄFER, *Die Tradition der mittelalterlichen Bischofssepulturen in Canterbury und York*, Europäische Hochschulschriften, III/716 (Frankfurt/M.: Lang, 1996), 330 pp. £36.00

Schäfer has approached the study of the English church between the beginning of Conversion in the late sixth century and the Reformation from an original angle. She has studied the burying places of the archbishops both of Canterbury and of York through these many centuries. As she shows, the assembly of data on this matter reveals patterns which pose rather interesting questions. Why was it that the archbishops of Canterbury, who had consistently been buried in the church built by Augustine in what came to be called St Augustine's Abbey Canterbury, were from the time of the death of archbishop Cuthbert (760) buried in the Baptistery dedicated to St John which was part of the Cathedral, while from the time of the death of Odo (958) they were, with a handful of exceptions, buried in the Cathedral itself? Why was it that no such consistent tradition appears in York until the burial of Ealdred in York minster initiates the general rule of interring bishops there? In her careful assemblage Schäfer performs an important service, in particular for German readers, which extends beyond the apparently rather narrow bands of her subject. She provides a detailed guide to the history of the archbishops, and one which also sheds interesting light on the history of the Church in England as a whole. For example, she shows how in the later Middle Ages a bishop might be buried in one place, but chiefly commemorated in another, for example in an Oxford College of his own foundation. It is the more to be regretted that for all her careful work she appears to have paid no attention to the authoritative collection of chronological data relative to the archbishops in the *Handbook of British Chronology*. While the divergencies between her lists and those of the *Handbook* are not major, they are quite numerous, and her work would have been tidier and more authoritative had she been aware of the existence of the *Handbook*, which, almost unbelievably, appears not to have been the case. Nevertheless, her book has significant value.

Bärbel Brodt

[31] KLAUS HILLINGMEIER, *Untersuchungen zur Genese des englischen Nationalbewußtseins im Mittelalter von 1066 bis 1453*, Akademische Abhandlungen zur Geschichte (Berlin: Verlag für Wissenschaft und Forschung, 1996), 258 pp. DM 88.00

The author has provided a very methodical, though necessarily relatively brief survey of a broad theme: the development of English national consciousness between the Norman Conquest and the collapse of the English empire in France in 1453. He sees the intervening centuries as tending to build and reinforce the sense of national identity in varied ways and from varied directions. The development of a school of English or half-English historians in the twelfth century he sees as related to a sense of English history which helped to transcend the social and emotional divisions intrinsic in the Norman Conquest. A peculiar but very influential element here was the appearance of the body of legendary historiography associated with Geoffrey of Monmouth and relating in particular to King Arthur. A public and religious expression of English self-awareness was the cult of Edward the Confessor in the royal abbey of Westminster, a cult whose power was symbolized and expressed in the thirteenth century when for the first time since the Conquest a king of England gave one of his sons an English name: the future Edward I. National consciousness naturally depends in large measure on competition; the author brings out the significance, from the twelfth century at the latest, of English hostility to the Welsh and the Scots and that of the nationalistic forces fostered by war with France in the later Middle Ages. While there is little that is original in this book, it represents a competent survey with a wide, though occasionally slightly imperfectly described, bibliographical apparatus.

Bärbel Brodt

[32] HANS-GEORG VON MUTIUS (ed. and trans.), *Rechtsentscheide mittelalterlicher englischer Rabbinen. Aus dem Hebräischen und Aramäischen übersetzt und erläutert von Hans-Georg von Mutius,* Judentum und Umwelt/ Realms of Judaism, 60 (Frankfurt/M.: Lang, 1995), 145 pp. £ 21.00

Between their arrival in England in the later eleventh century and their expulsion in 1290, Jews played an important role. The appearance of this volume of translated *responsa* from eleven rabbis in England makes available an important and interesting source to that large majority of students of medieval England unacquainted with Hebrew or Aramaic. The selected texts mostly relate to the thirteenth century. They deal for the most part with family law with special reference to the position of women. Others, however, relate to Jewish law concerning, for example, debt. Although most of the cases dealt with naturally arose in England, some came from the Continent. Of particular intellectual interest is the high sophistication of Jewish law in matters small as well as great.

Bärbel Brodt

[33] HANS EBERHARD MAYER (ed.), *Die Kreuzfahrerstaaten als multikulturelle Gesellschaft: Einwanderer und Minderheiten im 12. und 13. Jahrhundert,* Schriften des Historischen Kollegs: Kolloquien, 37 (Munich: Oldenbourg, 1997), xii + 187 pp. DM 88.00

There is no shortage of books on the Crusades in general and on England, the land of King Richard I – the so-called Lionhearted – in particular. This one, however, stands out. It contains the revised papers read at the *Historisches Kolleg* in 1994, which dealt with the topic of immigrants and religious minorities in the Crusader-states during the twelfth and thirteenth centuries. This topic is an interesting one, and so far it has not received the attention it deserves. The eleven authors (a misspelling of Jonathan Riley-Smith's name in the table of contents really should not have occurred) argue on the whole very convincingly that it was only thanks to the immigrants and their influence, and to a certain degree shaping by the nobility, the church, the central administration, the economy, and last but not least the arts, that the Crusader-states were able to maintain a 'European' level of development. This positive image is sadly reversed in those papers which also deal with the religious and social minorities in these kingdoms – the prevailing picture is that of conflict with the Latin conquerors; only rarely was there more than a very fragile symbiosis, born out of necessity rather than acceptance. 'Multicultural' the society might have been; united it was not. The book contains a wealth of information about individuals, but it is – by its very nature – not an easy book to read. It requires a good deal of specialized knowledge of the subject, as well as considerable language skills.

Bärbel Brodt

[34] BÄRBEL BRODT, *Städte ohne Mauern: Stadtentwicklung in East Anglia im 14. Jahrhundert*, Publications of the German Historical Institute London, 44 (Paderborn: Schöningh, 1997), 401 pp. DM 48.00

So what, then, makes a town a town: a borough charter, population size, the presence of religious orders, political autonomy, guilds, economic importance, or all of these things? In Germany the answer would be comparatively simple: towns are characterized by a charter and – a wall. In England, the situation is far more complicated. In a detailed case study, Brodt examines the development of nineteen towns and settlements with urban characteristics in fourteenth-century East Anglia. The book covers their internal political organization, including a prosopography of office holders, as well as the other aspects of 'urbanity' mentioned above. It concludes that there were no fixed criteria for what constituted a town in medieval England – all characteristics of a settlement have to be considered to reach a final evaluation. Brodt argues that the fiscal policy of the Crown, which taxed boroughs at a higher rate than villages, encouraged prosperous villages which could easily have qualified as towns not to seek formal recognition as municipal corporations, because this brought financial disadvantages with it. The investigation of the political élite of the towns under examination demonstrates, moreover, that the Black Death of the mid-fourteenth century did not bring about a fundamental break in continuity in the urban élite, which suggests that the impact of the disease may have been overstated.

Andreas Fahrmeir

[35] VOLKER LEPPIN, *Geglaubte Wahrheit: Das Theologieverständnis Wilhelms von Ockham*, Forschungen zur Kirchen- und Dogmengeschichte, 63 (Göttingen: Vandenhoeck & Ruprecht, 1995), 365 pp. DM 98.00

The Nominalist, Venerable Inceptor, and Invincible Doctor William Ockham was a brilliant thinker, who substantially redefined the nature of philosophical-theological debate for his successors. Volker Leppin's massive study, which is based on his Heidelberg theological Ph.D. thesis, provides a close analysis, in demanding prose, of major aspects of William of Ockham's thought. Leppin is concerned to identify the main elements in Ockham's thought and to explain their interrelationships. His work has an interest which extends beyond that of pure intellectual history in so far as much of Ockham's work has important political significance because of his relationship to the cause of Louis the Bavarian. In considering Ockham's consequentially complicated relationship to the Papacy, Leppin argues that the condemnation of 51 of his propositions at Avignon in 1326 did not affect his later work to the degree sometimes contended. This work contains complex and sophisticated arguments, the full worth of which will be accessible only to readers with a considerable knowledge of the subject.

Bärbel Brodt

[36] HERBERT EIDEN, *"In der Knechtschaft werdet ihr verharren..."*. *Ursachen und Verlauf des englischen Bauernaufstandes von 1381*, Trierer Historische Forschungen, 32 (Trier: THF, 1995), 529 pp. DM 92.00

The ill-fated so-called Peasants' Revolt of 1381 has stimulated a large number of studies from all over the world, some of which are ideologically biased. Eiden is a fairly neutral observer; his book is dilligent rather than original. Its great merit is the wealth of archival sources Eiden has used in his attempt to link up disturbances, local riots, and uprisings in no fewer than twenty-six English counties and a number of urban centres, above all in London, under the general heading of the Peasants' Revolt. It is difficult to deny the possibility that the events which began in Essex and Kent in the last days of May 1381 spread as far as Yorkshire, since the grievances were the same all over the kingdom. Eiden has traced some 3,554 persons who were actively involved in the various disturbances – 1,214 in Norfolk, 954 in Essex, 456 in

Kent, 299 in Suffolk, 242 in Cambridgeshire, and finally, 389 in the remaining twenty-one counties. These are indeed telling figures. While there is no doubt that disturbances in 1381 were almost country-wide, there is no less doubt that they were overwhelmingly concentrated in the South-East. An interesting feature of his analysis is the emphasis which he lays on the speed and effectiveness of communication among dissidents. A very strong feature of this work is the excellence of the indexes.

Bärbel Brodt

[37] SARAH McNAMER (ed.), *The Two Middle English Translations of the Revelations of St Elizabeth of Hungary, ed. from Cambridge University Library MS Hh. i.11 and Wynkyn de Worde's printed text of ?1493*, Middle English Texts, 28 (Heidelberg: Winter, 1996), 136 pp. DM 58.00

The present volume is a critical edition of the two Middle English translations of *The Revelations of St Elizabeth of Hungary*, and the Latin version which is their source. The *Revelations* enjoyed a wide circulation in the fourteenth and fifteenth centuries and bear witness to the influence of continental texts on devotional currents in late medieval England. They will be of special interest for the study of women's writing, piety, and the cult of the Virgin Mary. Presented mainly as a dialogue between Elizabeth and the Virgin Mary, the *Revelations* transport powerful images of female mysticism. In her introduction, McNamer discusses the uncertain authorship and the history of these texts and provides useful clues, including a glossary, for their interpretation. Especially helpful for students new to this period is the selected bibliography at the end of the edition. This volume will be a welcome source for university teachers and students of medieval gender history.

Dagmar Freist

[38] KARL MICHAEL EISING, *Aspekte des englischen "de facto"-Gesetzes vom 14. Oktober 1495 (11 Henry VII c. 1)*, Ius vivensis: Rechtsgeschichtliche Abhandlungen, Abteilung B, 2 (Münster: Lit, 1995), xvi + 123 pp. DM 48.80.

In this work the author studies and elaborates the importance of a Statute promulgated in Parliament in 1495, sometimes called the 'de facto' Statute. The proem to the Statute summarizes its purpose: 'An Acte that noe person going with the Kinge to the Warres shalbe attaynt of treason.' The purport of the Act was that no one should be punished as guilty of high treason or anything else for following the king in times of war. The intention of this legislation was obviously to safeguard the position of Henry VII himself, but by its very nature it had and has a more general constitutional weight and interest. Eising provides a clear and orderly analysis. (It is a pity that the title of his book contains an error. 14 October 1495 was not the date of the Statute, but rather the date when the Parliament which promulgated the Statute first met.)

Bärbel Brodt

Sixteenth to Eighteenth Centuries

[39] HEINZ DUCHHARDT (ed.), *Der Herrscher in der Doppelpflicht. Europäische Fürsten und ihre beiden Throne*, Veröffentlichungen des Instituts für Europäische Geschichte Mainz. Abteilung Universalgeschichte, Beiheft 43 (Mainz: Verlag Philipp von Zabern, 1997), 276 pp. DM 52.00

As Duchhardt points out in his introduction to this collection of twelve articles on six monarchs who, between the fifteenth and the eighteenth centuries, were rulers in two kingdoms, biographies of kings and queens are currently very much *en vogue*. This book, however, provides more than just biographical details. It deals with the complicated and intricate subject of the *Personalunion*, and the problems, challanges, and possibilities which originated from it. Amongst the monarchs who held either successive or, indeed, parallel thrones were James VI and I and William III, the former being king of Scotland from 1588 and of England from 1603, the latter Governor-General of the

Netherlands from 1672 and king of England from 1689. The most intriguing thing about this collection is that each monarch is dealt with in two articles, written by leading experts, each respectively covering the time in office in just one country from a rather 'nationalistic' perspective (Jenny Wormald [345] and Conrad Russell [314] on James VI and I; Arie T. van Deursen [263] and James R. Jones [283] on William III). This approach is highly stimulating as well as controversial, for the resulting picture is not always one of agreement. Both Wormald and Russell agree, however, that the conditions of monarchy in England were very different from those in Scotland; Wormald in particular stresses the differences between the centre of the realm and its periphery, and points towards the power of the General Assembly of the Scottish Church. In England, however, the king was the chief executive, the Supreme Governor of the Church. Although in England the king was the possessor of hereditary wealth and the leader of his subjects in war and peace, his authority here was constitutionally limited by tradition. The English Parliament was more independent than that of Scotland. In both essays (maybe it would have been better to refrain from a translation) James is portrayed as a highly intelligent ruler who did not provoke his leading subjects too far, and as one who was ready to withdraw unpopular opinion. James was a learned theologian, and possibly the best symbol of his on the whole successful British rule is the King James Bible. Unlike so many other contemporary unions, the Anglo-Scottish one was to survive. William III, on the other hand, was unique in a different way: in both nations he gained his power through revolution, and he conquered one of his kingdoms, Ireland, in the manner of a medieval monarch, as Jones rightly points out, by defeating James at the Battle of the Boyne in 1690. In England William was never a congenial king and his popularity diminished further after his wife's death in 1694 and as memories of the causes of the revolution of 1688 faded. His original attempt to govern by employing more or less non-party men as his ministers failed; he could not be called a 'Tory king', but he also disliked the Whigs because they intended to limit monarchical authority. At least he was reconciled with Anne, thus safeguarding his succession. The four essays under consideration here are stimulating and learned, and they all provide good bibliographies.

Bärbel Brodt

[40] ERK VOLKMAR HEYEN (ed.), *Öffentliche Verwaltung und Wirt-schaftskrise/Administration publique et crise économique*, Jahrbuch für europäische Verwaltungsgeschichte, 7 (Baden-Baden: Nomos, 1995), 388 pp. DM 108.00
ERK VOLKMAR HEYEN (ed.), *Verwaltung und Verwaltungsrecht in Frankreich und England (18./19. Jh.)/Administration et droit administratif en France et Angleterre (18e/19e s.)/Administration and Administrative Law in France and England (18th/19th c.)*, Jahrbuch für europäische Verwalt-ungsgeschichte, 8 (Baden-Baden: Nomos, 1996), 347 pp. DM 108.00

The *JEV* is an annual publication of a particularly useful kind. Each volume is devoted to a collection of scholarly essays on a particular theme in the history of administration. The publication is the respon-sibility of the Deutsche Forschungsgemeinschaft and the Centre Na-tional de la Recherche Scientifique, but a large proportion of the con-tributions are in English and English summaries are provided for all the others. In this regard a detail of some passing interest is that while the title of volume 7 is given in German and French, that of volume 8 is given in English too. Volume 7 deals with public administration and economic crisis, with contributions ranging from eighteenth-cen-tury France to the former GDR and present-day Eastern Europe. To the student of the history of the United Kingdom the most important essay is that by C. Zimmermann **[346]** which, although exclusively concerned with the administrative history of Württemberg in relation to famines (1770-1847), provides a highly instructive comparative di-mension to the Irish potato famine and its handling by British govern-ments. Volume 8 is concerned with administration and administra-tive law in France and England in the eighteenth and nineteenth cen-turies. It is curiously imbalanced in so far as there are contributions outlining the relationship between administration and law in Eng-land from the Middle Ages to the nineteenth century, but there are no corresponding contributions for France. However, there is a great deal of thoughtful and thought-provoking analysis of the two systems (or perhaps one should say a system and a quasi-system) of administra-tive law. A particularly interesting essay is that by Vida Azimi **[255]**, relating to the work of the nineteenth-century jurist Laboulaye on English administration. His German counterpart was, above all, Gneist who is discussed among others by Erk Volkmar Heyen **[402]**. These two contributions admirably illustrate the truism that one of the best ways into comparative history is the study of the history of comparative history. The only criticisms one can make of these volumes is that the standard of proof correction is not quite all that it might be, and the linguistic standard of some of the English summaries is not always the highest. What does Heyen mean when he says: 'The English notorious lack of thinking and developing administrative institutions on clear principles was criticised and seen as the reason for its inaccessibility by foreigners'?

Bärbel Brodt

[41] HARMUT BERGHOFF and DIETER ZIEGLER (eds), *Pionier und Nachzügler? Vergleichende Studien Großbritanniens und Deutschlands im Zeitalter der Industrialisierung. Festschrift für Sidney Pollard zum 70. Geburtstag*, Arbeitskreis Deutsche England-Forschung, 28 (Bochum: Brockmeyer, 1995), vii + 315 pp. DM 54.80

The Festschrift in his honour deals with Sidney Pollard's life-long interest in the comparative economic performance of Britain and Germany. The contributors have been chosen according to their expertise in this field. Edited by two of his former Ph.D. students, the book is prefaced by a sympathetic biographical sketch **[159]**. We learn that Siegfried Pollak, as he was first known, escaped from Nazi-infested Austria at the age of thirteen, on one of the now famous *Kindertransporte*. Later on Pollard served in the British army, before setting out on his splendid career as an economic historian at the University of Sheffield.

Answers were sought in particular to three central questions. First, what are the long-term causes of Britain's industrial decline in comparison with Germany? Second, is any new insight to be gained about Germany's so-called 'deviation' (*Sonderweg*) from the developmental path of western Europe? Third, what are the mechanisms of interaction between imitation and adaptation in all matters concerning the transfer of technology and know-how in general (for example, management skills). As far as the overall analytical model of 'pioneer and late-comer' is concerned, it is important to stress the question-mark at the end. The essays, usefully summarized in the introduction, all give a slightly different answer to this question: they range from textile industries, via banking, co-operatives and philanthropy, academic cross-fertilization, to the formation of wealth. They also bear witness to Pollard's concern that economic history should not be studied in isolation but should encompass politics as well as culture and society. The relationship between the first industrial nation and, as it were, the first under-developed country, which was soon to out-perform its master, was a very complex one. This is perhaps the most important result of these studies. In many ways the late-comer was in a better starting position, being able to learn from the trial-and-error approach of Britain. The period under investigation is mainly the nineteenth century. But in view of the decline of the nation-state, in the long run the topics covered in this volume appear to be more relevant than inter-governmental relations in the traditional sense. It remains to be said that this volume would have been more appropriately placed with a publisher of more international standing and a greater distribution network.

Lothar Kettenacker

[42] URSULA MACHOCZEK, *Die regierende Königin – Elizabeth I. von England: Aspekte weiblicher Herrschaft im 16. Jahrhundert* (Pfaffenweiler: Centaurus, 1996), xii + 507 pp. DM 88.00

Bearing in mind the typical Renaissance ideas on the nature and position of women, it seems at least amazing that the sixteenth century saw fifteen women as regent or queen in their own right. One of them, maybe the most famous, and almost certainly the subject of the most biographies, was Elizabeth I of England. Machoczek's recent addition to these biographies is indeed welcome. It deals first and foremost with the specific conditions of female rule resulting from the different contemporary concepts of sovereign and females; the sovereign with his godly right to rule, the female with her duty of subordination. These conditions also resulted in a different education for the female heir to a throne, made her political activities different from those of a male counterpart, and the question of marriage a very complicated one indeed. Machoczek impresses most by her balanced and wide-ranging use of contemporary sources; and she also places the reign of Elizabeth into its historical context, thus illuminating Elizabeth by apt comparisons with the role of ruling women in other centuries or countries. Elizabeth was well educated; this helped her in the adroit way in which she dramatized her position as a female sovereign. In its balanced judgement and range of reference, this work compares very favourably with the superficially similar one published by Carole Levine some two years ago.

Bärbel Brodt

[43] PETER KIRCHEISEN, *London: Das Leben in Englands Metropole im 16. und 17. Jahrhundert* (Frankfurt/M.: R. G. Fischer, 1995), 199 pp. DM 39.80

This book is a richly illustrated general history of sixteenth and seventeenth-century London, directed at readers unfamiliar with English history rather than at specialists. It describes the government of the City, economic developments, festivals and everyday life, as well the relationship between the City and the political developments of England in this period.

Andreas Fahrmeir

[44] RAINGARD EßER, *Niederländische Exulanten im England des 16. und frühen 17. Jahrhunderts*, Historische Forschungen, 55 (Berlin: Duncker & Humblot, 1996), 271 pp. DM 92.00

This book is an extremely interesting study of the Dutch emigrant community in sixteenth and seventeenth-century Norwich, originally submitted as a Ph.D. thesis at the university of Cologne. Eßer uses Norwich, home of a large community of Dutch emigrants, as a case-study to test general assumptions about the nature of sixteenth-century emigration from The Netherlands to Britain. Clearly making the most of the available sources, Eßer discusses the development of the Dutch parishes, education and cultural activities, patterns of settlement, the interaction of the foreign with the native community, the immigrants' economic activities, and the contacts the Norwich community maintained with The Netherlands. The picture that emerges is above all one of a successful experiment in the settlement of immigrants. The children of the more successful Dutch families in Norwich attended the English-speaking grammar school, and in 1618 a second-generation immigrant was awarded the Norwich scholarship to Corpus Christi College, Cambridge. The legal integration of the Dutch seems to have created few problems, even though several contentious issues were brought before the Privy Council, which tended to back the immigrants rather than the Norwich council. Eßer challenges conventional views above all in two respects. First, she argues that the exclusive emphasis on the religious motivation for migration to England in older works obscured other, mainly economic motivations. Second, she points out that the Dutch migrants in Norwich did not introduce new technology to the textile trade. By contrast, they adapted to the traditional structures in place. If they conducted their business more successfully than their English competitors, this was not due to a technological revolution. Rather, native textile manufacturers seem to have been willing to allow the Dutch newcomers to take over textile production, while seeking to maintain control over the supply of raw materials.

Andreas Fahrmeir

[45] ARMIN REESE, *Europäische Hegemonie versus Weltreich: Außenpolitik in Europa 1648-1763*, Historisches Seminar, N. F., 7 (Idstein: Schulz-Kirchner, 1995), 190 pp. DM 35.80

This is a comprehensive textbook, addressed to teachers and students of, and all those interested in, the eventful period between the Treaty of Westphalia and the Treaty of Paris. The book is divided into three main sections: a general overview of the historical development; contemporary sources (instructions to legates, actual texts of treaties, pamphlets etc.); and finally a very brief discussion of current themes and theories. An equally brief bibliography rounds off the volume, of which the second section is clearly the best. The well-presented collection of contemporary documents (in one case both the original and translation is provided, the other sixteen are given in German only) illustrates the complex power-relationships extending from Silesia to Canada, and notably enhances the value of this work as a teaching manual.

Bärbel Brodt

[45] HEINZ DUCHHARDT, *Balance of Power und Pentarchie 1700-1785*, Handbuch der Geschichte der Internationalen Beziehungen, 4 (Paderborn: Schöningh, 1997), xviii + 448 pp. DM 148.

This is the first published volume of a projected nine-volume compendium on international relations from 1450 to 1990. The collection should be complete by 1999. The compendium aims to respond to the newly-aroused interest in the history of international relations, especially since there is no modern general work on the topic in the German language. The present book, which covers the period of the pre-revolutionary eighteenth century, centres around the two concepts of 'balance of power' and the rule of the five mightiest powers in Europe: Britain, France, Austria, Russia, and Prussia. In contrast to the preceding and following centuries (especially after the Congress of Vienna), in this age the circle of powers was open to all options and coalitions. The idea of a 'universal monarchy', such as that of Louis XIV in France and his attempt to establish French supremacy in Europe ultimately failed in 1714. This was the year when the concept of a dominant super-power finally made way for a multipolar system of states in which former powers such as Spain were becoming second-rate. Conflicts were not only settled in Europe, but increasingly in the new continents. India and America were the battlefields for the numerous wars between Britain and France, and it was often here, in the colonial settlements, that conflicts actually started. Consequently, because the politics of international relations became such a central issue, philosophical thinking about the mechanics of internationalism increased dramatically. The antagonism between France and Britain, for both countries the dominant factor in the eighteenth century and after, is very well covered in this volume. It is divided into two parts: the first describes the main factors, conditions and participants of European international relations until the aftermath of the American war; the second discusses key features such as the development of a British-French entente. In Germany the history of the eighteenth century unfortunately receives less attention than, for example, that of the nineteenth century. Therefore a comprehensive volume that, as one of its many merits, puts British continental and colonial policies into the context of the rivalry among the European powers, is a welcome and important contribution.

Benedikt Stuchtey

[47] RAIMUND OTTOW, *Markt – Republik – Tugend. Probleme gesellschaftlicher Modernisierung im britischen politischen Denken 1670-1790*, Politische Ideen, 5 (Berlin: Akademie, 1996), 459 pp. DM 98.00

This magisterial Hamburg dissertation, based on extensive English and Scottish manuscript and printed sources, appears in the relatively new and prestigious series 'Politische Ideen', edited by Herfried Münkler. Since the end of the Cold War, the history of political ideas has gained new importance, providing a theoretical framework of past ideas for current political constellations. In the context of the history of British ideas, the present volume investigates the market economy that emerged from 1670 onwards in what Ernst Schulin, some thirty years ago, called 'Handelsstaat England'. The author studies the idea of the bourgeois society that emerged as a theoretical concept during the Enlightenment and was later to become a classic social model which, though always prominent, was certainly not uncriticized. The relationship between market, state, society, and individual, as well as the nature of politics, changed as result of the socialization of the market in early modern times. Once the classic idea of politics had gone, a distinction emerged between the economic 'bourgeois' and the political 'citoyen', reflecting the tension between market and republic. The book discusses how republican concepts and those of natural law initially ran parallel, and how they were later brought together in the Scottish Enlightenment. Thus economy and state, merchant and citizen co-existed on the basis of the idea of virtue. This separated morality from law and postulated the primacy of justice over what is morally right. The result was a socialization of 'moral sentiments': the market needed to be discovered by political theory. This process is shown within the framework of the ideas of William Temple, John Locke, Francis Hutcheson, David Hume, Henry Home, James Steuart, Adam Smith, Adam Ferguson, and others. The question is posed as to whether the developing 'commercial culture' was connected to certain political forms; which role culture played in mediating between politics and economics; and which political consequences were drawn from the dynamics of social conditions. In a broader sense the author investigates how intellectual traditions were transformed under the pressure of social transformation.

Benedikt Stuchtey

[48] ANDREAS PRÄUER, *Zwischen Schicksal und Chance: Arbeit und Arbeitsbegriff in Großbritannien im 17. und 18. Jahrhundert auf dem Hintergrund der "Utopia" des Thomas More*, Schriften zur Wirtschafts- und Sozialgeschichte, 52 (Berlin: Duncker & Humblot, 1997), 328 pp. DM 112.00

This 1996 Munich dissertation offers a wide-ranging overview of concepts of work in Britain between the publication of Thomas More's *Utopia* and Adam Smith's *Wealth of Nations*. Its two main sections deal with different perceptions of 'work', as a burden, a duty, or a chance, and different types of work, such as science, trade, industry, or war.

Andreas Fahrmeir

[49] DORIT GRUGEL-PANNIER, *Luxus: Eine begriffs- und ideengeschichtliche Untersuchung unter besonderer Berücksichtigung von Bernard Mandeville*, Münsteraner Monographien zur englischen Literatur, 19 (Frankfurt/M.: Lang, 1996), 346 pp. £39.00

This book is a revised version of a Münster Ph.D. thesis. It focuses on the concept of luxury from the point of view of the history of ideas, with special reference to the concept in the work of the English author Bernard Mandeville (*c.* 1670-1733). In his *Fable of the Bees, or Private Vices Made Public* (1723) he considers vice to be just as necessary for a state to flourish as hunger is for humans to thrive. The first chapter of Grugel-Pannier's book is a detailed philological reconstruction of the concept of luxury. This is followed by a critical presentation of influential concepts of luxury which played an important role in the English debate in the seventeenth and eighteenth centuries. With reference to his precursors, Mandeville's concept of luxury is then analysed from systematic points of view, for example, in an economic context. Particular emphasis is given to the question of whether the provocative formulation 'private vices, public benefits' is really at the root of his concept of luxury and his notions of economy. Although it is characteristic of Mandeville that his judgements cannot be clearly pinned down, the extent to which he was orientated towards the nation in his defence of luxury, which for him is synonymous with prosperity, is clear. The self-seeking pursuit of private interests – Hobbes' influence is obvious – promotes the good of the nation. The study shows that Mandeville not only propagates the independence of economy from ethics, but also gives it primacy over ethics. Obsessed with the utilitarian principle, his work reflects capitalist values and the claim to power of the new economic forces. This is particularly interesting since Mandeville's works were by no means reserved for specialist readers, but addressed a broad lay public with a variety of interests.

Sabine Freitag

[50] INSA CHRISTIANE HENNEN, *"Karl zu Pferde". Ikonologische Studien zu Anton van Dycks Reiterporträts Karls I. von England*, Europäische Hochschulschriften, 28/225 (Frankfurt/M.: Lang, 1995), 276 pp. £35.00

This 1994 Trier dissertation in art history offers a perceptive analysis of Anthony Van Dyck's portraits of Charles I on horseback against the background of the King's self-presentation as a divine monarch and sole ruler. Hennen argues that a proper understanding of Van Dyck's works of art is possible only if they are analysed in the context of the history of their composition, their initial hanging as part of a wider iconographic arrangement, and their public impact. This is exemplified by a detailed study of the portrait *Charles I and St Antoine* and the spatial significance of its position in relation to other works hanging in St James's Gallery, which forms the core of the book. Abraham van der Doort's *Catalogue of the Collections of Charles I* and an anonymous manuscript (*c.* 1640) in the Victoria and Albert Museum allow a complete reconstruction of the painting's hanging context and its significance. The author analyses these portraits as part of the pictorial propaganda of the period designed to manifest the monarch's sovereignty and divine right as well as his role as the guarantor of a *pax universalis* like Elizabeth I and Henry IV of France. Hennen supports her interpretation by drawing iconographic comparisons with portraits and monuments of other European rulers on horseback and their impact, as well as by referring to political events of the period that might have influenced the composition of the portraits. Of interest to cultural historians are the cross references she makes to various masques of the 1630s which represented the King in the same light, and an analysis of court culture as the primary target of this type of propaganda. The King's gradual withdrawal from public appearances is mirrored in the self-representation of the monarch which was not aimed at the

general public. The growing rift between court and country, the dis-
cord among courtiers which undermined the court's political cred-
ibility, and political stagnation had an impact on Van Dyck's work in
Britain. He was unable to create another coherent room decoration
that would have appealed to the court and could have offered the
ideal of consensus. His *Garter Procession* tapestry sequence was rejected
by Charles I. Similarly, Van Dyck's second portrait of Charles I on horseback was probably never used as part of a closed pictorial programme.
Hennen concludes that the iconographic programme of the King's first
court painter failed to respond to a changing reality but reiterated familiar topoi which became devoid of meaning. Out of touch with his
people and convinced of his own greatness, the King can be seen as a
victim of his own propaganda. It is a pity that the reproductions of
eighty-one paintings and sculptures at the end of the book are of poor
quality.

Dagmar Freist

[51] IMMO MEENKEN, *Reformation und Demokratie. Zum politischen
Gehalt protestantischer Theologie in England 1570-1660*, Quaestiones:
Themen und Gestalten der Philosophie, 10 (Stuttgart: frommann-
holzboog, 1996), 380 pp. DM 168.00

This fascinating (and carefully produced) book, a Trier Ph.D. thesis,
examines the political substance of Protestant theology in England
between 1570 and 1660. Meenken looks at some of the roots of modern democracy which can be traced back to the Reformation. To this
end, Presbyterianism, Congregationalism, and Baptism are studied in
one chapter, which the author convincingly calls 'Entwürfe der
fortgeschrittenen Reformation', models of the advanced Reformation.
The following chapter discusses the elements of political emancipation in the theology of Anglicanism. It is a particular merit of the work
that these chapters are preceded by a well-informed historical outline; also the *Begriffsgeschichte* and the meaning of the terms 'Puritanism' and 'democracy' are explained. An extensive section deals with
previous and current research questions such as, for example, the
historiographical and theological discussion about Puritanism or the
role of the Levellers. The concluding comprehensive bibliography of
50 pages includes many titles from the late sixteenth and the seventeenth centuries, but as far as Anglicanism is concerned, Meenken con-

centrates on three classical theological writers only: Richard Hooker's *Of the Laws of Ecclesiastical Polity*, William Chillingworth's *The Religion of Protestants. A Safe Way to Salvation*, and Jeremy Taylor's books pleading for practical Christianity. A summary of the complicated context of the book's major thesis can only remain superficial. The comprehensive and systematic manner in which Puritanism and religious radicalism on the one hand, and episcopal Anglicanism on the other are confronted, show the different qualities of these religious beliefs as a basis for democratic ideas. Here, as the author himself states, English history is particularly revealing, because Reformation and Revolution partially coincided. Puritanism, which could well be considered democratic in terms of its institutional structure and procedure, was essentially authoritarian and even intolerant as regards the theoretical concepts on which it was founded as a religious system. Anglicanism, on the other hand, despite its undemocratic episcopal background, represented certain fundamental individual and social values that were reflected in a practical and somehow universally applicable faith. Values such as human dignity and achievement indicated a tendency away from dogma and towards the criteria of modern democracy.

Benedikt Stuchtey

[52] FRANK ENGEHAUSEN, *Von der Revolution zur Restauration. Die englischen Nonkonformisten 1653-1662*, Heidelberger Forschungen, 30 (Heidelberg: Winter, 1995), 500 pp. DM 98.00

The beginning of the Restoration, when Charles II returned to England in the spring of 1660, was marked by rapturous celebrations and pageants for the King. As Hans-Christoph Schröder has put it, the Commonwealth just seemed to 'slip into monarchy'. This apparent domestic consensus puzzled contemporary observers, and continues to occupy researchers today. By analysing the political views of religious Nonconformists, the author of the present work attempts to show why supporters of the 'good old cause' mounted no serious revolt when the monarch returned and soon curtailed religious freedoms despite promises of toleration. The work is largely based on the petitions, programmatic writings, and open letters by Nonconformists assembled in the Thomason Tracts, one of the most significant collection of seventeenth-century pamphlets and tracts. The author comes to the conclusion that the monarchy was restored 'not out of its own strength, but with the approval of its former enemies' (p. 252). Disappointment about the lack of religious toleration and of a will to reform, and the political fragmentation of the 1650s combined with a belief in Providence and the positive expectations for the future which the King raised (among other things by the Declaration of Breda), meant that the vast majority of religious Nonconformists, while they remained sceptical, accepted the King's return without resistance. When these hopes were disappointed by the resumption of religious persecution and the imposition of a rigorous uniformity on the state church with the dismissal of thousands of Nonconformist clergy, there were isolated revolts. Yet even radical Nonconformists distanced themselves publicly from violent resistance. Instead, the author suggests, they found compensation for their defeat in millenarian ideas.

The main merit of this work is the differentiated overview it offers of Nonconformist reactions to the various power constellations between 1653 and 1662, something which has not been done in this form before. However, it must be asked whether the outcome justifies the length of this study, in particular as it leaves a number of serious gaps which require further work in social history and the history of mentalities. These include an assessment of the domestic political mood during the first two years of the Restoration which were awash with rumours of armed uprisings, the King's breach of confidence towards religious minorities, and the discrepancy between how Nonconformists saw themselves and how they saw others. A more comprehensive understanding of this transitional period would require questions to be asked, for example, about the social composition of Nonconformists and the reception of their writings among a broader public.

Dagmar Freist

[53] ULRICH BACH, *Englische Flugtexte im 17. Jahrhundert. Historisch-pragmatische Untersuchungen zur frühen Massenkommunikation*, Anglistische Forschungen 254 (Heidelberg: Winter, 1997), 528 pp. DM 128.00

This *Habilitationsschrift* was submitted to the English Faculty of Düsseldorf university in 1990, and it is important to remember that it is not the work of a historian. This massive study seeks to examine some 500 pamphets dating from 1640 to 1660, without being much concerned with their historical background. Rather, the author looks at their reception by literate as well as illiterate contemporaries, using very elaborate structural and linguistic schemes and models which make little sense to the non-expert. It is hardly a secret that pamphlets were used for the purposes of religious-political persuasion and polemics. Bach does not intend to add much to the historical dimension of popular culture; his field is that of 'items' and of 'italics', of 'grammar' and of 'metaphor'. It is a very useful compilation of texts, and will be received by historians as such and little more.

Bärbel Brodt

[54] MICHAEL HASSELS, *Von der Dynastie zur bürgerlichen Idealfamilie. Studien zum fürstlichen Familienbild des Hauses Hannover in England*, Europäische Hochschulschriften, XXVIII/257 (Frankfurt/M.: Lang, 1996), 271 pp. £34.00

As so often the subtitle gives more away than the main title: the House of Hanover is the clear object of attention. Furthermore, 'Familienbild' is to be understood in the literal sense. The author examines the changing composition and meaning of English royal family portraits in the course of the eighteenth century. Paintings of royal personages therefore constitute the source material for this dissertation, which is more of a contribution to art history than to history in a conventional sense. Almost one third of this book consists of illustrations: some eighty pages, often with more than one picture on a page, and all in black and white.

However, these paintings serve a purpose beyond their meaning for the art historian in the context of their genre. According to Hassels they were of a specific historical relevance at the time, in as much as they demonstrated the perception, not least the self-perception, of monarchy. While royal portraits always serve to enhance the monarch's elevated position, as foreigners the first Hannoverians had an even greater need to legitimize their rule. Hassels makes observations which are of particular interest to the political and social historian: the divine right of kings, greatly undermined by the Glorious Revolution and the ascent of parliament, was upheld in the realm of allegorical painting. It was kingship rather than parliament which enthralled the public and satisfied their spiritual needs. The pictorial emphasis on divine providence helped the Whigs in their propaganda battle against Tories and Jacobites who disputed Hanoverian legitimacy.

Long before Victoria and Albert came to symbolize the ideal middle-class family, the trend had already been established by royal fam-

ily portraits at the time of Gainsborough. George III disliked pompos-
ity and preferred to be painted as a family father in private and informal surroundings, thereby creating a role-model for the emerging
middle classes.

Lothar Kettenacker

[55] DANIEL BRÜHLMEIER, HELMUT HOLZHEY, and VILEM
MUDROCH (eds), *Schottische Aufklärung: "A Hotbed of Genius"* (Berlin: Akademie, 1996), 156 pp. DM 84.00

The characterization of Enlightenment Scotland as a 'hotbed of genius' goes back to the eighteenth century itself. The country did not
criticize slavery in the American colonies, but its intellectuals (Hume,
Smith, Ferguson, Millar, Hutton, Watt, Adam, Ramsay, Robertson,
Hutcheson, Burnet, and many more) fought for social and economic
change, and Scotland was undoubtedly among the first representa-
tives of the European Enlightenment. Historiography, philosophy,
poetry, political economy, social science, geology, modern biology,
medicine, architecture and other subjects were hotly discussed by the
educated classes, who embodied a strong optimism and the feeling
that new opportunities and independence in thought and judgement
were guaranteed. A recently published anthology of the Scottish Enlightenment, edited by Alexander Broadie (Edinburgh: Canongate,
1997), reflects this well-known phenomenon, showing that the centre
of British cultural and intellectual creativity moved from London to
Scotland in the years after 1750. Due to the Union of 1707, which
brought economic prosperity and stability to Scotland, the Scottish
literati soon took the lead in the European modernization movement.
And intellectuals did not hide in their ivory towers, but played a central role in public life; Hume was a successful diplomat. The present
book, the result of a series of lectures at the 'Wissenschaftshistorisches
Kolloquium Zürich', does not and cannot claim completeness: the
development of chemistry, for example, is missing. The book's aim,
however, is not encyclopaedic but exemplary, and this allows other
issues to be included, such as the reception of the Scottish Enlightenment in France [309] and Germany [334], and the connections between
the Enlightenment and visual art [330].

Benedikt Stuchtey

[56] ULRICH J. ORTNER, *Die Trinitätslehre Samuel Clarkes. Ein For-schungsbeitrag zur Theologie der frühen Aufklärung*, Bamberger Theologische Studien, 4 (Frankfurt/M.: Lang, 1996), 365 pp. £39.00

This 1995 Bamberg dissertation in theology fills a gap in our knowledge of the theologian and philosopher Samuel Clarke by looking closely at his *Scripture Doctrine of the Trinity* and the controversies it provoked. Ortner intertwines his theological analysis with a biography of Samuel Clarke and an account of his later involvement with the Anglican Church. He shows how individual friendships, for instance that with John Moore, influenced both Clarke's career and his thinking. Similarly, leading intellectuals of the seventeenth century who were closely attached to Clarke, among them Isaac Newton and William Whiston, left their traces in Clarke's *œuvre*. Although the book is a contribution to the theology of the English Enlightenment, historians interested in church history will find those sections relating to Clarke's criticism of the Anglican Church and the Book of Common Prayer useful.

Dagmar Freist

[57] HANS UTZ, *Schotten und Schweizer – Brother mountaineers. Europa entdeckt die beiden Völker im 18. Jahrhundert*, Scottish Studies: Publications of the Scottish Studies Centre of the Johannes Gutenberg Universiät Mainz in Germersheim, 17 (Frankfurt/M.: Lang, 1995) 169 pp. £22.00

In this study, Hans Utz presents travel accounts and impressions of both Scotland and Switzerland on the basis of little-known source material. Contributing to the history of the Grand Tour in the eighteenth century, the author examines attitudes of travellers to both countries around 1800. From a comparative perspective, he concludes that they both responded to contemporary visions of an apparently lost idyll that had vanished with the first wave of modernization in other regions and countries. This 'invention' of the Highlander or Swiss mountaineer, respectively, was readily accepted by the Swiss and the Scots, notwithstanding its divergence from reality. Ultimately, this myth has had a long-term relevance for the shaping of national identity in Switzerland and Scotland.

Ulrike Jordan

Nineteenth Century

[58] DIRK SCHUBERT, *Stadterneuerung in London und Hamburg: Eine Stadtbaugeschichte zwischen Modernisierung und Disziplinierung* (Wiesbaden: Vieweg, 1997), xii + 704 pp. DM 98.00

Unlike most academic studies, Dirk Schubert's book is not only equipped with a bibliography and endnotes, but also with 'end-pictures' – *c.* 100 pages with 376 illustrations, to which the reader is referred by numbers in the text's margins. Considering the usual prices for German academic works in paperback, this well-produced volume can therefore only be described as a bargain.

Stadterneuerung in London und Hamburg is the published version of a *Habilitationsschrift* submitted to the research centre 'City, Environment and Technology' of Hamburg's Technical University in 1994. Its topic is the development of 'urban planning' both on the theoretical and practical level. Schubert argues that the modern concern with urban planning and urban improvements originates in the debate on housing for the lower classes, and can therefore best be studied in two of the leading cities of their day, London and Hamburg, which are in turn representative of broader trends in Britain and Germany. Far from being the single preoccupation of municipal authorities, the improvement of certain districts was part of a larger concern with modernization and the 'disciplining' of the 'lower classes'. For, considered dispassionately, the urban areas described as slums by nineteenth-century middle-class observers can also be interpreted as the most rational response to the demands of the modern economy: they provided cheap housing in the vicinity of the major employers.

In spite of the numerous differences between London and Hamburg (land tenure, political structure), developments in the two cities were at first remarkably similar, thus confirming Schubert's thesis. In spite of grander plans, improvements in the nineteenth century were at first limited in scope. Only the shock of the 1892 Hamburg cholera epidemic and the growing criticism of the housing situation for those on low incomes in London led to the development of larger schemes.

However, unless they were part of general improvements to a district, as in the London Kingsway project, the cost could be prohibitive. Moreover, building new accommodation did nothing to solve the underlying problem, as the former residents could not afford the rents for new flats or houses and were thus only displaced. The housing crisis which followed the First World War put a stop to modernization plans, which were only resumed in the 1920s. It was not until the 1930s that urban reform in England and Germany diverged significantly. Whereas in England the investments in new housing were part of a rationally conceived attempt to provide employment through investment, in Germany the housing question was integrated into the National Socialist regime's racial concepts of society. After the Second World War, large-scale destruction in both London and Hamburg radically altered the problems urban planners faced, from improving existing real estate to constructing entirely new settlements.

Andreas Fahrmeir

[59] VOLKER THEN, *Eisenbahnen und Eisenbahnunternehmer in der Industriellen Revolution: Ein preußisch/deutsch-englischer Vergleich*, Kritische Studien zur Geschichtswissenschaft, 120 (Göttingen: Vandenhoeck & Ruprecht, 1997), 512 pp. DM 78.

This weighty volume deals with an important aspect of the comparative history of industrialization in Prussia and Germany : the railways and railway businessmen in the age of expansion in the mid-nineteenth century. The author takes his cue from a comparison of economic, legal, political and entrepreneurial preconditions and subsequent railway development in these countries. As a contribution to a critical evaluation of the 'special path' theory, applied to railway entrepreneurs, Volker Then concludes that German businessmen developed strategies not dissimilar to those of their English counterparts operating within a completely different political and legal framework. The social strata participating in this rapidly growing industry were very different as well: while in the German states and Prussia the middle classes and the state shared a mutual interest in railway expansion and use, in England the landed gentry took part in this as well. In spite of massive differences in the conceptualization and realization of railway policies, however, the author finds his thesis of broadly parallel international developments supported by evidence. The similarity of regions rather than national characteristics is a key element in his analysis - a supposition echoed by the recently emphasized concept of a 'Europe of regions'.

Ulrike Jordan

[60] CHRISTIANE EISENBERG (ed.), *Fußball, Soccer, Calcio: Ein englischer Sport auf seinem Weg um die Welt* (Munich: Deutscher Taschenbuch Verlag, 1997), 234 pp. DM 29.90

Soccer is one of the most popular and best-known games in the world. In 1994 some 179 countries were members of FIFA, the Fédération Internationale de Football Association, exceeding the number of member states of the UNO. Soccer originated in England and it is thus fitting that Tony Mason opens this collection of nine essays with an account of the history of the game there **[422]**. He argues that soccer started off as a game played by a small élitist group, mainly consisting of members of public schools with the notable exception of Rugby, of course. Within a few decades, however, the game had become an integral part of the 'culture' of the working classes. 'Culture' features prominently in this book. The notion that the English, while creating an Empire, intentionally used the game of soccer to promote a *Kulturimperialismus,* is forcefully rejected by Mason and his co-authors who stress that the game attracted different groups of people with different social and religious backgrounds and served as a means for social integration. At the turn of the last century, in particular during the last few years before the outbreak of the First World War, a close symbiosis developed between the game and nationalism; after the war soccer became a well organized mass phenomenon, and very competitive indeed. From the 1960s on, it became big business, televised and sponsored. The players have become professionals who are 'bought' and 'sold' by the clubs. Mason concludes that professional soccer in England is now on its way to becoming part of the *Popkultur.* It is still the people's game, although the question of international success seems to have become the most important one in the eyes of the fans. Whether this will lead to a 'break in the continuity', as Mason laments, remains to be seen.

Bärbel Brodt

[61] JOHANN BRAZDA, ROBERT SCHEDIWY, and GERHARD RÖNNEBECK (eds), *Pioniergenossenschaften am Beispiel der Konsumgenossenschaften in Großbritannien, Schweden und Japan*, Forschungen zur Wirtschafts-, Finanz- und Sozialgeschichte, 4 (Frankfurt/M.: Lang, 1996), 301 pp. £36.00

This book is best described as a collection of three separate reports on consumers' associations in Britain, Sweden, and Japan respectively. It contains neither an extensive introduction nor a comparative conclusion. The essay on British co-operatives, by Franz Müller [431], focuses on the economic development of consumers' associations. From relatively humble beginnings in the nineteenth century, these organizations, which were successful as retailers, less so as producers, captured a significant share of the UK food market, some 21 per cent in 1960. Their success was in part due to the way in which they solved the problem of control and profit sharing – the former was based on the principle of 'one member, one vote', while the latter was distributed not according to the amount of capital invested in the society, but according to the value of goods purchased from it, thus effectively allowing members to purchase goods at cost. From the 1960s the market share of consumers' organizations began to decline in spite of reforms aimed at centralization and increasing efficiency following a 1955 commission report. In 1991 consumers' associations had dropped to tenth place on the list of major British food retailers, while average wages indicate that the working conditions of their employees have become almost indistinguishable from those offered by their private competitors.

Andreas Fahrmeir

[62] MICHAEL PRINZ, *Brot und Dividende: Konsumvereine in Deutschland und England vor 1914*, Kritische Studien zur Geschichtswissenschaft, 112 (Göttingen: Vandenhoeck & Ruprecht, 1996), 404 pp. DM 78.00

This Bielefeld *Habilitationsschrift* is dedicated to the study of consumers' associations in Germany and England in a comparative perspective. Its two main sections discuss the development of consumers' co-operatives in the two countries, their membership, economic activities, and links with political parties and movements. For both the German and the English co-operatives, Prinz has undertaken extensive research in German and British archives. He argues that, on the one hand, the similarities in the development of such associations from comparatively humble beginnings to major players in the food market indicate that the economic forces of industrialization had a greater impact on the development of 'consumer culture' than political ones. The time lag between the development of such associations in Germany and England is therefore due to the later onset of industralization in Germany.

On the other hand, a number of differences in the status of consumers' organizations in the two countries can only be explained in political terms. First and foremost, consumers' co-operatives became much more respectable, powerful, and accepted by all political parties in England than in the German states. In England, consumers' associations attracted a substantial middle class membership – in German states, the middle classes generally avoided them or founded their own, more exclusive buyers' associations. Second, political developments in Germany had far greater influences on the evolution of consumers' co-operatives than in England, partly because they were considered to be political as well as economic associations. The period of repression following the revolution of 1848, for instance, led to the virtual disappearance of consumers' associations in the German states for a number of years.

Andreas Fahrmeir

[63] JOHANNES EUE, *Die Oregon-Frage: Amerikanische Expansionspolitik und der pazifische Nordwesten, 1814-1848*, Nordamerika-Studien / North American Studies, 3 (Münster: Lit, 1995), 414 pp. DM 58,80

The Oregon Question, the dispute between Great Britain, the United States, and other powers over the territories in the American Northwest, has usually been considered mainly as a diplomatic incident. By contrast, this Cologne dissertation stresses the domestic dimension of the crisis. While American administrations were not particularly concerned about guarding their mainly theoretical rights during the 1810s and 1820s, and were willing to leave the question open for the time being, the start of immigration into Oregon after 1843 turned Oregon into a subject of domestic disputes. Therefore, while the important decisions were made by the executive throughout, the interest of Congress in these questions was rather limited before the 1840s. Eue argues that Congress was far more radical in its demands for an American show of strength than the executive. This was only partly due to concerns about maintaining good relations with Britain, which demonstratively increased its naval expenditure. American administrations also saw no need for decisive action, as the theory of 'manifest destiny' indicated that the Oregon territories could only become American in the long run. For the American side of the story, as it were, Eue has worked extensively in various repositories across the United States; his account of British policies is based exclusively on printed materials.

Andreas Fahrmeir

[64] GÜNTHER HEYDEMANN, *Konstitution gegen Revolution: Die britische Deutschland- und Italienpolitik 1815-1848*, Publications of the German Historical Institute London, 36 (Göttingen: Vandenhoeck & Ruprecht, 1995), 404 pp. DM 120.00

This Bayreuth *Habilitationsschrift* is a study of British policy *vis-à-vis* Germany and Italy between the Congress of Vienna and the European revolutions of 1848. To some extent, the title of the book is the motto of British politics: in order to avoid revolution it is necessary to allow political reforms and to grant constitutions. British politicians could follow this maxim from their country's position of superiority in Europe. The consequence for the German and Italian states, which constituted the most unstable factors in the European system and caused most of its crises, was that they moved slowly but surely along the road towards modernization. Britain was perceived as a model in this, and, from the opposite perspective, the differences, similarities, and peculiarities of the German and Italian developments became obvious. However, in the end it was Austria and relations between Vienna and London that stood at the centre of British politics of Europe: the Habsburg Empire, incapable of constitutional reform, could not be convinced of the need for parliamentary modernization and representation. Thus Britain contributed not only to the inevitable decline of the Habsburg Empire, but also to the political disintegration of the fragile European state system after 1815. It soon became clear that those who had been allies during the Napoleonic Wars did not have much in common once peace had been achieved – above all their constitutional differences were too great. However, as the author shows, British attempts to influence the order of 1815 by advocating moderate reforms pushed the constitutional question on the Continent too far, and consequently, by the mid-nineteenth century, Britain gradually withdrew from direct involvement in European politics in order to pursue what was later to be called a policy of 'no intervention'. The first fifty years of the nineteenth century thus show how closely European politics still dovetailed. Austria was certainly *the* central European power which sought to maintain the *status quo* of 1815 for the sake of uniting the European monarchies and the multitude of the nationalities under its control. After 1848 it became increasingly clear that Vienna was a retarding element in European politics. The diplomatic and political aspects of Heydemann's thesis are rightly extensively elaborated, although a discussion of economic questions, for example, would have been helpful as well.

Benedikt Stuchtey

[65] RAINER POMMERIN and MICHAEL FRÖHLICH (eds), *Quellen zu den deutsch-britischen Beziehungen 1815-1914*, Quellen zu den Beziehungen Deutschlands zu seinen Nachbarn im 19. und 20. Jahrhundert, 3 (Darmstadt: Wissenschaftliche Buchgesellschaft, 1997), lxxxii + 229 pp. DM 98.00

This is the first volume of an edition of sources on Anglo-German relations planned to run to two volumes. The sources assembled here can represent only a small selection of the wide range of material available and suitable for documenting the complex and changing relations between Britain and Germany in the 'long' nineteenth century. There is no question that the choice of documents here was dictated more by their representative character than by their completeness. Eighty-five sources presented in chronological order describe developments in relations between the two states from the post-Napoleonic period to the 1848 revolution, from the nation-state to the 'new course' in German policy, and finally, the growing antagonism between the two countries leading up to the First World War. A substantial introduction presents the context of the sources, and a ten-page abstract provides a summary of it in English. A comprehensive subject index allows the reader to locate specific sources by topic.

Sabine Freitag

[66] RAYMUND SCHUSTER, *Das kirchliche Amt bei John Henry Newman:*
Eine historisch-systematische Untersuchung seines Priesterbildes im Kontext,
Europäische Hochschulschriften, XXIII/526 (Frankfurt/M.: Lang,
1995), 322 pp. £35.00

At the centre of this 1993 Freiburg dissertation in theology lies an analysis of John Henry Newman's conception of church office. The author
chooses a biographical, chronological approach which he combines
with systematic questions about Newman's theological views on liturgy, prayer, Holy Communion, the doctrine of the Holy Trinity, and
church office before and after his conversion to Catholicism. This study
is based on a number of previously little known documents, among
them Newman's ordination sermon 'On the Ministerial Order, as an
existing divine institution' (1831), which is reproduced in the appendix. The book thus promises to throw new light on the perception of
Newman, and on the relationship between the Anglican High Church
and the Catholic Church as it developed in the nineteenth century
under the impact of the New Oxford movement and the life and work
of Newman.

Dagmar Freist

[67] CLEMENS ZIMMERMANN, *Die Zeit der Metropolen: Urbanisierung*
und Großstadtentwicklung, Europäische Geschichte (Frankfurt/M.: S.
Fischer Taschenbuchverlag, 1996), 192 pp. DM 18.90

One of the key dates in the history of the city of Manchester is 16
August 1819, when eleven workmen were killed during a demonstration on the Peterfield, an event which is famously named 'Peterloo' in
allusion to Waterloo. While the latter stands for the nation's glory, the
former is a symbol of the emerging crisis caused by the steadily growing industrial cities. Soon Manchester became a centre for the great
social movements, the mass-strikes of 1842 and Chartism. And it was
also one of the most modern cities in England, if not in the world, as
the centre of technological innovation. In Germany, Elberfeld in the
Ruhr region was called the German 'Manchester', Lyon would be the
corresponding French example. Zimmermann's book clearly demonstrates the national impact of growing urbanization while also indi-
cating the international comparability of metropolises: Manchester as
the 'classical industrial town' is put into context with St Petersburg,

Munich, and Barcelona, and the account is rounded off by an informative introduction to some general characteristics of urbanization in the nineteenth century: theatres, boulevards and stately homes, new means of transport and communication, street-lighting – on the other hand, dirt, slums, industrial restlessness, and new diseases. All this and much more contributed to a highly ambivalent image of the modern city on the part of admirers and critics alike. In this process Manchester played a crucial role in Europe, so that it is very plausible that the author puts it first. The book is part of a successful Fischer Verlag series, 'Europa entdecken', which explores Europe from various perspectives. The series deals, amongst other things, with intellectuals, political movements, and the entertainment culture. Günther Lottes' *Stadtwelten. Urbane Lebensformen in der Frühen Neuzeit* (1999) would provide an interesting parallel for the early modern period.

Benedikt Stuchtey

[68] MICHAEL TOYKA-SEID, *Gesundheit und Krankheit in der Stadt: Zur Entwicklung des Gesundheitswesens in Durham City 1831-1914*, Publications of the German Historical Institute London, 38 (Göttingen: Vandenhoeck & Ruprecht, 1996), 371 pp. DM 106.00

The struggle against, and attitudes towards disease are key components in the social history of Victorian England. Toyka-Seid's book, describing and analysing the position in Durham City 1831 to 1914, is a most useful contribution. The author emphasizes that the debate about public health in the city was conducted by groups whose nature and composition varied from time to time. In this shifting and progressing debate party and faction politics played a relatively small part. The urge to improve public health was an issue above and beyond party politics. He also lays stress on the extent to which reforming initiatives in Durham had substantial working-class support. A case in point is the establishment and maintenance of the Durham County Hospital. This and other initiatives in the field of public health led to a significant decrease in mortality rates in Durham during the second half of the nineteenth century. The precise allocation of responsibility for such improvement amongst a range of reforms is, the author emphasizes, essentially impossible.

Bärbel Brodt

[69] MICHAEL HENKER *et al.* (eds), *Ein Herzogtum und viele Kronen: Coburg in Bayern und Europa. Katalog zur Landesausstellung 1997 des Hauses der Bayerischen Geschichte und der Kunstsammlungen der Veste Coburg in Zusammenarbeit mit der Stiftung der Herzog von Sachsen-Coburg und Gotha'schen Familie und der Stadt Coburg. Veste Coburg und Schloß Callenberg, 3. Juni bis 28. September 1997*, Veröffentlichungen zur bayerischen Kultur und Geschichte, 36/97 (Regensburg: Pustet, 1997), 385 pp. DM 58.00

The Duchy of Saxe-Coburg and Gotha was a small state in Thuringia. By an extraordinarily fortunate series of marriages in the nineteenth century, the ruling family ended up related to practically every other European royal family, one of the most important such alliances being, of course, Prince Albert's marriage to Queen Victoria. In 1920, the southern part of the Duchy became part of Bavaria, and its history was the topic of the 1997 Bavarian *Landesausstellung*, which is documented in this catalogue. The exhibition was divided into two parts. One, shown in the Veste Coburg, covered the history of Coburg from the Reformation to the twentieth century, the marriage politics of its ruling house, and the Coburg contribution to the Great Exhibition of 1851 in London. The second part, put on display in the recently restored Schloß Callenberg, was devoted to the activities of the ducal court and its relatives in the nineteenth century, with great emphasis on Albert and Victoria: neo-Gothic buildings and interior design, 'princely living', travels and hunting, feasts, and 'noble dilettanti'. The volume of essays accompanying the catalogue **[153]** is already out of print.

Andreas Fahrmeir

[70] WILFRIED ROGASCH (ed.), *Victoria & Albert. Vicky & the Kaiser: Ein Kapitel deutsch-englischer Familiengeschichte* (Ostfildern-Ruit: Hatje, 1997), 310 pp. DM 88.00

This is the beautifully produced catalogue of an exhibition at the German Historical Museum Berlin devoted to Anglo-German royal family relations between 1837 and 1914. The picture-story starts with the first year of Queen Victoria's reign and ends with the total estrangement between the two countries before the outbreak of war. This also incorporates many years of attempted bridge-building between island

and Continent, as well as many years of tragic misconception and false perceptions. The catalogue is richly illustrated by paintings, water-colours, contemporary photographs, crown jewels, art and crafts. Victoria was the grandmother of Germany's last Emperor, her eldest daughter Vicky, the Princess Royal, was his mother, and the later kings Edward VII and George V were his uncle and cousin respectively. As has often been said, William II was raised as 'half an Englishman'. It was Edward in particular whom William held responsible for the breakdown in Anglo-German relations while he, from the perspective of a modern *Kaiserreich*, did not really understand the role which the monarchy in Britain had been playing for centuries. When Victoria made her grandson an admiral of the fleet, she gave him a honorary title, but this certainly did not mean what he thought: military respon-sibility in Britain. The Kaiser's enthusiasm for naval armament, which caused the arms race with Britain, is one of the symbols of his ambiva-lent relationship with his mother's homeland. Almost two-thirds of the book is devoted to scholarly studies about, to list but a few, royal individuals, the court, Albert and the World Exhibition of 1851 [405], and the function of the monarchy in Britain [370]. Most noteworthy is John Röhl's essay on William's relations with England [453]. The one disadvantage of the catalogue is that, as a reflection of the exhibition, it is too Prussia-orientated and does not take into account the fact that Queen Victoria had several German sons-in-law besides Frederick III (six of her nine children were married to German aristocrats). One of its main merits, however, is that it documents both sides of the royal coin – high politics as well as private fate.

Benedikt Stuchtey

[71] CHARLOTTE PANGELS, *Dr. Becker in geheimer Mission. An Queen Victorias Hof. Die Briefe des Prinzenerziehers und Bibliothekars Dr. Ernst Becker aus seiner Zeit in England von 1850 bis 1861* (Hamburg: Jahn & Ernst, 1996), 373 pp. DM 48.80

In this popular account Pangels seeks to illustrate every-day life at the courts of Queen Victoria. In so doing, she combines contemporary sources, mainly letters and diary entries, with her own narrative. The book is primarily concerned with the chemist Dr Ernst Becker who, from 1850 to 1861, was employed by Queen Victoria at the suggestion of her trusted advisor, Baron Christian Friedrich von Stockmar, as a librarian and also as tutor to her two eldest sons, Albert Edward and Alfred. Becker's letters to his family in Germany have been edited by Pangels and these present the reader with Becker's view of his life, his position, and indeed his assumed importance. The book's dramatic main title derives from Becker's role in trying to control the often ill-balanced temperament of the heir to Victoria's throne. During his childhood Prince Edward suffered from temperamental rages and fits, and Becker, who claimed some understanding of phrenology, pointed out to his family that this 'expertise' aptly qualified him to look after the Prince. Nobody, however, was to know about Edward's condition; Becker's mission was a 'secret' one. Despite this claim, Becker's main duty was looking after Prince Albert's library. He was just one of numerous lesser employees at Court, to some extent drawn into the inner circle thanks to his friendship with Stockmar. The author also includes other contemporary texts, ranging from a letter by Richard Wagner to his wife in which he describes his visit to England in 1855 and his own observations on the Queen's figure, to letters by Helmuth von Moltke, and Victoria's own diary. The book is well illustrated and an index is provided.

Bärbel Brodt

[72] BENEDIKT STUCHTEY, *W. E. H. Lecky (1838-1903). Historisches Denken und politisches Urteilen eines anglo-irischen Gelehrten*, Publications of the German Historical Institute London, 41 (Göttingen: Vandenhoeck & Ruprecht, 1997), 385 pp. DM 112.00

William Edward Hartpole Lecky was one of the most influential and popular Victorian historians and essayists, but is almost completely ignored in modern studies of British historiography. He was the author of four major historical works – *The Leaders of Public Opinion in Ireland* (1861, [2]1871, [3]1903), *History of the Rise and Influence of the Spirit of Rationalism in Europe* (1865), *History of European Morals from Augustus to Charlemagne* (1869), and *History of England in the Eighteenth Century* (1878-90), which, contrary to what its title suggests, deals extensively with the history of Ireland. The first two parts of Stuchtey's study, the revised version of a Freiburg PhD thesis supervised by Ernst Schulin, consist of a detailed analysis of Lecky's historical writings and their reception by the English-speaking public. At first greatly influenced by H. T. Buckle's notion that history was subject to scientific laws which could be discovered by historical research, Lecky moved on to a far more sceptical position stressing individuals' freedom of action and the complexities of historical phenomena, first made explicit in his histories of general historical tendencies.

His *History of England* was more closely connected to political questions than his earlier writings from the outset. Its great emphasis on Irish history as an integral part of the history of the British Isles and its detailed study of the sources at once set it apart from other works and immediately made it the best available source for politicians interested in the subject. W. E. Gladstone was one of those who made extensive use of it. Lecky's work was also intended as a detailed refutation of the distinctly anti-Irish interpretation of Irish history presented by James Anthony Froude in his *The English in Ireland in the Eighteenth Century* (1872-74), and Stuchtey places it in the context of the general historiographical implications of a 'victims' history'.

As Lecky presented as fair and neutral an account of Irish history as possible, and as the space devoted to Irish history in the eight volumes of what was ostensibly a history of England seemed to indicate a political agenda, his writings were frequently understood to advocate the introduction of home rule for Ireland, all the more so as the relevance of the Irish parliament of 1782 for the home rule discussion was difficult to overlook.

However, the political sympathies of the Protestant absentee landowner Lecky lay elsewhere. Fiercely critical of Gladstone's home rule plans, Lecky found himself obliged to descend from the ivory tower of academic publication and to become a political essayist and politician. The last section of Stuchtey's book is therefore devoted to Lecky's career as a 'public moralist' and M.P. for Trinity College Dublin, a position which he occupied from 1895 to 1902. Even though this phase of Lecky's life produced another major work, *Democracy and Liberty* (1896), a lengthy but not very well received conservative political tract, his position in parliament showed how difficult it was to reconcile independence of judgement and party politics. Lecky's position on Irish questions, which can perhaps best be described as that of an Irish Protestant nationalist unionist, was all but impossible to reconcile with that of any larger political group. Lecky's predicament is characteristic of Irish Protestants (the 'Protestant ascendancy') more generally, and Stuchtey's book is also intended as a contribution to the broader debate on the role of this group.

Future research on Lecky will not be able to pass Stuchtey's work by. Incidentally, it contains a complete list of Lecky's publications and speeches, as well as of his manuscript papers in libraries and repositories in Ireland, the United Kingdom, and the United States.

Andreas Fahrmeir

[73] JENS JÄGER, *Gesellschaft und Photographie. Formen und Funktionen der Photographie in England und Deutschland 1839-1860*, Sozialwissenschaftliche Studien, 35 (Opladen: Leske und Budrich, 1996), viii + 351 pp. DM 68.00

Jens Jäger presents us with an ambitious and comprehensive study of early photography in England and Germany. He has adopted a generous definition of the topic, which includes the social and educational background of photographers, the number and distribution of photographic studios, the social class of their customers, the content of photographs, and the uses to which the new technology was put. In his introduction, he quotes a comment on pictures produced by means of photography by Johann Gustav Droysen, who called them 'correct, but not true' (p. 2). Perhaps this suspicion of the new medium, which quickly gained major importance among those social groups able to afford it, explains why it has been neglected by historical scholarship for so long. Jäger suggests that it was mainly the comparatively high cost of early photography which prevented it from becoming even more popular. Photographic portraits quickly became a common feature of bourgeois or aristocratic homes. It was this association of photographs with the personal or private sphere which gave rise to doubts as to whether it would be proper to employ the same technique for creating, for instance, criminals records.

In addition to its broad range of topics concerning photography itself, Jäger's book is also a contribution to the steadily rising number of studies of the 'British' and 'German' paths to modernity. His main conclusion is that, allowing for the difference in living standards, which permitted photography to expand more quickly in England, photography was part of an international bourgeois culture which was used in similar ways for similar purposes in both countries. However, there were some subtle differences. Apparently, the discussion about the possible uses of photography covered a wider range of topics and was of broader appeal in England than in Germany, which may of course merely be a side-effect of the larger number of amateur enthusiasts. The main difference in content is the greater importance attached to landscape photography in England. In Germany, outdoor photos usually pictured buildings; in England, the emphasis was on photos of the countryside, supposedly as a means of making it accessible to the urban middle classes.

Andreas Fahrmeir

[74] PETER ALTER and RUDOLF MUHS (eds), *Exilanten und andere Deutsche in Fontanes London*, Stuttgarter Arbeiten zur Germanistik, 331 (Stuttgart: Hans Dieter Heinz / Akademischer Verlag Stuttgart, 1996), x + 491 pp. DM 54.00

Although in numerical terms they constituted only 0.5 per cent of the population of London, in the mid-nineteenth century the German emigrants – political refugees from the 1848-49 revolution and economic exiles – were the largest national minority in the British metropolis (apart from the Irish, a special case). This volume – a Festschrift for the 85th birthday of the Germanist, literary connoisseur, and doyenne of Fontane research Charlotte Jolles – brings this circle to life. It is not Fontane, the critical observer of contemporary events, or his years in England that take centre stage, but all those whom he met, or could have met, in London. These were mainly Germans of various sorts, rather than English people: poets, journalists, businessmen, teachers, governesses, diplomats. The circle of Germans in 'Fontane's London' was varied and diverse, and these characters are portrayed in a vivid and fascinating way in the individual contributions to the volume. The essays deal both with individual personalities, and with the problems they encountered as Germans in London. Issues such as job opportunities, survival strategies, choice of profession, problems of assimilation, intellectual activity, mixed marriages, and finally, perceptions of England, including a specifically female impression of London in the middle of the last century, are discussed in this book. Furthermore, it shows the extent to which the German colony contributed to the mutual understanding between the two peoples, and stimulated interest in German language, culture, and history amongst the English.

Sabine Freitag

[75] STEFAN NEUHAUS, *Freiheit, Ungleichheit, Selbstsucht? Fontane und Großbritannien*, Helicon: Beiträge zur deutschen Literatur, 19 (Frankfurt/M.: Lang, 1996), 444 pp. £44.00

Among the numerous Germans who came to England in the course of the nineteenth century, whether as emigrants or visitors or part-time residents, Theodor Fontane is certainly one of the most important and best known. Although a number of publications on Fontane and his relationship with England exist, Stefan Neuhaus has undertaken a further study on this inexhaustible topic by integrating literary investigations into the context of the intellectual history of Fontane's time. The author states that Fontane's descriptions of his travels should not be regarded as a mirror of his personal convictions and that many of his texts concerning England, including novels, are only a limited reflection of his private opinion. Consequently he differentiates strictly between author and person. Fontane's diaries and correspondence are analysed, and detailed studies are provided about the role played by England in novels such as *Cecile, Unwiederbringlich, Frau Jenny Treibel,* and *Stechlin*. Apart from Shakespeare it was predominantly Walter Scott's work which influenced Fontane and his perception of Britain. Neuhaus meticulously analyses Scott's impact and his picture of Scotland, and elaborates on how Fontane's admiration for this author developed. The result is a positive picture, an anglophile Fontane who regarded many aspects of Britain, whether social, political, or intellectual, as exemplary for his own country. The book is therefore a good companion to the very important collection of essays edited by Peter Alter and Rudolf Muhs, *Exilanten und andere Deutsche in Fontanes London* [74].

Benedikt Stuchtey

[76] SABINE SUNDERMANN, *Deutscher Nationalismus im englischen Exil: Zum sozialen und politischen Innenleben der deutschen Kolonie in London 1848-1871*, Publications of the German Historical Institute London, 42 (Paderborn: Schöningh, 1997), 281 pp. DM 78.00

This Berlin dissertation is a study of the political activities of German emigrants in London in the second half of the nineteenth century, based on the files of the Prussian political police and the newspapers and papers of the exiles. After a description of London's 'little Germany' as it evolved after 1849, including a brief overview of the legal situation of emigrants relative to their native and host country, employment opportunities or the lack thereof, charitable foundations and the emigrants' views of England and the English, the actual narrative sets in with a description of the 1859 Schiller festival. The first of the two central parts of the book covers the various German associations in London with a political edge, above all the London branch of the *Nationalverein* with its various offshoots, such as the German gymnasium and the German Legal Aid Association. The second deals in a systematic way with the organization of the German press in London and the emigrant community's responses to political crises: the Schleswig-Holstein affair and the attempt by Carl Blindt's stepson to assassinate Bismarck in 1866.

Andreas Fahrmeir

[77] KLAUS HILDEBRAND, *No Intervention. Die Pax Britannica und Preußen 1856/66-1969/70. Eine Untersuchung zur englischen Weltpolitik im 19. Jahrhundert* (Munich: Oldenbourg , 1997), 459 pp. DM 168.00

Klaus Hildebrand has only just completed a magisterial overview of German foreign policy between 1870 and 1945. Now he has returned to Britain's attitude towards Bismarck's Prussia on the eve of the Franco-Prussian War, which was to change the map of Europe and the international system in its wake. This topic had occupied the author since the early 1970s, long before a second German unification could be anticipated. Throughout the 1860s Britain was not averse to German unification. This is Hildebrand's main thesis. The ruling élite of statesmen and diplomats had no objections to a large market and a strong power in the midst of Europe keeping the balance between France and Russia. Moreover, in the 1860s Britain was much too preoccupied with its own domestic reforms to be in the mood for an interventionist foreign policy. No doubt the need to hold the Empire together was given priority over any European commitment. As a matter of fact, the ruling élite saw their country as the centre of a great maritime empire rather than as a primarily European power. Again and again Hildebrand makes the point that Britain's semi-detached attitude towards continental power shifts was no sign of weakness but proof of a cautious husbanding of resources. Nor did non-intervention amount to an abdication of responsibility to maintain peace at any price if the situation required. As in the case of the Belgian railway conflict with France, the Foreign Office did not shy away from a show of strength. Hildebrand dismisses the charge made by later historians that Britain should have intervened to prevent German unification. This was not perceived to be in Britain's interests. Britain was neither psychologically prepared, not militarily ready to go to war for the sake of preserving the existing order. It was felt that there was a greater chance of saving Europe from a major conflagration by not taking sides between France and Prussia.

Hildebrand stops short of analysing Britain's attitude during the Franco-Prussian War, which has been examined in detail by one of his research students (Thomas Schaarschmidt, *Außenpolitik und öffentliche Meinung in Großbritannien während des deutsch-französischen Krieges von 1870/71*, Fankfurt/M., Lang, 1997; cf. Ulrike Jordan (ed.), *Research on British History in the Federal Republic of Germany1989-1994*, London, German Historical Institute, 1995, no. 87). However, his lengthy conclusions are also a kind of epilogue in which developments after 1870 are briefly outlined. After all, public opinion in Britain did not take to the new German empire which had been forged on the battlefield. What was most worrying was the way in which German unification had come about, rather than the fact as such. From the British point of view peaceful change was always the more preferable and profitable option. The new German empire appeared to represent military despotism rather than the liberal ideas of the age. It had all the hallmarks of a potentially hegemonic power which could upset the balance of Europe. It took British statesmen and diplomats some time to grasp the fact that Bismarck was as interested as they were in maintaining the new *status quo*. More and more he was perceived as the man who could be relied upon to safeguard the peace, however odious his domestic policies might appear. The real question was whether those succeeding him would be able to restrain the ambitions of their countrymen.

Lothar Kettenacker

[78] GABRIELE METZLER, *"Großbritannien – Weltmacht in Europa"*. *Handelspolitik im Wandel des europäischen Staatensystems 1856 bis 1871* (Berlin: Akademie, 1997), 353 pp. DM 128.00

This dissertation presented to the University of Tübingen deals with Britain's influence on the changes which took place in the European system of states between the end of the Crimean War and the establishment of the German Kaiserreich, and asks what Britain's part in this process was. The author follows a current trend in research in that although studying foreign policy, she goes beyond bilateral relations and the political actions of diplomatic élites. She draws her methods from the repertoire of political economy. This means that her starting point is the individual who wants to maximize profits while also having an interest in keeping to a minimum the transaction costs involved in exchanging information, negotiating, exerting influence, and ultimately coming to a contractual agreement (cost-benefit ratio). The work is also indebted to the concept of bounded rationality, a notion which historians must repeatedly take into account. This states that rational action is never possible in an unadulterated form, but is always limited by unconscious abilities, habits, values, and available knowledge.

Thus well-equipped, the author asks whether it was precisely the outstanding significance of economic interests that allowed the gradual withering of the contractual duties of 1815 appear desirable to Britain. Thus the unification of Italy, and even more of Germany, may have suited Britain's concept of free trade. The thesis of this study is that after the Crimean War Britain, as the leading trading nation, began to supplement traditional diplomacy abroad with a trade policy that, although it began with purely commercial intentions, gradually came to have more and more political implications. For example, the inventor of the contract, Cobden, saw it as an instrument to secure peace in Europe. British trade policy, however, came up against its limits when most continental European states continued to use military force to solve their conflicts in the 1860s. And after the end of the American Civil War, British trade policy again turned more strongly towards its trans-Atlantic relations. Europe as a market, some of whose political relations were shifted to the level of economic exchange, became less attractive again, not least because almost all states went over to an increasingly exclusive policy of national autonomy. 'Change through trade' remained the strategy for a period of transition. The political economy approach succeeds in providing answers where traditional diplomatic history fails. Instead of taking recourse to an indeterminate and diffuse assumed British sympathy for liberal and constitutional states as the motive for its foreign policy engagements, it can be shown that Britain favoured these simply because they accorded more easily with the basic principles of free trade. It is easier to do business with constitutional states than with autocratic ones. And after all, Britain committed itself only where profits beckoned.

Yet this study also illustrates the interconnections between foreign and domestic policy. A prosperous state with growing foreign trade has an impact on economic and social structures, the domestic welfare of the country, and ultimately helps to stabilize social peace. In this context, the position of the Board of Trade is interesting. It increasingly began to rival the Foreign Office by taking over responsibilities in the country's foreign relations. The author's indication that within these two administrative authorities, the debate was conducted between the traditional, pre-industrial élites and the rising, economically successful middle classes is convincing. Although the methodology drawn from political economy appears at first to be mechanically applied, the author does not ascribe to it any exclusive explanatory powers. Precisely because British foreign policy had no clearly defined objectives let alone doctrines, the demonstration that economic factors had a concrete impact on British foreign policy is a contribution towards illuminating complex decision-making processes on foreign policy issues. This study also draws our attention to the fact that the complex network of relations between the economy and politics resulting from a whole bundle of specific interests was not always intended, or even completely perceived, by the actors involved. This book is an interesting and lively attempt to interpret British foreign policy from a new angle in relation to the changing European system of states.

Sabine Freitag

[79] HANS-HEINRICH JANSEN and URSULA LEHMKUHL (eds), *Großbritannien, das Empire und die Welt. Britische Außenpolitik zwischen "Größe" und "Selbstbehauptung", 1850-1990*, Veröffentlichungen Arbeitskreis Deutsche England-Forschung, 25 (Bochum: Brockmeyer, 1995), viii + 324 pp. DM 44.80

These contributions to the 1994 annual conference of the Arbeitskreis Deutsche England-Forschung look at British foreign policy between 1859 and 1990, paying particular attention to the mechanisms and strategies of British self-assertion. The structure of the volume follows the thematic emphases of the conference: the nineteenth century, the inter-war period, the aftermath of the Second World War, and party politics and international policy in the post-war period. In each essay the empirical approach is intended to encompass the 'how' and the 'why' of the British capacity for self-assertion. The volume brings together a number of interesting contributions.

During the first half of the nineteenth century Britain was cast in the role of an 'umpire' in Europe, largely because of the instability of domestic political conditions in most of the Continental European great powers. Starting from this point, it is possible to show that after 1848 Britain almost automatically developed this role into a claim to international leadership. Britain withdrew from the concert of Europe in pursuit of its own interests. Between 1856 and 1871, it consolidated this claim to leadership, even though it was involved in crises and conflicts all over the world. It maintained its international position less by diplomatic or military means than by expanding its trade policy, which was followed by the dissemination of political and ideological values (for example, a sense of mission). British foreign policy, motivated by economic factors, established a system of 'informal rule' on the basis of trade. Signs of crisis did not appear until the 1920s, caused by growing self-confidence in the British colonies, where British values had been successfully internalized, and by the fact that these manifestations of British foreign policy had become less socially acceptable.

In contrast to the nineteenth-century wars in which Britain had been involved, neither the First nor the Second World War resulted in territorial or economic gains. Britain had to manage its economic and financial resources ever more carefully, as it needed them for its own reconstruction, among other things. It therefore did not take the opportunity to help shape the world outside British territory, for example, by granting loans. After the Second World War in particular, Britain's position as a great power was no longer justified by its financial, economic, or military resources. It had to find new ways and means of asserting itself in an international context. Its superiority gone, Britain was forced to take an active part in international affairs in order to counter a deeply felt threat to its position in the world. In an attempt to achieve equality of rank with the USA and the Soviet Union, Britain assumed the role of a mediator. Negotiating power grew out of this mediating role, with the result that after 1945 Britain secured the right to have a say on the fundamental issues of international politics. Another factor was that increased institutional co-operation had changed the meaning of the word 'power', which no longer referred primarily to military superiority. Domestic policy, too, made an active foreign policy necessary because influence in international policy was intended not least to secure national interests. In this way Britain was largely able to compensate for the loss of economic and political power. At the same time, keeping symbols of British power intact (for example, the Empire/Commonwealth as a system of imperial currency and trade), and the creation of new, prestigious symbols (for example, its own nuclear force) played an important part in obscuring Britain's loss of significance.

Sabine Freitag

[80] IMMO SIEVERS, *AutoCars. Die Beziehungen der englischen und der deutschen Automobilindustrie vor dem ersten Weltkrieg*, Europäische Hochschulschriften, III/640 (Frankfurt/M.: Lang, 1995), 459 pp. £46.00

This 1993 Berlin dissertation is the first comprehensive, comparative study of the British and German car industries before the First World War. In two separate accounts the author presents various phases of the German and British car industries between 1861/63 and 1914, and their relations with each other. Sievers modifies the widely held view that the British car industry was mainly influenced by French technology. Especially at the beginning, the German car industry was the motor for developments in Britain. Not until 1914 did France become the undisputed leader of the European car industry, and did Britain supersede Germany in know-how and production numbers. In the comparative third part of the volume Sievers addresses the question of innovation and technology transfer which he analyses with reference to 'master patents', the role of individuals such as Frederick Simmons, the emergence of multinational firms, and the flow of information. His detailed analysis and well chosen quotations, the reproduction of drawings, photographs, and documents throughout the text, and an extensive appendix including letters patent make this book not only an important contribution to the history of technology but also an interesting read for the general reader.

Dagmar Freist

[81] JOHN BREUILLY, GOTTFRIED NIEDHART, and ANTHONY TAYLOR (eds), *The Era of the Reform League. English Labour and Radical Politics 1857-1872. Documents selected by Gustav Mayer*, Mannheimer Historische Forschungen, 8 (Mannheim: Palatium Verlag, 1995), xii + 369 pp. DM 98.00

This critical edition is the product of Anglo-German co-operation. It brings together documents about the radical and labour movement in England which the Berlin historian Gustav Mayer collected after his emigration to England in 1937. Before he left Germany, Mayer, a liberal Jewish historian, had already published numerous works on the German labour movement and had written a two-volume biography of Friedrich Engels. Although he lived as a private scholar in London, in 1937 Mayer started collecting the documents assembled in this edition in his capacity as an Associate Member of the International Institute of Social History in Amsterdam. They cast light on the period from the dissolution of the Chartist movement to the rise of the Labour Party.

Unlike Mayer, many historians believe that the period from 1857 to 1872 witnessed exclusively a reaction to the extended mass political agitation of the Chartist movement, and was largely marked by political apathy. Improvements in living conditions took the wind out of the movement's sails, and under the leadership of the moderate trade unionists, people distanced themselves from the radical behaviour of the Chartists. Eventually, they argue, the movement became irrelevant. Mayer, by contrast, investigates to what extent attempts were made from the 1850s to the 1870s to pick up the ideas of the 1830s and 1840s, to preserve them, and finally to bring them into the 1870s. The contrast with Germany, where the labour movement's development went in the opposite direction, motivated him to ask about continuity in England. Although Ernest Jones, leading advocate of Chartist socialism after 1850, did not, like Ferdinand Lassalle, succeed in maintaining a movement independent of middle-class Liberalism or the Conservatives, Chartism was not simply absorbed by the Liberal reform movements. The sources collected here make this clear. They illustrate how much working men influenced the reform debate of the 1860s, and demonstrate that trade unionists and reform leaders became an accepted part of the political culture of the 1860s.

This edition uses just one quarter of the material collected by Mayer, for which it provides notes and commentaries. Each of the volume's five chapters is preceded by an introduction, written by the three editors, in which they give more detail about the specific period covered by the chapter, and indicate continuities in the context where the material has gaps as the result of Mayer's limited access to documents at the time. The second chapter goes beyond the purely domestic British context. It presents documents which reveal British radicalism's relationship with other countries, in particular, the reactions of the radical reform movement to specific events abroad: the American Civil War, Garibaldi and the Italian question, and finally, the Polish rising of 1863. The source material consists largely of official government papers from the Home Office, reports of assemblies, and speeches and articles from contemporary newspapers and journals. A chronology of events and brief biographies of members of the movement bring this meticulously edited volume to a close.

Sabine Freitag

[82] KNUT HANSEN, *Albrecht Graf von Bernstorff. Diplomat und Bankier zwischen Kaiserreich und Nationalsozialismus,* Europäische Hochschulschriften, III/684 (Frankfurt/M.: Lang, 1996), 338 pp. £36.00

This doctoral thesis is a biography of Albrecht Graf von Bernstorff, scion of a famous noble family from Mecklenburg which has brought forth important Prussian civil servants, ministers, and diplomats. While reconstructing the individual stations of Bernstorff's life – educated at Trinity College, Oxford, attaché in Vienna, second secretary, then ambassador at the German embassy in London, and, after early retirement in 1933, Berlin banker – Hansen attempts to discover what formative influences and experiences made Bernstorff such a decided opponent of the National Socialists. This is a detailed attempt to get close to Bernstorff's personality with the aid of existent source material.

As a type, Bernstorff must be counted among those who were neither dazzled by the false splendour of the Wilhelmine empire, nor willing to submit to the new, brown regime. His moral frame of reference was provided by his family and his aristocratic origins, and his political attitudes were strongly shaped by his stay in England. Bernstorff was not a theoretician. Influenced by British pragmatism, he believed in common sense and followed the politics of the middle way. Human rights, the rule of law, freedom of opinion, free competition, and tolerance formed the cornerstones of his political thinking. In foreign policy he supported Germany's integration into the West, and in particular, its links with Britain and the USA, while he had his doubts about France. He regarded Anglo-German understanding as the basic precondition for any permanent peace in Europe. He called for a democratic Germany to be trusted after the First World War in London, where this trust was slow to grow. Eventually, Bernstorff was to be horrified at how much faith Britain put in the Nazis.

The age of panegyrical historiography is past. This biography, too, knows nothing of a hero. But through Bernstorff the author wants to draw attention to the great diversity of German resistance, which was not limited to the circle of the plotters of 20 July. Bernstorff did not take part in active resistance in the sense of trying to overthrow the regime. Yet his passive resistance ranged from the informal exchange of information in London to private assistance for those persecuted by the regime.

Ultimately, the murder of Albrecht von Bernstorff by the Nazis is one more horrifying example of the far reaching and cruel consequences that private denunciations can have in states not ruled by law.

Sabine Freitag

[83] JOST HINDERSMANN, *Der britische Spionageroman. Vom Imperialismus bis zum Ende des Kalten Krieges* (Darmstadt: Wissenschaftliche Buchgesellschaft, 1995), 250 pp. DM 45.00

Without doubt, the spy novel is one of the most popular literary genres in the English-speaking world, and, like the detective novel, largely associated with British authors. From the historian's point of view one important characteristic of both genres is that they can both have a very wide appeal (sometimes selling tens or even hundreds of thousands of copies), and also appeal to the highly educated and the intellectual in a way in which most categories of popular literature do not. Hindersmann does not attempt to question why this is the case; his task is to analyse some one hundred and fifty novels in their historical context. For him, spy novels are a reflection of contemporary history, and he argues that breaks in historical continuity are mirrored by breaks in the history of the spy novel, resulting in changes in the personification of evil. However, according to Hindersmann the relationship between contemporary history and spy novels is not a one-way street – spy novels often anticipate future historical events, like the fall of the Berlin Wall, or, indeed, the fairly recent coup in Moscow. Hindersmann also shows that the spy novel, originally a means of propaganda after the Second World War, can also become a vehicle for social criticism.

Bärbel Brodt

[84] DETLEF KLUSAK, *In Darkest England and the Way Out. Untersuchungen zum Beitrag der Heilsarmee zur englischen Armutsdiskussion 1880-1914*, Edition Wissenschaft, Reihe Geschichte, 33 (Marburg: Tectum, 1997), 4 microfiches, DM 88.00

With the advent of the Internet, one might have hoped that the most reader-unfriendly form of publishing, microfiches and microfilms, was on the way out. The reason why this is not the case is made clear in the publisher's information on microfiche one: microforms satisfy the publication requirement for German Ph.D. theses (the Internet does not), and they are much cheaper for the author than actual readable books, which generally require a high subsidy – although the purchaser does not appear to benefit from the lower production costs.

This 1997 Munich thesis is a study of William Booth's *In Darkest England and the Way Out* and of the Salvation Army's plans for moral reform of the poor. The main part of Klusak's work is an analysis of Booth's book, its contemporary reception, and its context. In particular, he contrasts William Booth's emotional approach with the more empirical investigation of social problems in Charles Booth's *Life and Labour of the London Poor*. The discussion of the Salvation Army's attempts to put its plans into practice by founding a model farm and setting up a model colony in a dominion as well as by encouraging emigration generally is comparatively brief. Klusak concludes that even though the Salvation Army may have been the only organization to attempt to work with the poorer sections of the British population, it ultimately failed to achieve any of its aims. The project of a colony overseas failed because of lack of funds, whereas assisted emigration schemes ended up benefiting groups other than those originally intended. Least surprisingly, its attempts to achieve moral reform turned out to have only short-term effects.

Andreas Fahrmeir

[85] ULRIKE JORDAN and WOLFRAM KAISER (eds), *Political Reform in Britain 1886-1996. Themes, Ideas, Policies*, Veröffentlichungen Arbeitskreis Deutsche England-Forschung, 37 (Bochum: Brockmeyer, 1997), 265 pp. DM 44.80

The German Association for the Study of British History and Politics (ADEF) organizes annual conferences on certain topics of mutual interest to which both German and British academics make their contribution. The proceedings are published in the Association's own publication series, edited by Gustav Schmidt: in this case the papers (in English) given at the 1996 conference on the general theme of reform movements in Britain in the course of the last century. Basically this book deals with three issues which, apart from the inter-war period, have occupied British politics up to the present day: first, the fate of the unelected institutions, that is, the House of Lords and the monarchy in the age of democratization, second, the emancipation of women, and finally, the debate on territorial reform and devolution of power. The three sections are preceded by two papers, one on the never-ending question of the nature of the British unwritten constitution, the other on party politics, especially the challenge posed by proportional representation. What worries Peter Caterall, Director of the Institute of Contemporary British History, is that the restraining power of parliament not longer seems to be guaranteed, and that new constitutional safeguards appear to be called for [496]. However, constitional issues such as devolution, Europe etc. are likely to be tackled piecemeal as in the past. When Wolfram Kaiser refers to 'radicalism' it is the Liberal Party and its political agenda which he has in mind. For

Andew Adonis the survival of the House of Lords is more astonishing than that of the Crown, the linchpin of the whole fabric of British politics and society [350]. He argues convincingly that it was the very weakness of the Lords that ensured their survival. Of the three papers on 'Women in Society and Politics', all by German feminist or gender historians, the one by Angela Schwarz is the most outstanding, dealing with stereotypes of femininity in late Victorian and Edwardian Britain [457]. While the other two contributions survey the increasing volume of modern, mainly English and American, literature on feminism, Schwarz examines original source material and makes the interesting observation that stereotypes about women's subordinate role were primarily based on cultural values and social norms, only to be subsequently reinforced and made more pernicious by Darwinian theories and the language of science. The cause of women's emancipation is always best served, as in this case, by exposing incriminating evidence rather than by mere propaganda. In terms of present-day politics the last section on 'Nationality Conflicts and Territorial Government' is no doubt the most relevant part of the book. Elfie Rembold surveys the debate on federalism before 1914, calling her essay 'Home Rule All Round', that is, Ireland, Scotland, and Wales [449]. One of the chief stumbling-blocks was the requirement for a written constitution, which was anathema to the ruling élite. This is also borne out by the following article on Scottish devolution [555]. Any form of devolution is perceived as a diminution of parliament, which is at the apex of the British consitutional system. James Mitchell admits that hitherto Britain has been regarded as a unitary state. However, he argues in favour of an alternative 'conceptual lens', that of Britain as a union state. While Scotland's distinct status has always been acknowledged, the position of the English regions appears to be the main impediment to any new constitutional arrangement. The Northern Ireland question cannot be conceived, according to Brian Girvin in the concluding article, as part of the debate on unitary versus union state [508]. It is clearly *sui generis* in as much as reform by institutional change has had little impact on its polarized society. The conflict cannot be solved by the traditional method of incremental reform. Only radical solutions, he argues, might achieve a lasting settlement of this thorny issue.

Lothar Kettenacker

[86] ADOLF M. BIRKE and MAGNUS BRECHTKEN (eds), *Politikverdrossenheit. Der Parteienstaat in der historischen und gegenwärtigen Diskussion. Ein deutsch-britischer Vergleich/Disillusioned with Politics. Party Government in the Past and Present Discussion. An Anglo-German Comparison*, Prince Albert Studies, 12 (Munich: Saur, 1995), 136 pp. DM 78.00

This volume contains the papers given at the thirteenth conference of the Prince Albert Society in 1994 in Schloß Rosenau. They deal with the topic of disillusionment with politics and growing scepticism about political parties. The focus is not so much on organizational aspects, but rather on the role of parties in the political culture of each particular era, and the crises of legimacy they went through, and are still going through, as a result of structural changes in society. The historical comparison shows that dissatisfaction with political parties is nothing new, either in Britain or Germany. One of the criticisms expressed most frequently was that the parties were not seeking the 'general good' in a way that transcended party loyalty, but took account only of particular interests and those of selective groups. Unlike today, it was not so much corruption scandals within political parties that damaged their reputation, but the realities of politics. These were largely beyond the parties' control, but did much to influence voters' attitudes. As usual, the present-day relevance of the conference theme is presented in a concluding podium discussion. Its results are summarized by Magnus Brechtken.

Sabine Freitag

[87] ADOLF M. BIRKE and MAGNUS BRECHTKEN (eds), *Kommunale Selbstverwaltung/Local Self-Government. Geschichte und Gegenwart im deutsch-britischen Vergleich*, Prince Albert Studies, 13 (Munich: Saur, 1996), 164 pp. DM 78.00

This volume contains the papers given at the fourteenth conference of the Prince Albert Society in 1995 in Coburg. The main theme is a comparison of the history and development of local self-government in Britain and Germany from the nineteenth century to the present. All the essays show that local self-government is constantly determined by its relationship with the central legislator and this was crucial in dividing up areas of responsibility. For example, the local communities may have been on the verge of collapse during the Weimar Republic because of a redistribution of finances and over-burdening, but under the totalitarian regime of the NSDAP they lost whatever independence they might have had. After the Second World War and unconditional surrender there was a lasting reform and restructuring of local self-government, implemented by the British occupying power, which contributed considerably to the process of democratization. At the same time, however, a trend towards centralization developed in Britain, perpetuated by the Labour governments which saw regulating for the whole country as a means of removing inequalities. The results of the podium discussion conclude the volume.

Sabine Freitag

[88] RUTH DROST-HÜTTL, *Die schottische Nationalbewegung zwischen 1886 und 1934. Nationalistische Ziele und Strategien im Wandel*, Veröffentlichungen Arbeitskreis Deutsche England-Forschung, 27 (Bochum: Brockmeyer, 1995), ii + 432 pp. DM 64.80

This comprehensive study of the Scottish nationalist movements between 1886 and 1934 was originally submitted as a PhD thesis to the University of Munich. On the basis of an impressive array of manuscript sources, as well as an extensive reading of nationalist publications, Drost-Hüttl offers a systematic analysis of the Scottish nationalist organizations, such as the first and second Scottish Home Rule Association, the Young Scots Society, the Scots National League, the National Party of Scotland, the Scottish Party, and the Scottish National Party. She describes their foundation, programmes, membership, activities and effects. She stresses the influence of the Irish model on the Scottish associations, but argues that their attempts to achieve a similar success were essentially doomed to failure, in part because plans for home rule were linked too closely to a general programme of imperial reform. From the late nineteenth century, advocates of Scottish home rule had proposed that the introduction of a Scottish parliament should go hand in hand with the transformation of Westminster into a central imperial parliament for the Dominions and the United Kingdom. By the 1930s, when the Dominions had achieved a large measure of independence, this plan had come to appear decidedly anachronistic. A concluding chapter outlines the development of the SNP and nationalist movements up to the present.

Andreas Fahrmeir

[89] CHRISTOPH CORNELIßEN, *Das "Innere Kabinett". Die höhere Beamtenschaft und der Aufbau des Wohlfahrtsstaates in Großbritannien 1893 bis 1919*, Historische Studien, 446 (Husum: Matthiesen Verlag, 1996), 420 pp. DM 118.00

The author of this Ph.D. thesis from Düsseldorf, published in a very renowned series, sets out to write a 'collective biography of the founding fathers of the British welfare state'. A sample are the higher echelons of the civil service, the Whitehall mandarins, in other words, who helped to launch and manage the system of social benefits, that is, above all, pensions, health, and unemployment insurance. Otto Hintze's more empirical approach rather than Max Weber's theoretical framework serves as a model. The introductory chapters deal with the creation and expansion of a modern bureaucracy (including useful statistical evidence) and with the institutional evolution of social services from the Department of Labour within the Board of Trade to the foundation of the Ministry of Health. After that the social background, the recruiting methods, and the social prestige of the administrative class are examined in detail, as are the formative influences provided by schools and universities and by the public discourse on social reform, including practical experiences in the East End of London (Toynbee Hall).

All this leads up to the main question: what was the impact of the Civil Service on the legislative process. All the major legislative initiatives before, during, and after the First World War are scrutinized with this question in mind. Two chapters are added, one on the international discourse on labour exchanges and the German example in particular, and one on two case studies regarding labour relations.

The result of this painstaking research based on a wide range of source material is not at all startling. A few hints must suffice. The top civil servants, often outsiders, were no 'secret dictators'. Democracy was never really endangered through manipulative bureaucrats. No 'official mind' existed or evolved which inspired or retarded legislation. The popular concept of 'socialism' was always qualified by terms such as 'limited' or 'practical'. Innovative ideas were developed by only a few of the leading spirits, with the bulk of the service following suit. Most of the service still clung to the traditions of political economy, relying more on self-help than on state intervention. These officials saw themselves as fair-minded umpires with a social conscience, above parties and vested interests.

Lothar Kettenacker

Twentieth Century

[90] CHRISTEL GADE, *Gleichgewichtspolitik oder Bündnispflege? Maximen britischer Außenpolitik (1909-1914)*, Publications of the German Historical Institute London, 40 (Göttingen: Vandenhoeck & Ruprecht, 1997), 247 pp. DM 78.00

Although it is a very British phenomenon and a crucial part of centuries of British history and political thinking, the term 'balance of power' has long been integrated into the language of theoretical and practical politics outside Britain as well. Christel Gade, in her Bonn Ph.D. thesis, does not follow the modern trend of using English expressions in German book-titles. Indeed, the question her book asks is neatly encapsulated in two German words – 'Gleichgewichtspolitik' and 'Bündnispflege': did British foreign policy, in the five years before the outbreak of the First World War, follow the maxim of balance of power, or did it pursue a policy of alliances? The author's answer is that officially (and in the language of political rhetoric) the concept of balancing the European powers served to legitimize political and diplomatic actions, but that in fact Britain had long-since embarked upon a policy of forming lasting alliances. The classical British principle of political non-intervention now had to be abandoned if Britain itself was not to become isolated. The worst scenarios for Britain were political isolation or a continental blockade. Alliances with Japan in 1902, France in 1904, and Russia in 1907, which emerged from negotiations on colonial issues, already indicated that the likelier the prospect of war became, the closer Britain was moving towards such commitments. So far historiography has generally accepted what politicians claimed at the time, namely that the mechanics of 'Pax Britannica' continued well into the twentieth century. In fact, as Gade convincingly demonstrates, this was not the case. The period of relative tranquility after the French Revolution was under threat, and thus also the stability of the empire, which is why alliances and ententes became more important than before. Although British politicians talked of a balance of European powers they produced a close web of alliances. In any case the traditional policy of balance of power was no longer an adequate guarantee of British security. The book is based on extensive archival research and also takes many printed sources such as memoirs and letters into account. It is a valuable contribution to research on the period leading up to the First World War.

Benedikt Stuchtey

[91] WOLFGANG KRUSE (ed.), *Eine Welt von Feinden. Der Große Krieg 1914-1918*, (Frankfurt/M.: Fischer Taschenbuch Verlag, 1997), 255 pp. DM 24.90

For a long time international research has focused on the Second World War at the expense of the First. In recent years efforts can be observed to restore the balance, since it has been recognized that in many ways the First World War was the more momentous event in the twentieth century: not only was it the first war affecting the whole population, but its historical consequences also had a world-shattering impact, not least because of their connection with the Second World War. This collection of essays, published in a popular German paperback edition, is a good testimony to this new historiographical evaluation. The aim of the contributors, except for one all German and fairly young, that is, not yet established, is to take a fresh look at the war, to acquaint the reader with recent research, and to present the First World War as an international phenomenon by no means confined to politicians and soldiers. The traditional aspects such as armaments, alliances and alignments, colonial rivalries, war aims and strategies are synthesized in one of seven chapters. There are other more interesting chapters on war and society – a whole chapter being devoted to the role of women – on public morale and soldiers' fighting spirit, on propaganda, and so forth. One of the most distinguishing features of the First, in comparison to the Second World War, was its cultural impact, with regard to both the intellectual mobilization and the outburst of artistic achievements. This chapter provides really new insight: it starts off by exploring the alleged popular enthusiasm for the war at its outbreak – the reaction was much more ambivalent – and ends with a discourse on the crisis of civilization brought about by the long-drawn-out war and its ethical implications. While conditions in Germany are in the foreground, the authors never lose sight of what happened in France and Britain at the same time. Russia is covered in a separate chapter on Socialism, Anti-War Movements, and Revolutions. At the end of the twentieth century it makes sense to get our perspective right and to be reminded that the points for the century's catastrophic history were set right at the beginning.

Lothar Kettenacker

[92] DAVID VON MAYENBURG, *Schule, Berufsschule, Arbeitsmark. Die englische Debatte um die Elementarschulreform (1914-1939)*, Münchener Studien zur neueren und neuesten Geschichte, 16 (Frankfurt/M.: Lang, 1996), 307 pp. £36.00

This study examines attempts to reform the elementary school system in England and Wales between 1914 and 1939. It is based on the records of the British Ministry of Education, and proposes to answer questions relating to the aims, success, and proponents of reform in this area. Overlapping concerns with general problems of the era under consideration, such as child labour, juvenile job losses, and the level of British industry, are taken into account as well. In particular, the debate about the economic viability of education strikes today's readers as of special ongoing relevance.

Ulrike Jordan

[93] BERND LEUPOLD, *"Weder anglophil noch anglophob". Großbritannien im politischen Denken Konrad Adenauers. Ein Beitrag zur Geschichte der deutsch-britischen Beziehungen*, Europäische Hochschulschriften, III/754 (Frankfurt/M.: Lang, 1997), 367 pp. £40.00

This revised version of a Freiburg dissertation is based on the premise that Konrad Adenauer personally controlled the foreign policy of West Germany 'to a degree unusual in western democracies' (p. 11). Therefore, his personal perceptions of other states were of exceptional importance. Adenauer's personal relationship with Great Britain is the subject of this study. This book is based on Adenauer's personal statements as well as his practical politics, beginning with his first intensive contact with British officials during the occupation of the Rhineland while he was mayor of Cologne after the First World War through to the end of his term of office as German chancellor. In line with Adenauer's statement that what he most admired about the British national character was 'English pragmatism' (p. 289), Leupold's study indicates that Adenauer's relationship with Britain was determined by changing political situations and was a function of his political interests. In contrast to Adenauer's attitude to France and the United States, which Leupold characterizes as emotional, he concludes that the first West German chancellor's perception of Britain remained deeply ambivalent, perhaps as a result of the enduring influence of stereotypes which were part of the standard educational fare of Wilhelmine Germany.

Andreas Fahrmeir

[94] MATTHIAS PETER, *John Maynard Keynes und die britische Deutschlandpolitik. Machtanspruch und ökonomische Realität im Zeitalter der Weltkriege 1919-1946*, Studien zur Zeitgeschichte, 51 (Munich: Oldenbourg, 1996), 343 pp. DM 88.00

This dissertation analyses the structural conditions and conceptual formulation of Britain's foreign and security policy *vis-à-vis* Germany and the influence of the national economist John Maynard Keynes on the British attitude. The emphasis is on the Second World War. The work closes a gap in the hitherto inadequately researched relationship between Keynes and Germany, which does not do justice to the significance that German policy actually had for his work.

The aim of the dissertation is to discover recurring motives amongst those Foreign Office officials involved in the decision-making process, and to look specifically at the significance of economic forces in foreign policy. As regards Keynes, who took part in the Versailles peace negotiations as a government official and, moreover, was an independent adviser to the British government, the key questions are as follows: to what extent do Keynes's ideas on policy towards Germany reflect the general process of transformation in the twentieth century? What lessons are learned for solving problems of security policy in the inter-war period and, in particular the period after 1945? Furthermore, how does Keynes's concept of stabilization relate to traditional

British notions of security? And what is the reaction of those decision-makers in the Foreign Office and the Cabinet committed to the primacy of foreign policy?

The insight Keynes drew from the crisis of liberalism and the classical national economy was that economic science should be geared towards contemporary structural change. He put forward the view that national economy must include social and political aspects of human behaviour. In other words, economic theory and historico-political practice are unified, under contemporary conditions of modernization, to form economic policy.

The question of Germany assumed a key position in Keynsian theory. Even during the Versailles peace negotiations he had come to the far-sighted conclusion that security *against* Germany could only be achieved in the form of security *with* Germany. During the discussion on economic security, part of British planning for Germany during the Second World War, Keynes therefore insisted that Britain needed a completely new approach to reparations. His concept of 'internal stabilization' was at odds with the Foreign Office for whom maintaining power was all-important, and security policy, as in the nineteenth century, was still a matter of power politics. Subsequently, Keynes's concepts of stabilization were constantly misrepresented. This was basically because the interaction between economy and security was not correctly identified. In other words, the question of how to deal with Germany's economy was seen purely as part of London's power-political calculations, not against the background of a contemporary situation that was funadamentally quite different.

Marita Baumgarten

[95] WOLFGANG GICK, *Die Entwicklung der Geldtheorie bei John Maynard Keynes*, Nomos Universitätsschriften, Wirtschaft, 23 (Baden-Baden: Nomos, 1995), 119 pp. DM 58.00

This is the shortened version of a doctoral thesis accepted by the Faculty of Social and Economic Science at the Leopold-Franz University in Innsbruck. It attempts to cast light on the genesis of monetary theory as developed by the British political economist John Maynard Keynes. The origins of this theory have remained a controversial subject to the present day. By adding to the history of dogma, the author hopes to contribute to the criticism and re-assessment of the exegesis of Keynes.

In contrast to the generally held view that monetary theory is merely an extension of the quantity theory of money, the author argues that Keynes's monetary theory had an independent existence. He attempts to demonstrate this by investigating the origins of monetary theory, clarifying the individual stages of its development, and identifying possible influences. Gick comes to the conclusion that the connection between Keynes and his teachers and contemporaries was much stronger than assumed by the schools which have grown up since Keynes. Alfred Marshall's methodology and mostly oral comments on monetary theory, for one, must have made a strong impression on Keynes. But it was only Knut Wicksell's approach to exchange economics that allowed Keynes to separate himself from the quantity theory of money. And not until he accepted a concept of interest was Keynes able to establish his own macro-economic monetary theory, which later came to fruition in his General Theory, a purely monetary theory of capital. Of equal significance, however, for the long development from monetary theory to the General Theory was the Stockholm school, which went back to Wicksell.

Sabine Freitag

[96] CONSTANZE BAUMGART, *Stresemann und England* (Cologne: Böhlau, 1996), 331 pp. DM 78.

Gustav Stresemann is one of the most controversial politicians of the Weimar Republic. Was he peaceable, democratic, pursuing a policy of *rapprochement*, precursor of European integration, or was he, behind this mask, an entrenched nationalist and Wilhelmine monarchist? Historical research has produced a differentiated picture of this Weimar politician and German Foreign Minister, which makes it increasingly difficult to categorize him definitively one way or the other. This book, a Cologne dissertation, now provides a further contribution to the image of this complex personality by focusing on Stresemann's concept of, and relationship with, England.

The book proceeds chronologically. It presents, firstly, a reconstruction of Stresemann's perception of England before he became an active politician. Before the First World War the young industrial lawyer and Reichstag deputy saw England as Germany's greatest economic competitor, its major opponent in world politics and thus as its arch enemy *par excellence*. He therefore considered that defeating England should be Germany's primary war aim. During the war Strese-mann's admiration for the capability of the English system of govern-ment, the strength, efficiency, and competence of this Western democ-racy, grew. In the author's opinion, this admiration contributed sig-nificantly to Stresemann's move towards parliamentarism in the spring of 1917. After the war, Stresemann's statements about England were totally unpolemical. This was due, in part, to his experience of Britain at the Versailles Peace Conferences where, in contrast to France, Brit-ain took an extremely moderate stance. Subsequently, Stresemann was influenced by the knowledge that Britain, as a trading and exporting nation, had a vested interest in keeping Germany's economy intact as an export market. Indeed, Germany's economic potential was the only instrument of power he had left. The intermediary role played by Brit-ain between Germany and France was of crucial importance to Stresemann since, as one of the Allies, Britain was in a better position than Germany to have a moderating influence on French demands. Thus, while pursuing its own interests, Britain also supported Ger-man ones. However, the close entente between England and France, never seriously called into question by the British, and always their top priority, set certain limits on their ability to support Germany.

In this book too much is made of Britain's role as 'honest broker'; it is portrayed as far too harmonious and selfless. The same applies to Stresemann's opportunities to influence British decisions and to his personal high esteem for the island state. The book underlines once again the politician striving for balance and *rapprochement*, seeking to reintegrate Germany into the international system. Baumgart believes that in the 1920s Stresemann was further than ever removed from be-ing a secretly aggressive politician whose aim was to put Germany into a position of world domination.

Sabine Freitag

[97] GABRIELA TEICHMANN, *Britischer und deutscher Wohnungsbau in den Zwischenkriegsjahren. Ein Vergleich*, Europäische Hochschul-schriften, III/740 (Frankfurt/M.: Lang, 1997), 296 pp. £36.00

After the First World War, Britain and Germany were confronted with a housing crisis. The situation in both countries had some similarities. The available buildings were overcrowded and many were in an un-satisfactory condition. At the same time, rising construction costs made the building of new dwellings unprofitable. In both countries, moreover, left-wing parties were the first to make solving the housing crisis part of their agenda.

This Hanover dissertation describes in some detail the measures taken by British and German governments. Whereas in Britain the state undertook to subsidize and organize the construction of new council houses and flats, and a substantial programme of slum clearance and resettlement was implemented, in Germany building societies were much more important. Nevertheless, British council housing proved to be less popular, and less accepted, than its German equivalent, the *sozialer Wohnungsbau*. Teichmann suggests that there were several reasons for this. Because of greater facility in obtaining mortgages, for British people council housing, which was constructed above all with an eye to keeping costs low, was more frequently merely a step on the way to home ownership. Moreover, in Germany there does not seem to have been much private competition to the *sozialer Wohnungsbau*, and the experience of living in flats was not as unusual for German families as for their British counterparts, who objected very much to being resettled in council blocks.

Andreas Fahrmeir

[98] HARTMUT WALRAVENS, *Asia Major (1921-1975). Eine deutschbritische Ostasienzeitschrift: Bibliographie und Register*, Orientalistik-Bibliographien, 2 (Wiesbaden: Harrassowitz, 1997), 166 pp. DM 86.00

Asia Major was a pioneering journal of East Asian studies published by Berlin scholars and a Leipzig publisher, Bruno Schindler. In 1935, the publisher was forced to emigrate to England, and publication ceased. An attempt at revival in Nazi Germany was made in 1944. In 1949-50, the first volume of a 'new series' appeared, once again published by Schindler. The new journal closed down in 1975 due to financial difficulties. Walravens's bibliography provides a short introduction to the history of the journal, a chronological list of articles, and an index of authors and subjects.

Andreas Fahrmeir

[99] BERND FECHNER, *Mission in der Industrie. Die Geschichte kirch-licher Industrie- und Sozialarbeit in Großbritannien*, Erfahrung und Theologie: Schriften zur praktischen Theologie, 25 (Frankfurt/M.: Lang, 1995), 266 pp. £31.00

This study investigates the role of church-based services in British industry from the inter-war period to the 1980s. Since the end of the Second World War, these services have been established in various West European countries. In the UK in particular, structures of industrial church councils, notably in the steel works of Sheffield and in the tertiary sector establishments of south London, came into existence. Based on this development, the Industrial Mission as pioneered in Britain advanced to the status of an export article, which came to influence the self-image of church work in many industrial areas of the world. Over the period under investigation, questions of social ethics and theology surface. These highlight problems of church modernization and are discussed broadly in this study.

Ulrike Jordan

[100] DETLEV CLEMENS, *Herr Hitler in Germany. Wahrnehmungen und Deutungen des Nationalsozialismus in Großbritannien 1920 bis 1939*, Publications of the German Historical Institute London, 39 (Göttingen: Vandenhoeck & Ruprecht, 1996), 468 pp. DM 128.00

This study looks at the British view of Hitler as it evolved from 1920 to the beginning of the Second World War, and thus contributes to the growing body of literature on that question (cf. Angela Schwarz, *Die Reise ins Dritte Reich*, 1993). Clemens's perspective, however, adds the crucial early phase from 1920 on to the period under consideration, thereby tracing the shift from minority opposition phenomenon to mass power politics. His study is predominantly based on Foreign Office records, which are characterized by highly comparative analyses of the First and Second World Wars. Consequently, Clemens explores the view of Germany after the First World War before addressing the evolution of the British view of Hitler and National Socialism. Here the book's title is slightly misleading in that it – laudably – focuses on the view of the National Socialist Party (NSDAP) as much as on Hitler's personality. The chronological steps are conventional (1920-22, 1923, 1924-30, 1930-33 and onwards); the findings well thought-out. Clemens argues that until 1939 National Socialism and its *Führer* remained a contradictory, difficult-to-grasp problem for its British observers. From 1920, the British regarded the NSDAP as a party on the anti-democratic right in Bavaria, and from 1922 saw it in relation to fascist Italy. In short, Hitler was regarded as 'the Bavarian Mussolini' (p. 439). This dimension of Italy as role model persisted in the British view until the mid-1930s. From 1923, when a 'Hitler coup' was envisaged, the British view of the Hitler movement and the NSDAP as a political force separate from the spectrum of anti-democratic parties deepened. However, the 1920s, when the British attempted a trust-based co-operation with the Weimar Republic, saw the development of a correspondingly more positive view of Germany. The events of the crucial years after 1930-31 only slowly led to an evaluation of the situation as a 'reverting to type' on the part of the Germans (p. 44), and the early years of the Nazi dictatorship produced a contradictory mixture of alarming observations and the persistence of 'wait and see' tactics. The author shys away from arguing explicitly that there was an official British fabrication of a view of Hitler and the NSDAP which ignored vital knowledge and its consequences. However, he succeeds in reconstructing the multi-layered, conflicting levels of analysis as they were presented to Hitler's contemporaries in Britain.

Ulrike Jordan

[101] DETLEF WÄCHTER, *Von Stresemann bis Hitler. Deutschland 1928 bis 1933 im Spiegel der Berichte des englischen Botschafters Sir Horace Rumbold*, Europäische Hochschulschriften, III/736 (Frankfurt/M.: Lang, 1997), 287 pp. £34.00

This Ph.D. thesis supervised by Klaus Hildebrand at the University of Bonn investigates conditions in the brief but dramatic period from 1928 to 1933 on the basis of the reports sent to the Foreign Office by the British ambassador Sir Horace Rumbold (1869-1941). Rumbold, who had been in the diplomatic service for decades, took up his last active post in Berlin in 1928. He was thus a direct witness of the increasingly troubled and unstable conditions in Germany, which deteriorated shortly thereafter partly in response to the impact of the world-wide recession, up to Hitler's seizure of power. On the political agenda were getting troops out of the Rhineland, revision of reparations payments, a German-Austrian customs union, and international disarmament. Against this background Rumbold's reports hold up a mirror to Anglo-German relations in the period under investigation.

This volume asks questions which must always be raised in connection with the diplomatic service. Could diplomats on the spot have any influence at all on Foreign Office policy? What images of Germany did diplomats bring with them, and how much was revised or confirmed by daily experience? How much depended on the personal talents of individual diplomats – their ability to make contacts and obtain information, their analytical capacity, gift for observation, negotiating skills, and feel for political developments?

Detlef Wächter shows that astonishingly, the British government, pursuing its own political imperatives and interests, only in a few cases acted on the advice of its ambassador in Berlin, despite the fact that Rumbold's reports were based on information from well-informed sources – the political élite in the German government, individual Nazi Party members, the diplomatic corps of other countries, the *Reichswehr*, and the Prussian government. Thus Rumbold advised his government that it was absolutely necessary to give the government of the Centre Party Chancellor, Henrich Brüning, immediate support. Rumbold believed that Germany's domestic stability largely depended on Brüning's policies, which were based on the rule of law. Rumbold also came to advocate and support Germany's demands for revision, but his appeal in London was unsuccessful.

Wächter's attempt to leave Rumbold's reports in their contemporary framework, and not to judge them with the benefit of hindsight, works well. The case of Rumbold illustrates how difficult it was even for an experienced top diplomat to assess the contemporary political situation. While he rejected the rise of the National Socialist Party, not least for aesthetic reasons, and criticized the coarse behaviour of its functionaries, he was nevertheless impressed by its efficiency. British supporters of the policy of appeasement, however, could feel vindicated by Rumbold's reports, as he was convinced that Germany would long be busy putting its own house in order, and would therefore avoid conflict abroad.

Sabine Freitag

[102] FRANK OTTO, *Die Keynesianische Revolution in Großbritannien (1929-1948). Zur Entwicklung der Finanzpolitik im Spannungsfeld von wirtschaftswissenschaftlicher Herausforderung, politischem Reformwillen und institutioneller Beharrungskraft* (Berlin: Duncker & Humblot, 1996), 335 pp. DM 98.00

This doctoral thesis in political economy describes and analyses a debate about British economic and financial policy, conducted over twenty years between the Treasury on the one side, and a group of liberal reformers around the political economist John Maynard Keynes on the other. The Treasury was orientated by the traditional principles of nineteenth-century cameralism, and followed orthodox financial policy. It insisted on the balanced budget rule and tried to prevent a deficit in public finances. The liberal reformers, by contrast, called for the state to pursue deficit spending in order to lift the economy out of recession by stimulating overall demand and reducing unemployment. From 1929, the Treasury increasingly felt compelled to defend its policies publicly against the alliance of reformers. An analysis of the Treasury view is one of the focal points of this study. Beyond this, it shows that the preconditions and profound changes required for a paradigm shift in favour of the Keynesian school were not created until after the Second World War. At the same time, however, it emphasizes a connection with the financial and economic crisis faced by Britain during the 1970s, whose origins, according to the author, can be traced back to the late 1940s. This is a well structured study, written in clear and accessible language. It is well worth reading.

Sabine Freitag

[103] MARKUS HUTTNER, *Britische Presse und nationalsozialistischer Kirchenkampf. Eine Untersuchung der "Times" und des "Manchester Guardian" von 1930-1939*, Veröffentlichungen der Kommission für Zeitgeschichte, Reihe B, 67 (Paderborn: Schöningh, 1995), 814 pp. DM 108.00

This voluminous study concentrates, more narrowly than its title might suggest, on the role of the British press in reporting and commenting on the German Catholic Church's relations with the National Socialist state. The chosen newspapers are *The Times* and the *Manchester Guardian*. These are investigated for the period 1930 to 1939, which covers the critical presidential years of the late Weimar Republic and the ascendency and consolidation of Nazi power up to the outbreak of war in September 1939. On more than 800 pages, this study provides a detailed account of the historical, political, and cultural framework of reporting on this essential question of German domestic policy. In addition, it contains further material on the history of the newspapers in question. Following both a quantitative and a textual analysis of the evaluation of church-state relations as mirrored in the foreign press, the author arrives at the conclusion that the liberal *Manchester Guardian* stands out in the entire spectrum of foreign newspapers in attempting to base its analysis of the National Socialist state on an evaluation of the church struggle in Germany. In this view, the phenomenon of anti-religious and anti-church structures in NS ideology dominates the struggle of the German churches, whereas *The Times* saw the concrete anti-church measures as the expression of an extremist wing in the Nazi hierarchy. The London-based paper followed an interpretation that stressed the quasi-religious character of ideology, which came to serve as a substitute for church and Christian religion. All in all, this well-researched book illuminates an important question, albeit a considerably smaller one than it postulates.

Ulrike Jordan

[104] CHARMIAN BRINSON, *The Strange Case of Dora Fabian and Mathilde Wurm. A Study of German Political Exiles in London During the 1930s*, Publications of the Institute of Germanic Studies, University of London, 67 (Frankfurt/M.: Lang, 1997), 418 pp. £38.00

This study by Charmian Brinson, specialist in exile studies, narrates an important, if almost forgotten episode in the history of political refugees from Nazi Germany in Britain. Readers should not be mistaken: the slightly mystifying main title belies the thorough scholarship and background knowledge contained in this book. Brinson not only reconstructs the biography and last weeks in the life of the two socialist emigré women Dora Fabian and Mahilde Wurm, who were found dead in their London flat in April 1935, but gives an insight into the fabric of the exile community in London in the first years of emigration. Both women were important actors on the socialist political scene in Germany and in exile, and their still unexplained end opens up important issues relating to the network of emigrés, surrounded by the increasingly Nazified German community and Embassy, and the English public. Threats to the emigrés' lives and activities ranged from the actions of Nazi spies such as Hans Wesemann to the ambivalent attitude of English individuals and institutions, for example, the Labour Party. This is a period which so far has been relatively little explored by those working on political exile, since they have tended to look at countries that developed a livelier and more numerous community of mostly left-wing emigrés (France, Czechoslovakia, etc.) This book, which reads very well, is thus a welcome addition to our insight into German political exile.

Ulrike Jordan

[105] MARCO BERTOLASO, *Die erste Runde im Kampf gegen Hitler? Frankreich, Großbritannien und die österreichische Frage 1933/34. Einer [sic!] Untersuchung der Außenpolitik der Westmächte in den ersten 18 Monaten des "Dritten Reiches" auf der Grundlage diplomatischer Akten* (Hamburg: Kovac, 1995), 299 pp. DM 98.00

This study examines the diplomatic dimensions of French and British policy towards Austria in 1933-34. The author regards the Austrian question as a test case for the evolving early appeasement policy. In this context, he is fully aware of the multi-faceted use of the term and its application to present phenomena, which complicate the historical analysis of the inter-war period. However, Bertolaso postulates that the underlying policy existed even before the term was coined. While the analysis of appeasement usually addresses the period 1938-39, culminating in the Munich Agreement of 1938, the example of Austria allows a tolerant view of German expansionist policy that was not yet coloured by a fear of military conflict. The unsuccessful *coup d'etat* by the Austrian Nazis on 25 July 1934, ending in the murder of Chancellor Dollfuß, forced the Western powers into a clearer definition of their attitude towards the alpine republic. Bertolaso succeeds in illuminating the contradictory and partly paralysing factors which contributed to the Western failure to intervene – even by co-operating with Germany's rival in Austria, Fascist Italy – in Austrian affairs in the light of Nazi claims to political influence: Germany was not held directly responsible for the *coup*, Anglo-French conceptions differed markedly in important areas, and a 'third way' in the Austrian question (neutrality, restoration of the Habsburg monarchy) did not prove viable in international debate. This micro-study at diplomatic level adds considerably to our understanding of the roots of the elusive phenomenon of appeasement policy.

Ulrike Jordan

[106] JUTTA RAAB-HANSEN, *NS-verfolgte Musiker in England. Spuren deutscher und österreichischer Flüchtlinge in der britischen Exilkultur*, Musik im "Dritten Reich" und im Exil, 1 (Hamburg: von Bockel, 1996), 530 pp. DM 68.00

This important study of refugee musicians in Great Britain makes use of hitherto unknown sources and contributes greatly to our understanding of this aspect of cultural history. The author explores in detail the process of seeking refuge and work as a persecuted musician from Germany or Austria. A great deal of empirical data has been unearthed, and the result is a history of the (often problematic and contradictory) integration of these artists into British musical life. The backdrop of this analysis, namely British attitudes and policy towards refugees and immigrants from Germany and Nazi-occupied countries, is known to historians. On this basis, Raab Hansen adds considerably to our knowledge of the refugees' own initiatives in the musical field, for example within the framework of the Freie Deutsche Kulturbund and the Austrian Centre. She focuses on three refugee musicians in particular, whom she presents in longer portraits: Berhold Goldschmidt, Ernst Hermann Meyer, and Maria Lidka. There are also short biographical sketches of a further 298 musicians.

Ulrike Jordan

[107] MICHAEL DOCKRILL (ed.), *Europe within the Global System 1938-1960. Great Britain, France, Italy and Germany. From Great Powers to Regional Powers*, Veröffentlichungen Arbeitskreis Deutsche England-Forschung, 30 (Bochum: Brockmeyer, 1995), 169 pp. DM 44.80

One might wonder whether it is a sign of the global economy or of European regionalism that the proceedings of a conference at King's College London in April 1992 should be published in English by a somewhat obscure German publisher. Five out of the nine papers are by British historians. This is not surprising because Britain's declining role in international affairs furnishes the prime example for the book's overall theme. Britain, threatened by financial exhaustion and the transfer of power in India, tried to defend its foothold both in Europe and in the global system. Why was India so readily abandoned while Britain's position in the Middle East was tenaciously maintained? The three authors, Brasted, Bridge, and Kent [601], contributing to one paper, argue that Britain's global status depended much more on informal empire and influence than on the preservation of formal control. The transfer of power could be seen as a deliberate commitment to self-government, whereas being 'kicked out of Egypt' would appear to be outright humiliation. As regards Europe, Great Power status implied that Britain was legitimately concerned with the whole of Europe, not only those parts in which it had special interests. Again, this was mere pretence because the Red Army controlled Eastern Europe. Most articles reveal the discrepancy between claim and reality. Anthony Adamthwaite shows how Britain was skilfully out-manœuvred by France when attempting to join the European club in the 1960s [482]. There was, he argues, no sustained policy-planning. De Gaulle's ideas about Europe, a confederation of states rather than a federation, are well-documented by the renowned French historian Georges-Henri Soutu. There are two articles by two Italian historians on the failure of their country's diplomacy *vis-à-vis* the Anglo-Americans at the end of the war, and its new role as a member state of the emerging Common Market. Gustav Schmidt examines the persistent rise of post-war Germany in the context of the Anglo-American special relationship, for which he coins the phrase 'From Third Factor to Third Actor' [580]. One cannot help but feel that in their more modest clothing as regional powers the old states of Europe have a much more useful and constructive role to play than in their former capacity as great, and for that matter imperial, powers.

Lothar Kettenacker

[108] CARSTEN KRESSEL, *Evakuierungen und erweiterte Kinderlandverschickung im Vergleich. Das Beispiel der Städte Liverpool und Hamburg*, Europäische Hochschulschriften, III/715 (Frankfurt/M.: Lang, 1996), 255 pp. £32.00

During the Second World War, women and children in both Britain and Germany were evacuated to the countryside for protection against heavy enemy bombing. This study examines the political and organizational implications in a broad comparison focusing on Liverpool and Hamburg. The author arrives at the conclusion that in both countries deeper conflicts lay at the heart of the success or failure of evacuation. The British debate about the welfare state and Germany's 'secondary war aims' of indoctrination and defence are examples of these conflicts discussed in the volume. By taking a comparative approach, this book closes an important gap in the research on the extended children's evacuation programme in Germany.

Ulrike Jordan

[109] HEIKE BUNGERT, *Das Nationalkomitee und der Westen. Die Reaktion der Westalliierten auf das NKFD und die freien deutschen Bewegungen 1943-1948*, Transatlantische historische Studien, 8 (Stuttgart: Franz Steiner, 1997), 341 pp. DM 76.00

Heike Bungert's study of the Western Allies' perception, assessment of, and reaction to the National Committee for a Free Germany, founded in 1943 by exiled German communists and prisoners-of-war near Moscow, throws light on important, yet hithero neglected areas of the history of anti-Nazi resistance, post-war planning and its aftermath. Until recently, the public and scholarly discussion was characterized by a lack of depth, often also by an ideologically informed approach. The author aims to help close this gap by following mainly an approach of diplomatic history with an emphasis on the multinational perspective which allows crosschecks and a balanced assessment in the sense of the new trends of 'international history'. Her findings add considerably to our knowledge of the topic and its wider ramifications. The Western Allies did, contrary to assumptions before her research, closely follow the Committee's activities. Especially the Americans regarded it as part of a world-wide network strategy, which accounts for its discussion at major war-time and post-war conferences. Of particular significance was the flawed Western perception of a continued post-war existence of the NKFD, a phenomenon which further illustrates the nascent phase of the Cold War. On a number of levels, the Western Allies attempted counter initiatives which developed their own momentum, as for instance the activities subsumed under the term of 'psychological warfare' and re-education programmes for prisoners-of-war. The author achieves a differentiated analysis of British, American, and French perceptions of the NKFD while at the same time clarifying the overall importance of the Committee in Allied thinking. In her view, it equals, if not surpasses, the role of the 20 July bomb plot resistance group in Western assessment and merits further research.

Ulrike Jordan

[110] HEINRICH OBERREUTER and JÜRGEN WEBER (eds), *Freundliche Feinde? Die Alliierten und die Demokratiegründung in Deutschland*, Akademiebeiträge zur politischen Bildung, 29 (Landsberg/Lech: Olzog, 1996), 240 pp. DM 32.00

This volume assembles essays which approach the 'democratization' of Germany after the Second World War from various perspectives. One section deals with the establishment of military governments and their policies. The main emphasis is on the American influence; there is no separate treatment of French policies. Another section of the volume covers the legacy of the Nazi era in so far as it appears in postwar German opinion polls. In his essay 'Spuren der NS-Ideologie im Nachkriegsdeutschland' Edgar Piel argues that the relatively long-term survival of attitudes associated with National Socialism among certain sections of the population finally gave way to a horror of the extreme right after the racist attacks of 1992.

Andreas Fahrmeir

[111] HEINRICH MAETZKE, *Der Union Jack in Berlin. Das britische Foreign Office, die SBZ und die Formulierung der britischen Deutschlandpolitik 1945/47*, Wissenschaftsforum Geschichte und historische Hilfswissenschaften, 1 (Konstanz: UVK - Universitätsverlag Konstanz, 1996), xvii + 472 pp. DM 78.00

At the end of the war the British had to revise their preparations for a condominium over Germany in alliance with the United States and the Soviet Union. The Soviets could not be made to play the part in the Control Commission once attributed to them by the Western Allies. The author of this Ph.D. thesis describes this painful learning process stage by stage. It is thus a valuable contribution to the unfolding history of the Cold War, which gives the impression of an unwelcome awakening in the West to the realities of the new day. With their plans in tatters, the British used their presence in Berlin for the purpose of observing and analysing what was going on in the East before actually making up their mind about how to respond. First, information was hard to come by: the horror stories of released prisoners of war about the Red Army's advance into Germany proved to be the first cold douche for Whitehall mandarins. Further signposts were unmistakable: the forced fusion of the two working-class parties into the SED, the imposition of a puppet regime in the Soviet-occupied zone, economic exploitation in the name of reparations, and the remake of the Russian zone according to the Soviet model. Rather than the platform for co-operation, Berlin turned into the Western outpost in a new political wilderness. British observers on the ground realized that the fate of Berlin and Germany were closely linked. While the Foreign Office believed Berlin to be untenable in the long run, Foreign Secretary Bevin remained steadfast in the face of Soviet intransigence. Fears grew among British observers that Berlin and the Soviet Zone were being built up as a springboard for the Soviet control of Germany as a whole. There is a fascinating chapter on the role of Jacob Kaiser as an unmanageable pawn in Soviet planning. For the British the crucial question was whether to hold on to Berlin against all odds, or to make the best of the new realities and form a West German state with US backing. The solution which Bevin favoured was an ingenious one, which was to prove him right forty years later: four-power control in Berlin, as both a symbol and a substitute for German unity which was being temporarily suspended in the Western zones to make way for a separate West German state. Berlin served, as it were, as a *pars pro toto* to honour the Potsdam Agreement which could not be maintained for the whole of Germany.

Lothar Kettenacker

[112] GUNTHER MAI, *Der Alliierte Kontrollrat in Deutschland 1945-1948. Alliierte Einheit – Deutsche Teilung?* Quellen und Darstellungen zur Zeitgeschichte, 37 (Munich: Oldenbourg, 1995), xiv + 536 pp. DM 198.00

This study fills a gap in our understanding of the structures and work of the Allied Control Authority (ACA) as a quadripartite body, bridging the numerous specialist approaches and providing an interpretative framework for future research. The author traces the ACA from its conception in 1943 to the founding of the two German states in 1949, ending with an epilogue that takes account of developments until 1990. The study provides a detailed and thoroughly source-based analysis of key political and economic problems of the era. Thus the question of interzonal policies, the revision of the Potsdam guidelines in summer 1946, the economic and financial entities which evolved after the outbreak of the Cold War, and eventually the end of the ACA as a decision-making body in 1947-48 are all broadly discussed. Ultimately, the author delineates the about turn mainly in Western positions between 1945 and 1948-49. The military, which had favoured zonal autonomy immediately after the war, spoke up for a centralized administration of Germany in 1948-49, whereas the diplomats, who had started out with the goal of European entities at the end of the Second World War, in 1949 favoured the division of Germany on the basis of ideology.

Ulrike Jordan

[113] THOMAS RÖLLE, *Der britische Einfluß auf den Aufbau des Nordwestdeutschen Rundfunks von 1945 bis 1948* (Aachen: Shaker, 1997), x + 289 pp. DM 98.00

The North-West German Radio Station (NWDR), which was established in the British zone of occupation in May 1945, was an important part of British cultural policy in Germany. As a mouth-piece for virtually uncensored German journalism after 'zero hour' this station, which was initially based only in Hamburg, fulfilled an important function in society. Thomas Rölle's study offers an interesting and reliable account of the NWDR in its formative phase, illustrating a facet of British occupation policy. It also provides an evaluation of Weimar broadcasting structures, principles, and policies, and their use or irrelevance for the founding of a new democratic radio station, as well as a survey of National Socialist policy in this area. Thus this slender volume bridges the gap between the 'unpolitical' approach of the Weimar period and the attempt to establish a democratic broadcasting culture along the lines of the BBC. To some extent the NWDR was bound up with the British occupation policy of re-education, or rather, education for democracy, as the occupiers themselves preferred to characterize it. But there was another strong factor behind the establishment of the NWDR, which played an imporant part in the editorial decisions taken, most of all in Berlin: the fight against Communist propaganda. However, fair and objective reports were the goal aimed at and largely achieved by the German staff and their British supervisors. Looking forward into the 1950s and 1960s, the author also hints at the subsequent attempts to politicize the broadcasting landscape in Germany.

Ulrike Jordan

[114] CHRISTEL ZIEGLER, *Lernziel Demokratie. Politische Frauenbildung in der britischen und amerikanischen Besatzungszone 1945-1948*, Studien zur internationalen Erwachsenenbildung: Beihefte zum Internationalen Jahrbuch der Erwachsenenbildung, 11 (Cologne: Böhlau, 1997), xii + 226 pp. DM 58.00

This study partially closes a gap in the historiography of the occupation years in the British and American zones. While the overall topic of democratization, (re-) education, and learning on a variety of levels has been the focus of a growing number of studies, the role of women in the Anglo-Saxon concept of political education has so far been neglected. Ziegler attempts to rectify this, and to a large extent she is successful in providing a reliable account of British and American efforts, supplemented by interesting glimpses of other countries' models and their influence (for example, Sweden). On the basis of the Control Commission records, she reconstructs the institutional and structural history of the early years of women's political education in Germany. With the aim of creating awareness and active participation in the political life of post-NS Germany, both the British and American authorities drew on their own models as well as German initiatives. The emphasis is clearly on the methods and conditions governing women's affairs and political education, not, however, on the deeper underlying aspects of expectancy and demand. Consequently, many questions remain unanswered. What mental framework did German women – after all, a significant element in Nazi domestic politics – bring to the new initiatives? Were they seen as a particularly useful means of individual reckoning with the Nazi ideology? The author does not contribute to our understanding of these questions, nor does she enlighten the reader much on the interaction of German, British, and American women. These, however, along with concepts and organizations, are the most vital aspects of this topic.

Ulrike Jordan

[115] GABRIELE CLEMENS, *Britische Kulturpolitik in Deutschland 1945-1949. Literatur, Film, Musik und Theater*, Historische Mitteilungen der Ranke-Gesellschaft, Beiheft 24 (Stuttgart: Steiner, 1997), 308 pp. DM 124.00

Britain's cultural and educational policy in its zone of occupation is generally seen as one of the success stories of these years, reflecting the benefits of the time-honoured principle of indirect rule in north-west Germany. In her study, Gabriele Clemens takes a fresh look at this aspect of occupation policy, placing it into the overall context. Not only does she avoid the pitfalls of an isolationist view of cultural policy (mistaking grass-roots policy for lack of direction), which has partly dominated the historiography on this topic, but she illuminates various areas of cultural activity from planning to realization. This anchoring in the planning phase is a welcome perspective, which demonstrates that the thought-out cultural programme starting in 1942-43 was one of the key aspects of the post-hostilities scenario.

In this sense, Clemens argues, cultural occupation policy, far from being a diversion from the dullness of post-war Germany, largely fulfilled well-defined tasks in the re-education of the Germans. Linked to this, the author maintains that Britain's cultural policy in Germany served British security interests, since it tackled Nazi and militaristic ideas at the root, establishing Western cultural values in a variety of ways. While this remained to a large extent an idealistic goal (because of the persistent interrelations between state bureaucracy and culture in Germany), Clemens demonstrates that British cultural policy followed another aim: that of advertising Britain and its way of life, albeit in a pre-industrial, idealized version. This, she argues, took the place of power politics in the age of the waning Empire and declining power. All in all, this study convinces the reader in its plausibility, clarity of structure and language, as well as comprehensive analysis of cultural policy 'under the Union Jack'.

Ulrike Jordan

[116] KLAUS LARRES, *Politik der Illusionen. Churchill, Eisenhower und die deutsche Frage 1945-1955,* Publications of the German Historical Institute London, 35 (Göttingen: Vandenhoeck & Ruprecht, 1995), 335 pp. DM 92.00

Winston Churchill was the only Western leader who seriously considered the possibility of a unified neutral Germany after Stalin's death in 1953 as a way of overcoming the Cold War and securing Britain's status as a world power. At a time when the integration of the Federal Republic of Germany into the West was making good progress, Churchill's political ideas for Germany were received with both approval and irritation. This excellent study looks at the motives underlying Churchill's foreign policy, his enthusiasm for summitry, and personal political encounters. In an in-depth analysis Larres combines a perceptive understanding of Churchill's personality and political philosophy with a detailed account of his policy making and the mixed reactions of both his own Foreign Office and the 'three Victorious Powers' around 1953. At a personal level it becomes clear that Churchill's enthusiasm for summitry was not born with Stalin's death in 1953 but went further back to his political experiences and successes between 1914 and 1945. Churchill's security policy, which he spelled out in his speech to the British parliament on 11 May 1953, has often been unjustly overlooked by contemporaries and historians; it receives special attention in this study. The reasons why Churchill pressed for a summit with Eisenhower and Malenkov in 1953 were fear of an escalation of the Cold War and the economic necessity for Britain to reduce its defence budget rather than a specific interest in Germany. The premier's initiatives for a summit eventually failed as the result of a combination of factors including Labour's foreign policy initiatives in Moscow, opposition within the British Foreign Office, the failure of the European Defence Community, Malenkov's dismissal, Churchill's health, and pressure from his colleagues to leave office. Looking closely at the reactions to Churchill's foreign and security policy, Larres can show that contrary to the widely shared perception of Eisenhower as generally interested in friendly gestures towards the Soviet Union the American president was, in fact, more interested in a propaganda victory over Moscow. Now available verbal utterances by Malenkov and Berija, however, suggest that between March and June 1953 the Soviet Union was seriously considering sacrificing the

GDR and accepting a unified Germany because of the difficult situation in East Berlin. Thus the realization of Churchill's summit idea might have led to an early end to the Cold War.

Based on a wealth of material including interviews and only recently accessible documents of the post-war period such as the private documents of Anthony Eden (Lord Avon), this book fills a serious gap in the study of Churchill's summitry which has hitherto been treated only in a few articles.

Dagmar Freist

[117] MARTIN KERKHOFF, *Großbritannien, die Vereinigten Staaten und die Saarfrage, 1945 bis 1954*, Historische Mitteilungen, Beiheft 22 (Stuttgart: Steiner, 1996), 251 pp. DM 88.00

This study examines the international aspects of the Saar question during the period between *c*. 1945 and 1955. The main emphasis is on the role of Great Britain and the USA in this process, a role that was on the whole restricted to indirect involvement only. The main aspects under review include the importance of the Saar in Anglo-American assessments of containment policy towards the Soviet Union, and US/UK policies aimed at minimizing the Saar question's potential to block a Franco-German *rapprochement* and West European integration. Moreover, the author examines discontinuities and fresh approaches in Anglo-American policies towards the Saar in general, including their repercussions on bilateral relations. Although eventually the planned Europeanization of the Saar failed, in his overall conclusion Kerkhoff stresses the important mediating function of the USA and Great Britain in the Saar question, and in the achievement of the ultimate agreement between West Germany and France.

Ulrike Jordan

[118] JÖRG LEITOLF, *Wirtschaft – Verbände – Integration. Britische Industrie und westeuropäische Integration von 1945-1975*, Veröffentlichungen Arbeitskreis Deutsche England-Forschung, 35 (Bochum: Brockmeyer, 1996), iv + 299 pp. DM 49.80

This work of political science analyses and describes the attitude of the Confederation of British Industry (CBI) and its predecessor organizations, the Federation of British Industries (FBI), the British Employers' Confederation (BEC), the National Union of Manufacturers (NUM), and the National Association of British Manufacturers (NABM), to Western European integration between 1945 and 1975, that is, in the period from the first concrete plans and negotiations to the confirmation of British entry to the European Community (EC) in June 1975 by a large positive majority in a referendum.

This study attempts neither to quantify the influence of these organizations on government policy, nor to construct causal connections such as, for example, that the industrialists' organizations forced the British government to enter the EC. Rather, it investigates an interest group which, while relevant to social policy, was outside or below the level of government. This examination reflects something of the domestic background of British policy towards Western Europe.

The process of opinion-formation on European integration was, in fact, far more pragmatic and free of ideology within British industrialists' organizations than within the government or the individual political parties. Far earlier than the government and political parties, these organizations came to the conclusion that Britain could not do without the growth markets and future markets which were located primarily within the EC, and that what was needed there was an environment as broad and as free of discrimination as possible. But unlike the comparable German institution, the Bund deutscher Industrie (BdI), which supported the European Economic Community (EEC) for political reasons in order to secure Germany's Western integration and support reconciliation with France, the CBI never regarded the EC as providing a new basis for British foreign policy. The organization refused to take a lead on this issue. The FBI and CBI did not see it as their job actively and publicly to encourage Britain to pursue a different foreign policy, especially as the heterogeneous interests gathered in this umbrella organization always made it difficult to obtain a clear vote. The author of this study comes to the conclusion that a political initiative more energetically pursued could certainly have produced earlier entry for Britain because the manufacturing industry's employers' organizations at least had a positive attitude towards it from an early date.

Sabine Freitag

[119] CHRISTOPH DARTMANN, *Re-Distribution of Power, Joint Consultation or Productivity Coalition? Labour and Postwar Reconstruction in Germany and Britain, 1945-1953*, Veröffentlichungen Arbeitskreis Deutsche England-Forschung, 31 (Bochum: Brockmeyer, 1996), viii + 398 pp. DM 59.80

In this comparative study, the author traces the development of labour participation in industry in Britain and Germany. Concentrating on the post-war period to 1953, he nevertheless includes the inter-war period in his investigation. Thus the long-term effects of traditional ideology can be put into the context of disparate developments after 1945. Dartmann delineates internal trade union policies as expressed in procedures, and the impact of external factors on labour relations in both countries before turning to key problems of a transnational character. These are, mainly, the export of industrial relations and labour participation in productivity. The overall conclusion of this study presents a very different picture in each of the two countries under review. While in Britain no measure regarding labour participation in industry was introduced in the inter-war to post-war period, in Germany co-determination was formally introduced in key industries (steel, coal) in 1951, and expanded, mainly by the Deutscher Gewerkschaftsbund, in years to come.

Ulrike Jordan

[120] WOLFRAM SCHNEIDER, *Die britische Iranpolitik im Zweiten Weltkrieg und der Ausbruch des Kalten Krieges*, 2 parts (Hamburg: Kovac, 1996), 752 pp. DM 198.00

This 1996 Marburg dissertation analyses Britain's policy towards Iran during the Second World War against the background of European foreign policy. Covering the time from the outbreak of the Second World War to the Truman Doctrine of 1946, the author looks in turn at diplomacy and warfare in Britain, France, Germany, the USSR, and the USA, and their engagement with Iran. By choosing to include the beginning of the Cold War in his analysis, Schneider hopes to fill a research gap in the history of British foreign policy. He argues, not surprisingly, that a key interest of the allies in their confrontation with Iran was oil. The conflict over Iran, according to the author, already foreshadowed friction among the allies which would lead to the Cold War at the end of the Second World War.

Dagmar Freist

[121] GUSTAV SCHMIDT (ed.), *Zwischen Bündnissicherung und privilegierter Partnerschaft. Die deutsch-britischen Beziehungen und die Vereinigten Staaten von Amerika 1955-1963*, Veröffentlichungen Arbeitskreis Deutsche England-Forschung, 33 (Bochum: Brockmeyer, 1995), x + 355 pp. DM 54.80

Historians of foreign affairs have recently criticized analyses of bilateral relations in the twentieth century as falling short of understanding the complexities of foreign policy in the modern world. Instead, it has been argued, the role of a 'third factor/third actor' in foreign affairs needs to be taken into account and the perspective of trilateralism should be introduced. The present volume is the first result of a joint project between the Department of War Studies, King's College, London, and the Chair of International Politics at the Ruhr University, Bochum, which aims to analyse the development and structure of 'three bilateral relations' and their convergence into a trilateral relationship, namely relations between the United States and Great Britain, the Federal Republic of Germany and the United States, and Great Britain and the Federal Republic of Germany between 1955 and 1963. Questions which were considered key issues in the interaction of all three powers were chosen for analysis: the economic and political aspects of the cost of stationing troops in Germany between 1955 and 1965 (Wolfram Kaiser [527]), Germany's role in the pound crisis and the sterling area in 1956-57 (Werner Wippich [598]), Anglo-German relations and the redefinition of international politics during the second Berlin crisis (Sabine Lee), plans for regional appeasement policies in central Europe between 1956 and 1962 (Thorsten Cabalo [494]), German, English and American interests behind the preamble to the Franco-German treaty of 1963 (Oliver Bange [485]), and finally, the critical attitude of the United States, Germany, and France to Britain's role in Europe (Gustav Schmidt [582]).

Dagmar Freist

[122] ASTRID RINGE, *Konkurrenten in Europa. Großbritannien und die Bundesrepublik Deutschland. Deutsch-britische Wirtschaftsbeziehungen 1949 bis 1957*, Studien zur modernen Geschichte, 48 (Stuttgart: Franz Steiner, 1996), 536 pp. DM 168.00

This Hamburg Ph.D. thesis traces economic relations between Britain, as an occupying power, and its potential rival West Germany from the time of the Marshall Plan to the foundation of the EEC. There were hardly two economies in post-war Europe which had, at the outset, more in common than Britain and the Federal Republic, mainly in three respects: size of territory, population, and state of industrialization. As one of the victorious powers and in possession of the industrial heartland of Germany, Britain was in a much stronger position. However, it was not Britain but the United States of America which called the shots. Since Bretton Woods the dollar had succeeded the pound as the world's leading currency. The dollar shortage had a stifling effect on both the German and the British economy. Britain was greatly indebted to the United States and its chief concern was to save dollars and thereby to maintain the value of the pound. Under Labour rationing and planning of imports and exports were not only believed to be more effective, but also carried more moral weight. Germany, with a reduction of its territory by 25 per cent, and an influx of 12 million refugees had no alternative but to stimulate exports in order to pay for foodstuffs and raw materials. As a consequence, Germany pushed in the same direction as the United States: liberalizing and intensifying international trade. It had no sterling area to fall back on. This meant first of all freeing itself from all restrictions imposed by the occupying powers which controlled all of Germany's foreign trade. British and German interests clashed during the Korean crisis due to the shortage of steel and coal which were needed for British rearmament and German industrial output. The beneficial result for Germany was that the level of steel production was raised. This, together with the European Payments Union, helped to accelerate Germany's recovery. The author sheds new light on two important questions: first, Britain was under constant pressure from the United States to improve Germany's terms of trade. Therefore the Foreign Office was not prepared to give in to special pleading by British industry and unions to curtail Germany as a competitor. The exception was ship-building – discussed at length – where discriminatory controls were maintained longer than elsewhere. Second, in the mid-1950s the emerging EEC was not a viable alternative to Empire-preferences and the sterling bloc, which were regarded as a safe haven for British industry and commerce. With the lifting of trade restrictions, customs were seen to be the last protective shield.

Lothar Kettenacker

[123] WOLFRAM KAISER, *Großbritannien und die Europäische Wirtschaftsgemeinschaft 1950-1961. Von Messina nach Canossa*, Studien zur Internationalen Geschichte, 2 (Berlin: Akakemie, 1996), 233 pp. DM 128.00

There are no lessons to be learned from history, otherwise British politicians and officials would wish to study what went wrong when Britain first faced the question of joining Europe on an uncharted journey. They would not have to master the German language because a more comprehensive account by the same author is now available in English (*Using Europe, Abusing the Europeans. Britain and European Integration 1945/63*, Houndmills, 1996). Therefore a few remarks about the original German thesis must suffice. The book is divided into two parts and six chapters dealing first with the British reaction to the initiative of the Six, and second with domestic and foreign policy problems accruing from Britain's approach to Europe. Kaiser makes extensive use of British sources, but does not include the archives of partner states.

Nor does he accept the widely held view that Britain, as it were, 'missed the bus' in 1956. Nobody of any influence wished to buy a ticket. Nor was it clear that the bus would reach its destination. By deliberately trying to torpedo the project ('embrace destructively'), and failing to do so by setting up a rival free trade area, Britain had compromised its own negotiating position. Both the application for EEC membership and its rejection, so Kaiser argues, were based on political rather than economic grounds, even though the fear of exclusion did cause concern. In 1955 the ruling élite believed that joining Europe would undermine Britain's status as an independent world power, especially *vis-à-vis* the Commonwealth, whereas six years later a leadership role within Europe was regarded as an indispensable prop and a means to enhance the special relationship with America. In other words, no genuine re-orientation towards Europe took place between

1955 and 1961. Whether a change of heart towards Europe did occur at a later stage is open to speculation.

Lothar Kettenacker

[124] MONIKA ROSENGARTEN, *Großbritannien und der Schuman-Plan. Politische und wirtschaftliche Faktoren in der britischen Haltung zum Schuman-Plan und zur Europäischen Gemeinschaft für Kohle und Stahl 1950-1954*, Europäische Hochschulschriften, III/766 (Frankfurt/M.: Lang, 1997), xx + 171 pp. £24.00

This M. A. thesis examines the influence of political and economic factors on the British decision not to join the European Coal and Steel Community. Its first section deals with the better known political factors which made joining such an organization difficult for Britain, primarily the commitments to the Commonwealth and scepticism concerning the transfer of national sovereignty to an international body. The second, more original section focuses on economic interests which suggested that Britain might actually be better off outside the nascent European Coal and Steel Union. British iron ore imports came mainly from Sweden and Algeria, which remained outside the union; lower labour costs, lower social insurance contributions, and the strategic position of British production sites close to the coast made British products more competitive than their continental rivals.

Andreas Fahrmeir

[125] SABINE LEE, *An Uneasy Partnership. British-German Relations between 1955 and 1961*, Veröffentlichungen Arbeitskreis Deutsche England-Forschung, 34 (Bochum: Brockmeyer, 1996), 337 pp. DM 59.80

In this book, which is largely based on the author's (British) Ph.D. thesis, Anglo-German relations between 1955 and 1961 are examined. Lee's study of the diplomatic and economic history of bilateral relations does not contain any surprising thesis or revision of current scholarship. Consequently, one of the main findings of her research is the fact that Anglo-German relations were determined by other bilateral relations, especially Franco-German, German-American, and Anglo-American, in this period. What the author terms 'personal chemistry', or the lack of it, for example between Adenauer and Macmillan, is explored as well. Lee looks back at the first post-war decade and the structural conditions of foreign policy-making in Foreign Office and Auswärtiges Amt, before turning to the core years under consideration: 1955 to 1958, the crisis of 1958/59 and the Berlin crisis. The fluctuations of Anglo-German relations, which ended in a slightly optimistic trend at the time Adenauer left office, are traced reliably. Based mainly on German and, to a lesser extent, British papers in the Bundesarchiv, the Archiv des Auswärtigen Amtes, the Public Record Office and others, the book also includes interviews with leading contemporaries.

Ulrike Jordan

[126] DANIEL HOFMANN, *Truppenstationierung in der Bundesrepublik Deutschland. Die Vertragsverhandlungen mit den Westmächten 1951 bis 1959*, Dokumente zur Deutschlandpolitik, Beiheft 8 (Munich: Oldenbourg, 1997), 281 pp. DM 98.00

Superficially the stationing of Allied troops on German soil and the costs incurred appeared to be a purely technical matter. However, originally the zoning of Germany for the purpose of occupation also looked innocuous, only to result in the solid division of the country for more than forty years. The first sentence of the book is a quotation from Adenauer on the decision taken by the London Conference in October 1954 saying that 'the occupation troops are about to become forces of defence'. This statement serves as a kind of leitmotiv for the whole book, which examines in detail the long-drawn-out process of negotations to find an acceptable, that is, non-discriminatory legal basis for the presence of Allied troops in Germany. If one remembers how keen Weimar governments had been to see the end of the regime of Allied occupation in the Rhineland, it is indeed astonishing that ten years after the Second World War the stationing of foreign troops was never questioned for a moment. The security of the young and otherwise defenceless Federal Republic depended on Allied protection. For the population of Berlin the miraculous transition from occupying to protecting powers had already occurred during the blockade of 1948. For the rest of the West Germans this happened with the accession of the Federal Republic to NATO in 1955. However, there is a history of intense negotiations about the status of Allied forces before and after that date. The problems and tensions arose from Bonn's desire to get rid of the relics of the occupation regime and at the same time to maintain and enhance the security of the Federal Republic, which for a long time had no army to speak of. Mainly because of the haggling over costs – 'burden-sharing' as it was dubbed – all participating governments had an interest in keeping the sensitive issue out of the limelight. Therefore the whole question, important though it was, has never really attracted the attention of historians it deserves. Bonn had already pinpointed all the crucial requirements by 1951. It then took the government nine years of patient negotiations to achieve these goals: a new, freely-negotiated treaty on the stationing of Allied troops, a legally binding guarantee to come to the defence of West Germany, a fair distribution of costs allotted to Allied troops and to the build-up of a German army, first within the European Defence Community, then as part of NATO, and finally, the protection of Allied forces in any emergency such as civil unrest. By 1959 satisfactory solutions to all these issues had been found. The Federal Republic had become a sovereign state, while Berlin and Germany as a whole had remained the prerogative of the four Powers. That this should have been a cause of relief rather than of resentment to most Germans is the final proof that Western integration had indeed produced a fundamental change of heart.

Lothar Kettenacker

[127] WOLFGANG-ULRICH PRIGGE, *Gewerkschaftspluralismus und kooperative Interessenvertretung in Großbritannien*, Veröffentlichungen Arbeitskreis Deutsche England-Forschung, 29 (Bochum: Brockmeyer, 1995), vi + 219 pp. DM 49.80

The perceived superiority of the *Einheitsgewerkschaft* as found in Germany (non-partisan industry-based unions open to all skills, grades, and specialisms in the branch of employment covered by the union) over the pluralistic model found in Britain (multi-unionism, in which more than one union competes for membership within a given group of workers within a factory) has come under question for a number of reasons. These include changing social and economic conditions and the apprehension of some countries about industry-based unions in the process of unifying the European labour market. Furthermore, central and eastern European countries are attracted to multi-unionism in reconstructing their work-force relations. Thus it is more than apt to compare the model of industial unionism which has, until recently, been represented as the ideal work-force organization, with the process of modernizing the crisis-ridden British trade-union sector. Prigge offers an empirical analysis of intra-organizational forms of co-ordination in the pluralistic organization of trade unions in Britain and draws comparisons with intra-organizational forms in industry-based organizations. He thus takes up an issue which has mainly been dealt with in the past from a theoretical standpoint only. Step by step the author traces the various aspects of the lack of co-ordination in intra-union relations in Britain and analyses the growing importance of co-operative representation as a result of internal conflicts, above all in the successful Electrical, Electronic, Telecommunication and Plumbing Union (EETPU). The key characteristic of co-operative trade union politics was 'single union agreements'. These were in stark contrast to the policy of the Trades Union Congress (TUC) which was able, however, to respond positively to the pressure for modernization by creating the mechanism of 'single table bargaining'. This allowed the co-existence of several trade unions in one company but offered at the same time a framework for co-ordination which helped to overcome the profound dysfunctionality of competitive unions. In conclusion, Prigge shows that the most recent development in British work-force relations is the modernization of multi-unionism through co-operative representation which, in fact, has made it possible for renegade unions such as the EETPU to reunite under the umbrella of the TUC.

Dagmar Freist

[128] ANDRÉ KAISER, *Staatshandeln ohne Staatsverständnis: Die Entwicklung des Politikfeldes Arbeitsbeziehungen in Großbritannien 1965-1990*, Veröffentlichungen Arbeitskreis Deutsche England-Forschung, 26 (Bochum: Brockmeyer, 1995), ii + 413 pp. DM 49.80

In *Staatshandeln ohne Staatsverständnis*, a political scientist analyses the influence of three factors on the development of British labour relations: 'policy', that is, the specific programmes of different parties at different times; 'politics', that is, what parties actually did; and 'polity', or the influence of the British political system and of British political and economic traditions. It delivers what it promises; the main section consists of a detailed description of state influence on labour relations in these crucial decades. Its main conclusions are threefold. First, British politics were more 'policy orientated' than is sometimes alleged. Rather than following the line which seemed most popular, parties largely adhered to their programmes once they had been firmly adopted. Also, until the 1970s differences were less between parties than between the different wings of Labour and the Conservatives and their respective advisers. As far as actual policies were concerned, governments were usually able to turn their political aims into legislation. However, all pre-Thatcher governments underestimated the practical problems of implementing them. Thatcher's governments, by contrast, solved this problem by leaving the implementation of the law to those concerned rather than to government. As stated in the title, Kaiser argues that a major problem faced by all British governments which attempted to regulate labour relations was the absence of a concept of an interventionist state, which made it difficult to sustain any argument for the regulation of labour relations. It is here that the influence of 'polity' was most apparent.

Andreas Fahrmeir

[129] WILLIAM E. PATERSON, PENNY HENSON, and PETER SHIP-LEY, *The European Policies of Labour and Conservative Party in Great Britain*, Konrad Adenauer Stiftung, Interne Studien, 109 / 1995 (St. Augustin: Konrad Adenauer Stiftung, 1995), 113 pp.

What role did the Labour Party play in the disputes surrounding the Treaty of Maastricht? What line of argument did Labour follow in the debate about Core Europe and its enlargement, about a common European foreign and security policy, and about economic and monetary union? These and related questions are taken up by Paterson and Henson in the first essay of this volume. Against the background of a historical analysis of the Labour Party's European policy, the authors show how Labour in opposition developed a pragmatic approach, especially in view of electoral strategies and party unity. Advocating the kingdom's exit from the European Union in their 1983 manifesto Labour later developed a pro-European position. Nevertheless, the authors conclude, the evolution of Labour Party policy on Europe has been inconsistent and contradictory. 'Like the Conservative Party, Labour has been deeply attached to a notion of Britain's unique role, centred on a special relationship with the United States' (p. 50).

    In the second contribution to this slim volume, Shipley gives a differentiated picture of the Conservative Party's European policy between 1979 and 1995, tracing the Conservatives' conversion from a 'party of Europe' to a party of Eurosceptics and the isolation of Great Britain in Europe. Margaret Thatcher's Bruges speech in September 1988 marked one turning point in the party's position on Europe. Another was John Major's strategy of decentralism. The party's growing reservations about European political and monetary union were initially shared by public opinion. However, since 1994 polls have shown a shift in opinion towards the markedly more pro-European Labour Party.

Dagmar Freist

[130] KLAUS DRIEVER, *Die Wirtschafts-Europäer. Irland in der EG/EU*, Nomos Universitätsschriften, Politik, 68 (Baden-Baden: Nomos, 1996), 303 pp. DM 89.00

This Freiburg political science dissertation investigates the most recent history of Ireland since the country became a member of the European Community in 1973. According to the author the Irish case can be taken as a typical example of an EC member state: like most members, Ireland is not one of the founders of the European Community. It is relatively small with comparatively large economic problems, and its European interests lie, according to Driever, more in economic benefits than in political and cultural integration. Are there any possible parallels with potential candidates from Eastern Europe who wish to join the EC? The book discusses how Irish policy on Europe responded to the different challenges posed to a nation-state within the economic and political community. It is astonishing how the Irish perception of Europe has changed in the course of the last thirty-five years. In the early 1960s only a small élitist group around Taoiseach (Prime Minister) Lemass supported the idea of a European federation, in 1973 it was a majority of the country, and today there is probably hardly anyone who would not agree that the European Community has meant a great political and socio-economic opportunity for Ireland. A country which was badly treated for hundreds of years could, at last, enjoy Europe's rich dinner-table towards the end of the twentieth century. However, the aim some Irish politicians and intellectuals had in mind was not really achieved, namely that their country should also participate in the political table talks. A one-dimensional fixation on economic integration alone characterized the profile of Irish interests in

Europe from the beginning. Therefore Irish policies on Europe seem to be unbalanced. They take into account neither the full dimensions of European integration, nor the fact that the Irish economy has become extremely dependent on the EC. Thus there is a fine line between opportunities and benefits on the one hand, and dangers, for example that of misperception, on the other. This is the reason why the author calls Ireland the country of the 'Wirtschaftseuropäer' who, in his opinion, do not appreciate the consequences of growing internationalism. But Irish history teaches us that nationalism has always been the decisive factor in this country, and it is still very much so in contemporary Ireland – Northern Ireland is an ever-present example. The tradition of nationalism plays an important role in political isolationism, which poses so many problems for European co-ordination.

Benedikt Stuchtey

[131] DAGMAR GALLENMÜLLER, *Die 'irische Frage'. Eine historische Studie zum gegenwärtigen Konflikt* (Frankfurt/M.: Lang, 1997), 194 pp. £27.00

The author points out that the number of publications on the Northern Ireland question has swollen to nearly 7,000 and has produced a virtual 'academic industry'. Therefore totally new insights could hardly be expected. However, there are few books in German pursuing the conflict up to the present. The introduction serves as a useful survey of the various approaches to the Irish question. The author opts for a historical explanation of the present conflict, referring specifically to Fernand Braudel, who once described mentalities as 'prisons *de longue durée*'. The habits of thought and action prevailing in Northern Ireland appear to be inspired by 'inherited folk memory'. The glorification of violence is intrinsically linked to, and apparently justified by, Irish historical consciousness, which is an amalgam of fact and fiction. This interpretative model has informed the structure of the book, which is divided into four parts, the longest dealing with Irish history up to 1921. The next chapter sketches in developments up to the renewed conflict in 1968-9, escalating up to 1972. Virtually half of the book is devoted to the various attempts to diffuse and eventually solve the problem of Northern Ireland from 1972 to 1994. The author argues that both Dublin and London hitherto neglected the long-term causes of the conflict. The British government in particular, traditionally allied to the Unionists, was always tempted to resort to *ad hoc* measures of a technocratic nature, which took no account of the psychological entrenchment on both sides of the divided community. However, the study ends on a cautiously optimistic note in view of the continued dialogue following the last cease-fire.

Lothar Kettenacker

[132] DANNY MORRISON, *Troubles. Eine politische Einführung in die Geschichte Nordirlands* (Münster: Unrast, 1997), 109 pp. DM 19.80

This is not, of course, a scholarly history of twentieth-century Northern Ireland. The author, Danny Morrison, was at one point director of Sinn Féin's public relations department and served a prison sentence for terrorist offences between 1990 and 1995. The book begins with a description of a demonstration in support of IRA prisoners on hunger strike outside the British embassy in Dublin in 1989, and ends with an indictment of all British governments as liars. It is a highly partisan account of the IRA's development and aims, effectively personalized by using 'My uncle Harry White' as its focal point, and suitably illustrated with pictures of British barracks, prisons, and police stations. It thus has some merits as a primary source of sorts, and in spite of its fiercely anti-British stance, its emphasis on dialogue as the only possible solution to the Northern Ireland problem holds out some promise for the future.

Andreas Fahrmeir

[133] CHRISTOPH KNILL, *Staatlichkeit im Wandel. Großbritannien im Spannungsfeld innenpolitischer Reformen und europäischer Integration* (Leverkusen: Deutscher Universitätsverlag, 1995), 332 pp. DM 68.00

This work deals with the change in the operation and the concepts of the English state. The author focuses mainly on developments in the 1980s and early 1990s. Knill is concerned to demonstrate the complex relationships and resulting dynamics between three levels – the European, the national, and finally the local one – by examining regulations on air pollution. He concludes that there was a marked transformation in administrative practice here – within the European framework English state organizations became more progressive and showed greater initiative than had previously been the case. Knill's thesis that this was to a large extent due to a new concept of the English state will, however, require further examination.

Bärbel Brodt

[134] GEOFFREY KEITH BARLOW, *The Labour Movement in Thatcher's Britain. Conservative Macro- and Microeconomic Strategies and the Associated Labour Relations Legislation. Their Impact on the British Labour Movement during the 1980s*, Europäische Hochschulschriften, XXXI/ 320 (Frankfurt/M.: Lang, 1997), 224 pp. £28.00

In this dissertation, the author (an Englishman who lived and taught in the GDR from the mid-1980s) examines the economic and industrial restructuring that took place in the era of Mrs Thatcher's prime ministership. Based on a variety of sources, the study approaches the core problems of the 1980s in a twofold manner. Firstly, Barlow inquires into the prime motivation for creating a large pool of unemployed labour. In this context, the alternatives of restructuring and reshaping the British economy have to be weighed up against the aim of fundamental change in work relations. Secondly, he examines the role of the Labour Party, whose ever-softening opposition to the Conservatives led to an erosion of economic structures. Barlow concludes with regard to the first problem that the Thatcher governments aimed at an overall strategy of a 'free' and unregulated market that went beyond much of what had been attempted in the 1970s. On the second point, the author evaluates the role of the Labour Party, which has reconsidered many positions, most of all the macroeconomic policies for full employment, as providing no real alternative to the Conservatives. Only Labour's stance on the European Union presents a meaningful political counter view. All in all, the book deals much more with Conservative policies and political philosophy than the title seems to imply.

Ulrike Jordan

[135] ULRIKE SCHMELTER-MÜHLE, *Krieg im Südatlantik. Die Politik der USA im Falklandkonflikt von 1982*, Europäische Hochschulschriften, XXXI/297 (Frankfurt/M.: Lang, 1996), 413 pp. £40.00

This book, the published version of a 1995 Bonn dissertation supervised by Manfred Funke, examines the policies of the United States of

America in the Falkland conflict. The nature of the topic has obliged the author to rely almost exclusively on official printed sources; her main interest is in high politics, not the military or the domestic sides of the Falkland War. After briefly sketching the background to the dispute over the 'Malvinas', she provides a meticulous summary of the negotiations between Washington, London, and Buenos Aires in 1982. Schmelter-Mühle argues that the comparatively cordial state of relations between the United States and Argentina led the Argentine government to believe that the United States would favour them, or at least remain neutral, in a military conflict with Britain. In these circumstances, they considered occupying the British islands in the South Atlantic as an opening gambit for diplomatic negotiations leading to a recognition of Argentine sovereignty, as the position of the United States would prohibit military intervention by a European power on the American continent. But while the United States suggested to Britain that they would be best placed to mediate between the two parties if they maintained a position of neutrality, and indeed did remain neutral during the first month of the conflict, they nevertheless abandoned that position in late April after attempts at mediation had failed. The fact that later bids by the United States and Peru to resolve the issue diplomatically were not successful either suggests, however, that the status of the United States did not make a great difference. The concluding part of the book traces the development of relations between the three countries from the end of the war to reconciliation.

Andreas Fahrmeir

EMPIRE AND COMMONWEALTH HISTORY

[136] WOLFGANG REINHARD, *Kleine Geschichte des Kolonialismus*, Kröners Taschenausgabe, 475 (Stuttgart: Kröner, 1996), viii + 376 pp. DM 34.00

Wolfgang Reinhard is one of Germany's leading experts on the history of colonialism. His magisterial *Geschichte der europäischen Expansion* in four volumes (1983-1990) covers the years from 1415 to 1989, structured according to the continents. The title of the present book sounds more modest, but the result is a scholarly account of what was both a European and a non-European historical phenomenom. Reinhard studies the expansion of Europe in the last six hundred years and the process of decolonization as comprehensively as the continental empires of Russia and the United States, or the specific colonialisms of China and Japan. However, no country in the world played as a central role in the world history of colonialism as Britain. Consequently the author devotes considerable space to the English / British side. The focus is on the continents that were colonized, with the result that the reader is informed equally about British trade in India and British colonial rule in Africa, to give only two examples, and thus the comparison with the colonialisms of other countries such as Holland or France is illustrated. The books opens with a *Begriffsgeschichte* of colonialism. Reinhard distinguishes between three types of colonies: *Stützpunktkolonien* (colonial bases), in the British case a world-wide net of naval bases; *Siedlungskolonien* (settlements), for example, the most important British settlements of North America and Australia; and *Herrschaftskolonien* (colonies ruled by a small minority of administrators, soldiers etc. without the need for settlement), for example, British India. Thus the book also offers some theoretical reflections, and puts British colonialism into a universal context.

Benedikt Stuchtey

[137] HENRIETTE BUGGE and JOAN PAU RUBIÉS (eds), *Shifting Cultures. Interaction and Discourse in the Expansion of Europe* (Münster: Lit, 1995), 218 pp. DM 68.80

The aim of this collection of essays is to show the cultural aspects of European expansion from the first colonial age. Originally given at a conference at the FU Berlin in autumn 1991, the contributions cover topics which range from Canada, Central America, Nicaragua, and Brazil to South India, South Africa, and the Philippines. Although the focus is clearly on the Spanish and Portugese in Central and Southern America, the British colonial experience – the original formation of a discourse, then the translation of culture, and finally the consolidation of an indigenous identity – is not wholly neglected. The most extensive essay in the first part of the book is by the co-editor Joan Pau Rubiés. She looks at sixteenth-century historians in their ethnological discourse, reflecting the duality of Christianity and civilization in the non-European context. Missonary 'cultural imperialism' with regard to India and South Africa is dealt with in the second part of the book, where attention is drawn to the instruments of mediation and translation between the different cultural conceptions. However, this point is not uncontroversial since, although missions were undoubtedly crucial for cultural exchange, they were probably not agents of 'cultural imperialism'. Therefore it seems to be more sensible to speak of cultural interaction, as developed in the third part of this volume. Here the question is asked as to how western / colonist and indigenous / colonized cultural patterns are transformed and under what conditions they are brought together in new forms of identity. Cross-cultural interactions and relations are increasingly shifting into the centre of research on imperial history, and these essays provide stimulating material for further discussion.

Benedikt Stuchtey

[138] VERA and ANSGAR NÜNNING (eds), *Intercultural Studies. Fictions of Empire*, Anglistik und Englischunterricht, 58 (Heidelberg: C. Winter, 1996), 224 pp. DM 35.00

This impressive collection of eight essays plus an informative introduction focuses directly on the problem of the complex relationship between literature and the construction of imperial identities. The editors take the British Empire and its fictions as both a historical and a literary paradigm. They do not pose the fashionable question about 'cultural studies' but rather adopt an intercultural perspective. In order to gain insight into how a national cultural heritage emerges, the cross-disciplinary approach looks at areas in which literature and imperialism strive for a common cause. Thus, as the editors say in their introduction, the ambivalent heritage of the age of empire requires constant reassessment, from the point of view of post-colonial criticism, of those literary works that significantly helped in building imperial identities and forming a matrix of colonialism as a part of our cultural memory. The volume is thus a vivid example of modern revisionism, and the essays look at the role of novels, poetry etc. in helping to paint a particular Victorian picture of the world. Edward Said may rightly be regarded as the founding father of this intellectual, revisionist approach. His book *Orientalism*, first published in 1978, not only showed the European way of representing the Middle East, but also reconstructed how the Western conception of the Orient shaped the whole tradition of its academic discipline. Since literature helped to stimulate the growth of the Empire, legitimizing its extension, constructing imperialist mentalities, and even inventing traditions, it is also a mirror of the decline of British imperialism in the late nineteenth century: a dialectic of the colonial discourse which is reflected in the variety of textual manifestations. The image of empire and its propaganda are two sides of the same coin. The imperial idea was thus founded on high quality literature, but even more so on popular fiction. John MacKenzie gives a historiographical overview of 'imperialism and popular culture' **[615]**. The essays that follow are studies of one or more novels and discuss the connection between British colonial literature and the construction and deconstruction of imperial thinking.

Benedikt Stuchtey

[139] BARBARA POTTHAST-JUTKEIT (ed.), *Familienstrukturen in ko-*
lonialen und postkolonialen Gesellschaften, Periplus Parerga, 3 (Münster:
Lit, 1997), iv + 136 pp. DM 58.80

This slim volume sheds a rare light on family structures in the so-
called Third World and their relation to European developments. The
collected essays cover the period from the early nineteenth to the twentieth centuries, and focus on African, Latin-American, Caribbean, and
Asian countries. While they discuss a variety of topics and problems,
there are a number of binding themes. These are, most importantly,
the relationship of the family (itself a changing concept) to state and
religious institutions and the overall colonial structure. One of the per-
vasive conclusions throughout the volume is a clear rejection of sim-
plified interpretations of social change. Instead, the complex interactions between family and institutions is the focus of analysis. This leads
to a critical appreciation of the theory of modernization and social
change, and to a concept of their delayed effects. While gender history is part of the methodological framework that characterizes these
essays, they present social history in the broadest sense.

Ulrike Jordan

[140] JAP DE MOOR and DIETMAR ROTHERMUND (eds), *Our Laws,*
Their Lands. Land Laws and Land Use in Modern Colonial Societies, Periplus
Parerga, 2 (Münster: Lit, 1995), 172 pp + 4 maps. DM 58.80

Dietmar Rothermund is one of the leading and most authoritative experts on the history of India. His contribution to the present volume, a
collection of conference papers originally delivered at the
Internationales Wissenschaftsforum Heidelberg in November 1991,
deals with 'Land-revenue law and land records in British India'. This
is a topic central to the concept of this book, namely that the land laws
which European colonial powers imposed on their colonies had a lasting influence even after decolonization. In other words, indigenous
customary land laws which had been the rule in pre-colonial times
were usually not reinstated once the new states had attained independence. This thesis is applied to several countries in Africa (Ghana,
Nigeria, Cameroon, francophone West Africa, Belgian Central Africa),
Latin America (Mexico, Surinam), and Asia (India, Indonesia). Thus
the volume, which is interesting from both a historical and an anthro-

pological view-point, takes the fruitful perspective of the periphery, not the traditional one of the former colonial powers. It is therefore a good reflection of the particular interests and problems with which the European powers were challenged in various ways when they conquered new lands. The reason why the legal heritage was retained may lie to some extent in the fact that many freedom-fighters who became influential in the new governments were themselves trained as lawyers and had studied colonial law. Consequently questions arise (to list but a few) concerning the control of land; the establishment of plantations; the effectiveness of European concepts of state control over property rights when applied to native societies; the policy of collecting land-revenue which, for example, was crucial for British India during the nineteenth century; the fiscal and economic interest in land; the question of private property and relations between landlords and tenants; the development of a land market; and the extension of colonial jurisdiction to indigenous law, mixing traditional with new customary legislation. The volume does not force a comparative approach that would put British colonial policy into context with French, German, Dutch, Belgian, Spanish, and Portuguese colonialism. Rather the peculiarities of each individual case, the functions of individual colonial land-laws, are developed, demonstrating, for example, that Spanish colonialism in America can hardly be compared to British colonialism in Asia or Africa.

Benedikt Stuchtey

[141] UDO J. HEBEL, *"Those Images of Jealousie". Identitäten und Alteritäten im puritanischen Neuengland des 17. Jarhunderts*, Mainzer Studien zur Amerikanistik, 38 (Frankfurt/M. etc. : Lang, 1997), xii + 390 pp. £36.00

This is a philologically orientated *Habilitation* thesis in American Studies presented to the Johannes Gutenberg University in Mainz. At its heart is an assessment and interpretation of literary accounts of Puritan New England between 1620 and the 1690s. Using approaches from neo-history, social psychology, and anthropology as well as comparative theories of relations between the self and the 'other', the author investigates texts by opponents and advocates of the Congregational state and church order. The cultural and poetic analysis of heterogeneous texts demonstrates that each account is an attempt to legitimize a particular group while casting doubt upon and criticizing the legitimation of the other, oppositional group. The study emphasizes the wide circulation of these images of the self and the other in the seventeenth century. Later, they served as a projection screen in the process of forming and revising American (national) identity. The jargon used in this linguistic, philological study occasionally gets in the way of reading and comprehension.

Sabine Freitag

[142] WILLI PAUL ADAMS and ANGELA ADAMS (eds), *Die Entstehung der Vereinigten Staaten und ihrer Verfassung. Dokumente 1754-1791*, Periplus-Texte, 2 (Münster: Lit, 1995), 472 pp. DM 34.80

These 175 translated documents, along with the introductions at the beginning of each chapter, present a documentary history of the founding of the American nation and the emergence of its constitution. The book is divided up according to the various spheres of conflict: first, the colonists' battle against England, the homeland, and their demands for political self-government; then the power disputes within the newly established parliaments and questions as to the form and division of power in the individual states; and finally the controversies about the establishment of a competent central government.

The sources selected include not only official texts such as the Declaration of Independence and the text of the constitution (given in the version valid after the later constitutional changes), but also the lively public debate in the American press, already free before the revolution, anonymous newspaper articles and pamphlets, parliamentary debates, political speeches, private letters, and diary entries. For each document there is a reference to the English original. Short introductory pieces put each source into its historical context. The bibliography offers a selection from the English and German literature on the subject up to 1995.

Without doubt, this volume, precisely because of the wide variety of historical sources, offers an excellent introduction to the USA's history of political ideas. According to the editors, the constitutional discussion documented here contradicts John G. A. Pocock's thesis of the overwhelming influence of community and virtue-orientated republicanism or civil humanism, which he sees as an alternative to the individualistic and interest-orientated liberalism of John Locke. Instead the sources show American political thought between 1776 and 1787 to be dominated far more by the Whig doctrine, predominant in English constitutional thinking from 1688, and formulated by Locke and others. Its three axioms were: legitimate rule based on the consent of those ruled (people's sovereignty), restricted governmental power divided among several institutions (constitutionalism and division of power), and the basic or human rights of the individual founded in natural law, which cannot be infringed by legislators or voting majorities.

Sabine Freitag

[143] MICHAEL MANN, *Flottenbau und Forstbetrieb in Indien 1794-1823*, Beiträge zur Südasienforschung, 175 (Stuttgart: Steiner, 1996), xii + 203 pp. DM 68.00

The author is an acknowledged German expert in the field of British colonial rule in India; in 1992 he has published a book on the Central Doab from 1801 to 1854 which can rightly be called a standard work on the topic (cf. Ulrike Jordan ed., *Research on British History in the Federal Republic of Germany 1989-1994*, London, 1996, no. 158). The present study is a contribution to environmental history as well as to the history of the colonial expansion of the East India Company (EIC). An enormous quantity of timber was required for the Royal Navy's expansion programme in the early nineteenth century. The construction of ships of 1,200 t. required whole forests and secure harbours, which were no longer available in New England after 1783. In the Revolutionary Wars and later the Napoleonic Wars the Navy therefore came to rely increasingly on an expanding shipbuilding industry that had developed in the Indian ocean in the eighteenth century. Bombay was to become a centre of high quality shipbuilding and the Malabar coast served as a rich source of timber. Here the author develops the interesting links with German forestry methods which played an important role through the German resident on the Malabar coast, Franz von Wrede. However, the task of controlling the timber trade single-handed was too great. The EIC therefore gave out a major licence to an Indian contractor and minor ones to either Indian merchants or European residents. One crucial issue in supplying the timber soon emerged, namely that of state or private ownership. Between 1810 and 1831 alone twenty-six ships were built for the Royal

Navy; while Bombay specialized in high quality and large vessels, Calcutta's task was to guarantee the construction of a large number of ships. As long as economic pressure at home and warfare abroad demanded a great quantity of timber, England followed a forest conservation policy in India. After 1840, however, this interest vanished.

Benedikt Stuchtey

[144] ISAAC PADINJAREKUTTU, *The Missionary Movement of the 19th and 20th Centuries and its Encounter with India. A Historico-Theological Investigation with Three Case Studies*, Europäische Hochschulschriften, XXIII/527 (Frankfurt/M.: Lang, 1995), xiii + 305 pp. £35.00

This doctoral dissertation examines the historical impact and theological aspects of the Catholic missionary movement in India from the second half of the nineteenth to the first half of the twentieth century. Although Christianity did and does not play a significant role in the religious multiplicity of India, the study reveals that there was considerable reflection in Europe, especially in Western theology, on problems arising from Indian missions. The study tries to find an explanation for this, and examines how missionaries dealt with political and social change in India at the turn of the century. As regards British colonialism and its interest in missions the author states that religious work was much less successful than educational: the people remained Hindus, but progressively accepted Western culture. In fact, if India experienced a renewal, it was not in Christianity but in its own religious culture, though under the impact of British rule. And according to the author the British remained neutral in religious matters despite the revolt of 1857. Thus change, which was seen by some Indian intellectuals as valuable in itself, came in the form of a deliberate movement for social and political reform, while preventing any serious interaction between Christianity and Hinduism.

Benedikt Stuchtey

[145] TILMAN DEDERING, *Hate the Old and Follow the New. Khoekhoe and Missionaries in Early Nineteenth-Century Namibia*, Missionsgeschichtliches Archiv: Studien der Berliner Gesellschaft für Missionsgeschichte, 2 (Stuttgart: Steiner, 1997), 205 pp. DM 76.00

This Cape Town University dissertation (with its rather unwelcoming title) studies the social transformation among Khoekhoe in early nineteenth-century, pre-colonial Namibia resulting from the interaction between European, especially British, missionaries and Africans. Dedering, whose work is based on extensive research in the Cape Archives, and the archives of Windhoek, Johannesburg, and Rhodes University Grahamstown, shows how the extension of the colonial frontier changed social relations in the indigenous societies and transformed their world-views. Further it becomes evident that the classic division – colonizers here, colonized there – is not sufficient if one takes into account that the so-called traditional societies had political and socio-economic agendas of their own. Thus missionary and colonial activities did not merely provoke reaction from the Africans but revealed that foreign challenges were often countered by initiatives on the part of the natives themselves. The period this study focuses on (*c.* 1780 to *c.* 1840) is particularly crucial for the process of social and economic transition in Africa, whereby indigenous patterns were reshaped. It concentrates on a region hitherto rather neglected by scholars, the Cape's north-western frontier. According to the author, this area has not been extensively researched because the term frontier has predominantly been associated with the eastern areas. The fact that Namibia became a German colony in 1884 (as South West Africa) and enjoyed German missionary influence through the Rhenish mission from the 1840s is also part of this largely forgotten history and, in a broader sense, of the history of the Cape.

Benedikt Stuchtey

[146] ROLAND LHOTTA, *Imperiale Verfassungsgerichtsbarkeit und Föderalismus. Das Judicial Committee of the Privy Council und der BNA Act*, Studien und Materialien zur Verfassungsgerichtsbarkeit, 63 (Baden-Baden: Nomos, 1995), 282 pp. DM 74.00

As the series title indicates, this Düsseldorf Ph.D. thesis is an investigation of the legal effects of the appeal process to the Judicial Committee of the Privy Council on the Canadian Constitution. It starts by surveying the history of the Judicial Committee of the Privy Council from its beginnings to the nineteenth century. The main part of the book is concerned with the legal technicalities of the appeals procedure to what had become the highest court of the British Empire, and the consequences of the court's decisions. Lhotta points out that, contrary to the centralist vision of Canada contained in the 1867 British North America Act, the Judicial Committee's decisions immediately tended to strengthen provincial rights because the Committee considered the federation of British North America as a 'compact in which the provinces also remained sovereign'. This political attitude on the part of the Judicial Committee, barely hidden in various moves through which it effectively granted itself the power to test Canadian legislation according to standards of 'common sense' or political expediency, made the appeals to London controversial in Canada. The resulting political polemics, the author argues, have caused some of the technical and legal justifications of the committee's stance to be misunderstood. Lhotta voices some doubts as to whether the Privy Council can really be considered a supreme court for Canada, as its judges were appointed by Britain and the court belonged to a higher-ranking political entity which looked, as it were, downwards from a superior position. In its functions, however, it was not dissimilar to an interventionist domestic supreme court.

Andreas Fahrmeir

[147] HERMANN JOSEPH HIERY, *Das Deutsche Reich in der Südsee (1900-1921). Eine Annäherung an die Erfahrungen verschiedener Kulturen,* Publications of the German Historical Institute London, 37 (Göttingen: Vandenhoeck & Ruprecht, 1995), 353 pp. DM 112.00

The German colonial empire in the South Pacific may have been a backwater and lasted only for some fourteen years: approximately as many square miles in area as the old Federal Republic, split into innumerable islands (the largest being Samoa), with a population equal to that of Wiesbaden, capital of Hesse, it was ruled by no more than 150 imperial officials, most of them middle class and with no career prospects. Yet apparently German rule left a deep impression on the indigenous population and even more surprisingly, a positive one. This is the puzzle the author sets out to explain in considerable and well researched detail. Why, he asks, should Germany wish to occupy these far-away islands? Not much was to be gained in economic terms; the volume of trade was virtually negligible. Strategic arguments turned out to be phoney too. Apart from the colonial craze as such, the romantic fascination with the South Seas, which captivated German public imagination, seems to have been the main driving force. The 'innocent savages' were to receive the blessings of German culture. However, on the spot it could only work through adaptation and interchange. The author examines this process on all levels of social communication such as general ethics, law and order, language, way of life in view of the climatic conditions, education and health care, and last but not least sexual relations between the overlords and their subjects. The much-needed co-operation of the indigenous élites could only be guaranteed by respecting local customs and traditions, as long as they did not harm the population (for instance, cannibalism). As a result, colonial administrators were often at odds with commercial interests and missionary zeal. Not racism, Hiery argues, but the degree of self-determination should be the yard-stick by which to judge colonial rule. Left to their own devices in this far-away corner of the world the German colonial administrators did a much better job than their German colleagues in Africa or, for that matter, than the successor states.

Maps, statistics, and illustrations supplement the text, which makes easy reading (that is, free of jargon), with useful information.

Lothar Kettenacker

[148] TOBIAS DÖRING, *Chinua Achebe und Joyce Cary. Ein postkoloniales Rewriting englischer Afrika-Fiktionen*, Transatlantik, Afrika – Lateinamerika, 6 (Pfaffenweiler: Centaurus, 1996), x + 231 pp. DM 89.80

The post-colonial rewriting studied in this book is an attempt to revise the image of a colony as constructed by English literature. This also calls into question the rhetoric employed for the representation of the cultural 'other'. Thus post-colonial rewriting firstly rehabilitates the indigenous cultural and historical traditions of former colonies. Secondly, it critically investigates literary canons with the result that Eurocentric concepts are certainly undermined, but also that nativist assumptions are sometimes questioned. The present study focuses on four novels. Two famous works by the English novelist

Joyce Cary (1888-1957), *The African Witch* (1936) and *Mister Johnson* (1939), are contrasted with what the Nigerian author Chinua Achebe (born 1930) wrote some twenty years later about the same historical and political context of colonial West Africa in *Things Fall Apart* (1958) and *No Longer At Ease* (1960). According to Döring, however, this process of rewriting is highly ambivalent. Achebe had to accept and then repeat the discourse of colonial hegemony in order to resist it. Nor can he free himself from the specific Nigerian situation: the politics of decolonization coupled with dependance on the English language, its textual tradition, and imperial education policies by which African authors are also moulded. Reconstruction of the colonial discourse and construction of a counter-discourse thus reflect the possibilities and limitations of the conflict between colonial hegemony and post-colonial resistance in cultural matters. The potential of a critical re-writing seems to lie, then, in a continuous decanonizing which in itself contributes to the cultural aspects of imperialism and anti-imperialism.

Benedikt Stuchtey

[149] HANS HECKLAU (ed.), *Ostafrika-Bibliographie. Kenia – Tansania – Uganda 1945-1993* (Munich: Saur, 1996), xvi + 278 pp. DM 168.00

This bibliography contains mostly English titles, but also a considerable number in German. It covers all aspects of natural features, population, society, culture, history, political life, common law, administration, economy, regional planning, and environmental affairs, and provides descriptions of countries and regions. In the history sections the colonial and post-colonial periods receive considerable attention. The bibliography is divided into four chapters: East Africa in general, Kenya, Tanzania, and Uganda. According to the editor the years between 1960 and 1980 were the most productive for East African geographical publications. The subsequent decrease in productivity was certainly due to political developments and civil wars, but also to the fact that governments only promoted research considered relevant to national economic development.

Benedikt Stuchtey

BOOKS NOT RECEIVED

[150] Elsbeth Andre, *Ein Königshof auf Reisen. Der Kontinentalaufenthalt Eduards III. von England 1338-1340*, Beihefte zum Archiv für Kulturgeschichte, 41 (Cologne: Böhlau, 1996), ix + 293 pp. DM 78.00

[151] Antje Hagen, *Deutsche Direktinvestitionen in Großbritannien, 1871-1918*, Beiträge zur Unternehmensgeschichte, 3 (Stuttgart: Steiner, 1997), 356 pp. DM 148.00

[152] Próinséas Ní Chatháin and Michael Richter (eds), *Irland und Europa im früheren Mittelalter. Bildung und Literatur / Ireland and Europe in the Early Middle Ages. Learning and Literature* (Stuttgart: Klett-Cotta, 1996), 318 pp. DM 228.00

[153] *Ein Herzogtum und viele Kronen. Coburg in Bayern und Europa. Aufsatzband* (Regensburg: Pustet, 1997), 224 pp. DM 54.00

[154] Freddy Litten, *Britische, amerikanische und französische Aktenpublikationen zu Westeuropa seit 1789. Ein Führer zu Mikroform-Beständen der Bayerischen Staatsbibliothek*. Mitteilungen, 21 (Munich: Osteuropa Institut, 1997), 58 pp. Price on application

[155] Donal O'Sullivan, *Furcht und Faszination. Deutsche und britische Rußlandbilder 1921-1933* (Cologne: Böhlau, 1996), 360 pp. DM 68.00

[156] Florian Henning Setzen, *Neutralität im Zweiten Weltkrieg. Irland, Schweden und die Schweiz im Vergleich*, Studien zur Zeitgeschichte, 14 (Hamburg: Kovac, 1997), 160 pp. DM 98.00

[157] Johannes H. Voigt, *Die Erforschung Australiens. Der Briefwechsel zwischen August Petermann und Ferdinand von Mueller 1861-1878* (Gotha: Perthes, 1996), 159 pp. DM 42.00

LIST OF ARTICLES

BRITISH HISTORY
General Studies

[158] Awbery, G. M., 'The English Language in Wales', in [10] Hildegard L. C. Tristram (ed.), *The Celtic Englishes*, Anglistische Forschungen, 247 (Heidelberg: Winter, 1997), pp. 86-99

[159] Berghoff, Hartmut and Dieter Ziegler, 'Sidney Pollards Lebensweg und Lebenswerk', in [41] Hartmut Berghoff and Dieter Ziegler (eds), *Pionier und Nachzügler? Vergleichende Studien zur Geschichte Großbritanniens und Deutschlands im Zeitalter der Industrialisierung. Festschrift für Sidney Pollard zum 70. Geburtstag*, Veröffentlichungen Arbeitskreis Deutsche England-Forschung, 28 (Bochum: Brockmeyer, 1995), pp. 1-14

[160] Birks, Peter B. H., 'More Logic and Less Experience: The Difference between Scots Law and English Law', in [21] David L. Carey Miller and Reinhard Zimmermann (eds), *The Civilian Tradition and Scots Law: Aberdeen Quincentenary Essay*, Schriften zur Europäischen Rechts- und Verfassungsgeschichte, 20 (Berlin: Duncker & Humblot, 1997), pp. 167-90

[161] Blaicher, Günther, 'Konstanten in der englischen Wahrnehmung Deutschlands', in [14] Hans Süssmuth (ed.), *Deutschlandbilder in Dänemark und England, in Frankreich und den Niederlanden: Dokumentation der Tagung Deutschlandbilder in Dänemark und England, in Frankreich und den Niederlanden, 15.-18. Dezember 1993, Leutherheider Forum*, Schriften der Paul-Kleinewefers-Stiftung, 3 (Baden-Baden: Nomos, 1996), pp. 251-66

[162] Blomeyer, Peter, 'Thomas Hobbes und Carl Schmitt: Essay über ein staatsphilosophisches Mißverständnis', in Ernst O. Bräunche and Hermann Hiery (eds), *Geschichte als Verantwortung. Festschrift für Hans Fenske zum 60. Geburtstag* (Karlsruhe: Wolf, 1996), pp. 1-10

[163] Bohrer, Karl Heinz, 'Epochenwandel auf englisch. Vom Erhabenen zum Banalen und wieder zurück', *Merkur*, 51 (1997), pp. 1045-50

[164] Cairns, John W., 'The Civil Law Tradition in Scottish Legal Thought', in **[21]** David L. Carey Miller and Reinhard Zimmermann (eds), *The Civilian Tradition and Scots Law: Aberdeen Quincentenary Essay*, Schriften zur Europäischen Rechts- und Verfassungsgeschichte, 20 (Berlin: Duncker & Humblot, 1997), pp. 191-224

[165] Chorus, Jeroen M. J., 'Civilian Elements in European Civil Procedure', in **[21]** David L. Carey Miller and Reinhard Zimmermann (eds), *The Civilian Tradition and Scots Law: Aberdeen Quincentenary Essay*, Schriften zur Europäischen Rechts- und Verfassungsgeschichte, 20 (Berlin: Duncker & Humblot, 1997), pp. 295-308

[166] Cottrell, Philip L., 'London as a Centre of Communications: From the Printing Press to the Travelling Post Office', in Michael Nordt (ed.), *Kommunikationsrevolutionen. Die neuen Medien des 16. und 19. Jahrhunderts*, Wirtschafts- und sozialhistorische Studien, 3 (Cologne: Böhlau, 1995), pp. 157-78

[167] Crossick, Geoffrey, 'And what should they know of England? Die vergleichende Geschichtsschreibung im heutigen Großbritannien', in Heinz-Gerhard Haupt and Jürgen Kocka (eds), *Geschichte und Vergleich: Ansätze und Ergebnisse international vergleichender Geschichtsschreibung* (Frankfurt/M.: Campus, 1996), pp. 61-76

[168] Eisenberg, Christiane, 'Pferderennen zwischen "Händler-" und "Heldenkultur". Verlauf und Dynamik einer englisch-deutschen Kulturbewegung', in **[41]** Hartmut Berghoff and Dieter Ziegler (eds), *Pionier und Nachzügler? Vergleichende Studien zur Geschichte Großbritanniens und Deutschlands im Zeitalter der Industrialisierung. Festschrift für Sidney Pollard zum 70. Geburtstag*, Veröffentlichungen Arbeitskreis Deutsche England-Forschung, 28 (Bochum: Brockmeyer, 1995), pp. 235-58

[169] Elvert, Jürgen, 'Nordirland als dreifache Peripherie', in Hans-Heinrich Nolte (ed.), *Europäische Innere Peripherien im 20. Jahrhundert / European Internal Peripheries in the 20th Century*, Historische Mitteilungen, 23 (Stuttgart: Franz Steiner, 1997), pp. 113-30

[170] Feenstra, Robert, 'The Development of European Private Law: A Romanist Watershed?', in [21] David L. Carey Miller and Reinhard Zimmermann (eds), *The Civilian Tradition and Scots Law: Aberdeen Quincentenary Essay*, Schriften zur Europäischen Rechts- und Verfassungsgeschichte, 20 (Berlin: Duncker & Humblot, 1997), pp. 103-16

[171] Gordon, William M., 'A Comparison of the Influence of Roman Law in England and Scotland', in [21] David L. Carey Miller and Reinhard Zimmermann (eds), *The Civilian Tradition and Scots Law: Aberdeen Quincentenary Essay*, Schriften zur Europäischen Rechts- und Verfassungsgeschichte, 20 (Berlin: Duncker & Humblot, 1997), pp. 135-48

[172] Görlach, Manfred, 'Celtic Englishes?', in [10] Hildegard L. C. Tristram (ed.), *The Celtic Englishes*, Anglistische Forschungen, 247 (Heidelberg: Winter, 1997), pp. 27-54

[173] Harvie, Christopher, 'The Challenge of the New Eastern Europe for British Studies and German Universities', in [25] Wolfgang Mackiewicz and Dieter Wolff (eds), *British Studies in Germany: Essays in Honor of Frank Frankel* (Trier: WVT – Wissenschaftlicher Verlag Trier, 1997), pp. 47-53

[174] Johnston, David, 'The General Influence of Roman Institutions of State and Public Law', in [21] David L. Carey Miller and Reinhard Zimmermann (eds), *The Civilian Tradition and Scots Law: Aberdeen Quincentenary Essay*, Schriften zur Europäischen Rechts- und Verfassungsgeschichte, 20 (Berlin: Duncker & Humblot, 1997), pp. 87-102

[175] Klippel, Friederike, 'Presenting the Past: English Cultures(s) in German English Language Textbooks since the Eighteenth Century', in [26] Jens-Ulrich Davids and Richard Stinshoff (eds), *The Past in the Present: Proceedings of the 5th Annual British and Cultural Studies Conference, Oldenburg 1994* (Frankfurt/M.: Lang, 1996), pp. 89-106

[176] Knight, Stephen, 'The Emergence of Robin Hood as a National Hero', in [20] Kevin Carpenter (ed.), *Robin Hood: Die vielen Gesichter des edlen Räubers / The Many Faces of that Celebrated Outlaw* (Oldenburg: Bis. Bibliotheks- und Informationssystem der Universität Oldenburg, 1995), pp. 45-53

[177]   Kress, Hans-Joachim, 'Geschichte', in [3] *Großbritannien – London*, Brockhaus: Die Bibliothek. Länder und Städte (Leipzig: Brockhaus, 1997), pp. 63-134.

[178]   Lehmkuhl, Ursula, 'Britische Formeln zur Macht: Eine empirische Bestandsaufnahme', in [79] Hans-Heinrich Jansen and Ursula Lehmkuhl (eds), *Großbritannien, das Empire und die Welt. Britische Außenpolitik zwischen "Größe" und "Selbstbehauptung" 1850-1990*, Veröffentlichungen Arbeitskreis Deutsche England-Forschung, 25 (Bochum: Brockmeyer, 1995), pp. 295-304

[179]   Lehmkuhl, Ursula, '"Größe" und "Selbstbehauptung" als Formeln britischer Weltgeltung: Einige theoretische und methodische Überlegungen', in [79] Hans-Heinrich Jansen and Ursula Lehmkuhl (eds), *Großbritannien, das Empire und die Welt. Britische Außenpolitik zwischen "Größe" und "Selbstbehauptung" 1850-1990*, Veröffentlichungen Arbeitskreis Deutsche England-Forschung, 25 (Bochum: Brockmeyer, 1995), pp. 3-29

[180]   Mestre, Jean-Louis, 'Juridictions judiciaires et annulation des actes administratifs dans la France d'Ancien Régime et en Angleterre', in [40] Erk Volkmar Heyen (ed.), *Verwaltung und Verwaltungsrecht in Frankreich und England (18./19. Jh.) / Administration et droit administratif en France et Angleterre (18e/19e s.) / Administration and Administrative Law in France and England (18th/ 19th c.)* (Baden-Baden: Nomos, 1996) = *Jahrbuch für europäische Verwaltungsgeschichte*, 8 (1996), pp. 37-54

[181]   Miller, David L. Carey, 'A Scottish Celebration of the European Legal Tradition', in [21] David L. Carey Miller and Reinhard Zimmermann (eds), *The Civilian Tradition and Scots Law: Aberdeen Quincentenary Essay*, Schriften zur Europäischen Rechts- und Verfassungsgeschichte, 20 (Berlin: Duncker & Humblot, 1997), pp. 19-74

[182]   Mommsen, Wolfgang J., 'Das Englandbild der Deutschen und die britische Sicht seit dem Ende des 18. Jahrhunderts', in [14] Hans Süssmuth (ed.), *Deutschlandbilder in Dänemark und England, in Frankreich und den Niederlanden: Dokumentation der Tagung Deutschlandbilder in Dänemark und England, in Frankreich und den Niederlanden, 15.-18. Dezember 1993, Leutherheider Forum*, Schriften der Paul-Kleinewefers-Stiftung, 3 (Baden-Baden: Nomos, 1996), pp. 215-34

[183] Ohlgren, Thomas H., 'Teaching Robin Hood at University: A Practical Guide', in [20] Kevin Carpenter (ed.), *Robin Hood: Die vielen Gesichter des edlen Räubers / The Many Faces of that Celebrated Outlaw* (Oldenburg: Bis. Bibliotheks- und Informationssystem der Universität Oldenburg, 1995), pp. 145-54

[184] Prinz, Michael, 'Von der Nahrungssicherung zum Einkommens-ausgleich. Entstehung und Durchsetzung des Selbsthilfemusters Konsumverein 1770-1914 in England und Deutschland', in Hannes Siegrist, Hartmut Kaelble, and Jürgen Kocka (eds), *Europäische Konsumgeschichte: Zur Gesellschafts- und Kulturgeschichte des Konsums (18. bis 20. Jahrhundert)* (Frankfurt/M.: Campus, 1997), pp. 717-46

[185] Rautenhaus, Heide, 'Robin Hood, vom Sherwood ins Klassenzimmer: Zur Behandlung des Mythos im Englischunterricht', in [20] Kevin Carpenter (ed.), *Robin Hood: Die vielen Gesichter des edlen Räubers / The Many Faces of that Celebrated Outlaw* (Oldenburg: Bis. Bibliotheks- und Informationssystem der Universität Oldenburg, 1995), pp. 155-63

[186] Robertson, J. J., 'The Canon Law Vehicle of Civilian Influence with Particular Reference to Scotland', in [21] David L. Carey Miller and Reinhard Zimmermann (eds), *The Civilian Tradition and Scots Law: Aberdeen Quincentenary Essay*, Schriften zur Europäischen Rechts- und Verfassungsgeschichte, 20 (Berlin: Duncker & Humblot, 1997), pp. 117-34

[187] Rodger, Alan, 'The Use of the Civil Law in Scottish Courts', in [21] David L. Carey Miller and Reinhard Zimmermann (eds), *The Civilian Tradition and Scots Law: Aberdeen Quincentenary Essay*, Schriften zur Europäischen Rechts- und Verfassungsgeschichte, 20 (Berlin: Duncker & Humblot, 1997), pp. 225-38

[188] Schofield, Roger, '"Montags-Kind, schön Angesicht". Zur Wahl des Wochentags für Taufen, Heiraten und Begräbnisse in England, 1540-1849', in Josef Ehmer, Tamara K. Hareven, and Richard Wall (eds), *Historische Familienforschung. Ergebnisse und Kontroversen Michael Mitterauer zum 60. Geburtstag* (Frankfurt/M.: Campus, 1997), pp. 83-102

[189] Schulze-Marmeling, Dietrich, 'Zur Geschichte Nordirlands', in [9] Dietrich Schulze-Marmeling (ed.), *Nordirland. Geschichte, Landschaft, Kultur und Touren* (Göttingen: Verlag die Werkstatt, 1996), pp. 21-130

[190] Sellar, W. D. H., 'The Resilience of the Scottish Common Law', in [21] David L. Carey Miller and Reinhard Zimmermann (eds), *The Civilian Tradition and Scots Law: Aberdeen Quincentenary Essay*, Schriften zur Europäischen Rechts- und Verfassungsgeschichte, 20 (Berlin: Duncker & Humblot, 1997), pp. 149-66

[191] Stenzel, Gudrun, 'Robin Hood und Maid Marian: Eine abenteuerliche Romanze?', in [20] Kevin Carpenter (ed.), *Robin Hood: Die vielen Gesichter des edlen Räubers / The Many Faces of that Celebrated Outlaw* (Oldenburg: Bis. Bibliotheks- und Informationssystem der Universität Oldenburg, 1995), pp. 87-96

[192] Stratmann, Gerd, 'British Studies and Teachability', in [25] Wolfgang Mackiewicz and Dieter Wolff (eds), *British Studies in Germany: Essays in Honor of Frank Frankel* (Trier: WVT – Wissenschaftlicher Verlag Trier, 1997), pp. 122-6

[193] Stuchtey, Benedikt, 'Geschichte und Kultur', in [4] *Irland – Dublin*, Länder und Städte, 3 (Leipzig: Brockhaus, 1997), pp. 91-150

[194] Visser, Daniel, 'Placing the Civilian Influence in Scotland: A Roman-Dutch Perspective', in [21] David L. Carey Miller and Reinhard Zimmermann (eds), *The Civilian Tradition and Scots Law: Aberdeen Quincentenary Essay*, Schriften zur Europäischen Rechts- und Verfassungsgeschichte, 20 (Berlin: Duncker & Humblot, 1997), pp. 239-58

[195] Wright, Vincent, 'The Development of Public Administration in Britain and France: Fundamental Similarities Masking Basic Differences', in [40] Erk Volkmar Heyen (ed.), *Verwaltung und Verwaltungsrecht in Frankreich und England (18./19. Jh.) / Administration et droit administratif en France et Angleterre (18e/19e s.) / Administration and Administrative Law in France and England (18th/19th c.)* (Baden-Baden: Nomos, 1996) = *Jahrbuch für europäische Verwaltungsgeschichte*, 8 (1996), pp. 305-22

[196] Zimmermann, Reinhard, 'The Civil Law in European Codes', in [21] David L. Carey Miller and Reinhard Zimmermann (eds), *The Civilian Tradition and Scots Law: Aberdeen Quincentenary Essay*, Schriften zur Europäischen Rechts- und Verfassungsgeschichte, 20 (Berlin: Duncker & Humblot, 1997), pp. 259-94

Sixth to Fifteenth Centuries

[197] Bake, John M., 'The Superior Courts in England 1540-1800', in Bernhard Diestelkamp (ed.), *Oberste Gerichtsbarkeit und zentrale Gewalt im Europa der frühen Neuzeit*, Quellen und Forschungen zur Höchsten Gerichtsbarkeit im Alten Reich, 29 (Cologne: Böhlau, 1996), pp. 73-111

[198] Barrow, Geoffrey W. S., 'The English Royal Chancery in the Earlier 13th Century', *Archiv für Diplomatik*, 41 (1995), pp. 241-8

[199] Bhattacharji, Santa, 'Pearl and the Liturgical "Common of Virgins"', *Medium Aevum*, 64 (1995), pp. 37-50

[200] Cluse, Christoph, '"Fabula ineptissima". Die Ritualmordlegende um Adam von Bristol nach der Handschrift London, British Library Harley 957', *Aschkenas*, 5 (1995), pp. 293-330

[201] Deliyannis, D. M., 'Church Burial in Anglo-Saxon England: The Prerogative of Kings', *Frühmittelalterliche Studien*, 29 (1995), pp. 96-119

[202] Dobson, Barrie and John Taylor, '"Rymes of Robyn Hood": The Early Ballads and the *Gest*', in [20] Kevin Carpenter (ed.), *Robin Hood: Die vielen Gesichter des edlen Räubers / The Many Faces of that Celebrated Outlaw* (Oldenburg: Bis. Bibliotheks- und Informationssystem der Universität Oldenburg, 1995), pp. 35-44

[203] Doe, Norman and James Young, 'Law and Administration in England from the Middle Ages to the 17th Century', in [40] Erk Volkmar Heyen (ed.), *Verwaltung und Verwaltungsrecht in Frankreich und England (18./19. Jh.) / Administration et droit administratif en France et Angleterre (18e/19e s.) / Administration and Administrative Law in France and England (18th/19th c.)* (Baden-Baden: Nomos, 1996) = *Jahrbuch für europäische Verwaltungsgeschichte*, 8 (1996), pp. 1-18

[204] Enright, Michael J., 'Veleda from a Comparative Perspective', in [152] Próinséas Ní Chatháin and Michael Richter (eds), *Irland und Europa im früheren Mittelalter: Bildung und Literatur / Ireland and Europe in the Early Middle Ages: Learning and Literature* (Stuttgart: Klett-Cotta, 1996), pp. 219-27

[205] Figueira, Robert C., 'Ricardus de Mores at Common Law. The Second Career of an Anglo-Norman Canonist', in L. Kolmer and P. Segl (eds), *Regensburg, Bayern und Europa. Festschrift für Kurt Reindel zum 70. Geburtstag* (Regensburg: Universitätsverlag, 1995), pp. 281-300

[206] Georgi, Wolfgang, 'Bischof Keonwald von Worcester und die Heirat Ottos I. mit Eghita im Jahre 929', *Historisches Jahrbuch der Görres-Gesellschaft*, 115 (1995), pp. 1-40

[207] Goetz, Hans-Werner, 'Johannes von Salisbury (ca. 1115/20-1180), *Historica pontificalis'*, in Volker Reinhardt (ed.), *Hauptwerke der Geschichtsschreibung*, Kröners Taschenausgabe, 435 (Stuttgart: Kröner, 1997), pp. 310-13.

[208] Haupt, Barbara, 'Wahrheit und Augenlust der Bücher. Zu Brandans "Reise"', *Zeitschrift für deutsche Philologie*, 115 (1996), pp. 231-7

[209] Holt, James C., 'Robin Hood: The Origins of the Legend', in [20] Kevin Carpenter (ed.), *Robin Hood: Die vielen Gesichter des edlen Räubers / The Many Faces of that Celebrated Outlaw* (Oldenburg: Bis. Bibliotheks- und Informationssystem der Universität Oldenburg, 1995), pp. 27-34

[210] Hunt, Tony, 'An Anglo-Norman Treatise on Female Religion', *Medium Aevum*, 64 (1995), pp. 205-31

[211] Jenks, Stuart, 'England und die kontinentalen Messen im 15. Jahrhundert und die Entstehung der Merchant Adventurers', in Peter Johanek and Heinz Stoob (eds), *Europäische Messen und Märktesysteme in Mittelalter und Neuzeit*, Städteforschung, Reihe A (Cologne: Böhlau, 1996), pp. 57-86

[212] Kapriev, Georgi, 'Menschliche Individualität und Personalität bei Anselm von Canterbury', in Jan Aertsen and Andreas Speer (eds), *Individuum und Individualität im Mittelalter*. Miscellanea Medievalia, 24 (Berlin: de Gruyter, 1996), pp. 355-70

[213] Keene, Derek, 'London im Jahre 1245: Eine Metropole, noch keine Hauptstadt?', in Wilfried Hartmann *et al.* (eds), *Europas Städte zwischen Zwang und Freiheit: Die europäische Stadt in der Mitte des 13. Jahrhunderts*, Schriften des Europa-Kolloquiums im Alten Reichstag (Regensburg: Universitätsverlag, 1995), pp. 141-54

[214] Kindermann, Udo, 'Zur Ästhetik der Schicksalsbewältigung in einer hochmittelalterlichen Logotherapie', *Das Mittelalter*, 1 (1996), pp. 43-50

[215] Kleinschmidt, Harald, 'Stirps Regia und Adel im frühen Wessex: Studien zu Personennamen in der Epistolographie, Historiographie und Urkundenüberlieferung', *Historisches Jahrbuch der Görres Gesellschaft*, 117 (1997), pp. 1-37

[216] Kraus, Thomas R., 'König Wenzel auf der Reise nach Reims und die Hoffnungen König Richards II. von England auf die römischdeutsche Krone 1397/98', *Deutsches Archiv für Erforschung des Mittelalters*, 52 (1996), pp. 599-616

[217] Leisi, Ernst, 'Chaucers "Canterbury Tales"', in Walter Buckl (ed.), *Das 14. Jahrhundert. Jahrhundert in der Krise*, Eichstätter Colloquium (Regensburg: Pustet, 1995), pp. 213-25

[218] Lottes, Günther, 'Von "tenure" zu "property". Die Entstehung des Eigentumsbegriffes aus dem Zerfall des Feudalrechts', in [19] Günther Lottes (ed.), *Der Eigentumsbegriff im englischen politischen Denken*, Veröffentlichungen Arbeitskreis Deutsche England-Forschung, 16 (Bochum: Brockmeyer, 1995), pp. 1-22

[219] MacEoin, Gearóid, 'Observations on some Middle-Irish Homilies', in [152] Próinséas Ní Chatháin and Michael Richter (eds), *Irland und Europa im früheren Mittelalter: Bildung und Literatur / Ireland and Europe in the Early Middle Ages: Learning and Literature* (Stuttgart: Klett-Cotta, 1996), pp. 195-211

[220] Mackey, James P., 'The Theology of Columbanus', in [152] Próinséas Ní Chatháin and Michael Richter (eds), *Irland und Europa im früheren Mittelalter: Bildung und Literatur / Ireland and Europe in the Early Middle Ages: Learning and Literature* (Stuttgart: Klett-Cotta, 1996), pp. 228-39

[221] McNamara, Martin, 'Early medieval Irish eschatology', in [152] Próinséas Ní Chatháin and Michael Richter (eds), *Irland und Europa im früheren Mittelalter: Bildung und Literatur / Ireland and Europe in the Early Middle Ages: Learning and Literature* (Stuttgart: Klett-Cotta, 1996), pp. 42-75

[222] MacQueen, Hector L., 'The Foundation of Law Teaching at the University of Aberdeen', in [21] David L. Carey Miller and Reinhard Zimmermann (eds), *The Civilian Tradition and Scots Law: Aberdeen Quincentenary Essay*, Schriften zur Europäischen Rechts- und Verfassungsgeschichte, 20 (Berlin: Duncker & Humblot, 1997), pp. 75-86

[223] Marsden, Richard, 'Job in His Place: The Ezra Miniature in the Codex Amiatinus', *Scriptorium*, 49 (1995), pp. 1-15

[224] Mentgen, Gerd, 'Die Vertreibungen der Juden aus England und Frankreich im Mittelalter', *Aschkenas*, 7 (1997), pp. 11-54

[225] Millett, Bella, 'The Songs of Entertainers and the Song of the Angels: Vernacular Lyric Fragments in Odo of Cheriton's "Sermones de festis"', *Medium Aevum*, 64 (1995), pp. 17-36

[226] Moran, Dermot, 'Eriugena's Theory of the "Periphyseon": Explorations in the Neoplatonic Tradition', in [152] Próinséas Ní Chatháin and Michael Richter (eds), *Irland und Europa im früheren Mittelalter: Bildung und Literatur / Ireland and Europe in the Early Middle Ages: Learning and Literature* (Stuttgart: Klett-Cotta, 1996), pp. 240-60

[227] Müller, Markus, 'Die Welfen und Formen höfischer Repräsentation im anglonormannischen Reich', in *Heinrich der Löwe und seine Zeit, Herrschaft und Repräsentation der Welfen 1125-1235. Katalogbuch zur Ausstellung Herzog-Anton-Ulrich Museum, Braunschweig 6. 8. 95 - 12. 1. 96*, vol 2 (Munich: Himer, 1995), pp. 377-86

[228] Müller-Oberhäuser, G., '"Cynna gemyndig". Sitte und Etikette in der altenglischen Literatur', *Frühmittelalterliche Studien*, 30 (1996), pp. 19-59

[229] Ní Chatháin, Próinséas, 'Ogham Terminology in Táin Bó Cauilnge', in [152] Próinséas Ní Chatháin and Michael Richter (eds), *Irland und Europa im früheren Mittelalter: Bildung und Literatur / Ireland and Europe in the Early Middle Ages: Learning and Literature* (Stuttgart: Klett-Cotta, 1996), pp. 212-6

[230] Nilgen, Ursula, 'Heinrich der Löwe in England', in *Heinrich der Löwe und seine Zeit, Herrschaft und Repräsentation der Welfen 1125-1235. Katalogbuch zur Ausstellung Herzog-Anton-Ulrich Museum, Braunschweig 6. 8. 95 - 12. 1. 96*, vol. 2 (Munich: Himer, 1995), pp. 329-42

[231] Palliser, David M., 'York – Englands zweite Stadt?', in Wilfried Hartmann *et al.* (eds), *Europas Städte zwischen Zwang und Freiheit: Die europäische Stadt in der Mitte des 13. Jahrhunderts*, Schriften des Europa-Kolloquiums im Alten Reichstag (Regensburg: Universitätsverlag, 1995), pp. 155-168

[232] Parker, Hugh C., 'The Pagan Gods in Joseph of Exter's "De bello troiano"', *Medium Aevum*, 64 (1995), pp. 273-7

[233] Picard, Jean M., 'Tailoring the Sources: The Irish Hagiographer at Work', in [152] Próinséas Ní Chatháin and Michael Richter (eds), *Irland und Europa im früheren Mittelalter: Bildung und Literatur / Ireland and Europe in the Early Middle Ages: Learning and Literature* (Stuttgart: Klett-Cotta, 1996), pp. 261-74

[234] Preissinger, Kurt, 'Die MacDonalds von Islay and Lords of the Isles. Schottische Adelige und gälische Fürsten', *Archiv für Kulturgeschichte*, 77 (1995), pp. 301-22

[235] Reichl, K., 'Satirische und politische Lyrik in der anglo-irischen Kildare-Handschrift (Hs. BL Harley 013)', in Christoph Cormeau (ed.), *Zeitgeschehen und seine Darstellung im Mittelalter / L'actualité et sa représentation au Moyen Age* (Bonn: Bouvier, 1995), pp. 173-99

[236] Reitemeier, Arnd, 'Ritter, Königstreue, Diplomaten. Deutsche Ritter als Vertraute der englischen und deutschen Könige im 14./15. Jahrhundert', *Zeitschrift für historische Forschung*, 24 (1997), pp. 1-24

[237] Renner, Steffen, 'Versuchten die Engländer im Kampf gegen Owain Glyndwr die walisische Sprache zu vernichten?', in Roland Martini (ed.), *Sprachenpolitik in Grenzregionen / Politique linguistique dans les régions frontalières* (Saarbrücken: Saarländische Druckerei, 1996), pp. 79-103

[238] Reuter, Timothy, 'Wilhelm von Newburgh (ca. 1135-1198/1208), *Historia rerum Anglicarum*', in Volker Reinhardt (ed.), *Hauptwerke der Geschichtsschreibung*, Kröners Taschenausgabe, 435 (Stuttgart: Kröner, 1997), pp. 724-26

[239] Richter, Michael, 'Giraldus Cambrensis (Girald von Wales, 1146-1223), *Werke zur walisischen und englischen Geschichte*', in Volker Reinhardt (ed.), *Hauptwerke der Geschichtsschreibung*, Kröners Taschenausgabe, 435 (Stuttgart: Kröner, 1997), pp. 227-9

[240] Richter, Michael, 'The Personnel of Learning in Early Medieval Ireland', in [152] Próinséas Ní Chatháin and Michael Richter (eds), *Irland und Europa im früheren Mittelalter: Bildung und Literatur / Ireland and Europe in the Early Middle Ages: Learning and Literature* (Stuttgart: Klett-Cotta, 1996), pp. 275-308

[241] Sarnowsky, Jürgen, 'Mord im Dom: Thomas Beckett 1170', in Alexander Demandt (ed.), *Das Attentat in der Geschichte* (Cologne: Böhlau, 1996), pp. 75-90

[242] Schneiders, Marc, 'The Origins of the Early Irish Liturgy', in [152] Próinséas Ní Chatháin and Michael Richter (eds), *Irland und Europa im früheren Mittelalter: Bildung und Literatur / Ireland and Europe in the Early Middle Ages: Learning and Literature* (Stuttgart: Klett-Cotta, 1996), pp. 76-98

[243] Schnith, Karl, 'Matthäus Paris (wohl bald nach 1200-1259), *Chronica Maiora*', in Volker Reinhardt (ed.), *Hauptwerke der Geschichtsschreibung*, Kröners Taschenausgabe, 435 (Stuttgart: Kröner, 1997), pp. 417-20

[244] Stevenson, Jane, 'Hiberno-Latin Hymns: Learning and Literature', in [152] Próinséas Ní Chatháin and Michael Richter (eds), *Irland und Europa im früheren Mittelalter: Bildung und Literatur / Ireland and Europe in the Early Middle Ages: Learning and Literature* (Stuttgart: Klett-Cotta, 1996), pp. 99-135

[245] Tilly, Michael, 'Der "Ewige Jude" in England. Die mittelalterliche Cartaphilius-Legende in ihrem historischen Kontext', *Zeitschrift für Religions- und Geistesgeschichte*, 47 (1995), pp. 289-303

[246] Udolph, Jürgen, 'Die Landnahme Englands durch germanische Stämme im Lichte der Ortsnamen', in Edith Marold and Christiane Zimmermann (eds), *Nordwestgermanisch. Reallexikon der Germanischen Altertumskunde*, supplementary volume 13 (Berlin: de Gruyter, 1995), pp. 223-70

[247] Wetzig, Karl-Ludwig, 'Jón Gerrekssons Ende oder Wie Island beinahe englisch geworden wäre', *Hansische Geschichtsblätter*, 114 (1996), pp. 61-104

[248] Wöhler, Hans U., 'Das "realistische" Individualitätskonzept Walter Burleys im geschichtlichen Kontext', in *Individuum und Individualität im Mittelalter* (Berlin, 1996), pp. 313-26

[249] Wood, Ian, 'Franken und Angelsachsen', in *Die Franken – Wegbereiter Europas: Vor 1500 Jahren: König Chlodwig und seine Erben* (Mainz: Von Zabern, 1996), pp. 341-5

Sixteenth to Eighteenth Centuries

[250] Altmann, Angelika, 'Edmund Burke und Thomas Paine: Zwei republikanische Denkansätze in der amerikanischen Verfassungsdiskussion', *Historische Mitteilungen (HMRG)*, 10 (1997), pp. 186-201

[251] Asch, Ronald G., 'Eigentum und Steuerwesen unter den frühen Stuarts von Bate's Case (1606) bis zum Case of Ship money (1637/38)', in [19] Günther Lottes (ed.), *Der Eigentumsbegriff im englischen politischen Denken*, Veröffentlichungen Arbeitskreis Deutsche England-Forschung, 16 (Bochum: Brockmeyer, 1995), pp. 57-80

[252] Asch, Ronald G., 'George Buchanan (1508-82), *Rerum Scotiarum Historia*', in Volker Reinhardt (ed.), *Hauptwerke der Geschichtsschreibung*, Kröners Taschenausgabe, 435 (Stuttgart: Kröner, 1997), pp. 71-4

[253] Asch, Ronald G., '"No Bishop no King" oder "Cuius Regio eius religio": Die Deutung und Legitimation des fürstlichen Kirchenregiments und ihre Implikationen für die Genese des "Absolutismus" in England und im protestantischen Deutschland', in Ronald G. Asch and Heinz Duchhardt (eds), *Der Absolutismus – ein Mythos? Strukturwandel monarchischer Herrschaft in West- und Mitteleuropa (c. 1550-1700)*, Münstersche historische Forschungen, 9 (Cologne: Böhlau, 1996), pp. 79-123

[254] Asch, Ronald G., '"The Politics of Access". Hofstruktur und Herrschaft in England unter den frühen Stuarts', in Werner Paravicini (ed.), *Alltag bei Hofe. 3. Symposium der Residenzen-Kommission der Akademie der Wissenschaften in Göttingen, Ansbach 28. Februar bis 1. März 1992*, Residenzenforschung, 5 (Sigmaringen: Thorbeke, 1995), pp. 243-66

[255] Azimi, Vida, 'Edouard Laboulaye et l'administration anglaise', in [40] Erk Volkmar Heyen (ed.), *Verwaltung und Verwaltungsrecht in Frankreich und England (18./19. Jh.) / Administration et droit administratif en France et Angleterre (18e/19e s.) / Administration and Administrative Law in France and England (18th/19th c.)* (Baden-Baden: Nomos, 1996) = *Jahrbuch für europäische Verwaltungsgeschichte*, 8 (1996), pp. 153-62

[256] Beppler, Jill, 'Augsburg – England – Wolfenbüttel. Die Karriere des Reisehofmeisters Hieronymus Hainhofer', in Jochen Brüning and Friedrich Niewohner (eds), *Augsburg in der frühen Neuzeit*, Colloquia Augustana, 1 (Berlin: Akademie, 1995), pp. 119-39

[257] Blaicher, Günther, 'Shakespeare als Dramatiker einer Zeitenwende', in Hildegard Kuester (ed.), *Das 16. Jahrhundert. Europäische Renaissance*, Eichstätter Colloquium (Regensburg: Pustet, 1995), pp. 131-47

[258] Bowen, Huw V., 'Diversity and Discontinuity: The Development of the Banking System in England and Wales, c. 1650-c.1830', in [22] Franz Bosbach and Hans Pohl (eds), *Das Kreditwesen in der Neuzeit / Banking System in Modern History: Ein deutsch-britischer Vergleich*, Prince Albert Studies, 14 (Munich: Saur, 1997), pp. 29-38

[259] Brühlmeier, Daniel, 'Die Geburt der Sozialwissenschaften aus dem Geiste der Moralphilosophie', in [55] Daniel Brühlmeier, Helmut Holzhey, and Vilem Mudroch (eds), *Schottische Aufklärung: "A Hotbed of Genius"*, Aufklärung und Europa. Beiträge zum 18. Jahrhundert (Berlin: Akademie, 1996), pp. 23-38

[260] Burk, Kathleen, 'Private Banks: The British Sonderweg', in [22] Franz Bosbach and Hans Pohl (eds), *Das Kreditwesen in der Neuzeit / Banking System in Modern History: Ein deutsch-britischer Vergleich*, Prince Albert Studies, 14 (Munich: Saur, 1997), pp. 47-56

[261] Burt, Roger, 'Proto-Industrialization and the British Non-Ferrous Mining Industries', in Ekkehard Westermann (ed.), *Vom Bergbau- zum Industrierevier*, Vierteljahrschrift für Sozial- und Wirtschaftsgeschichte, Beiheft 115 (Stuttgart: Steiner, 1995), pp. 317-34

[262] Cameron, Alan, 'Bank of Scotland, 1695-1891. Some Cautionary Notes on Free Banking in Scotland', in [22] Franz Bosbach and Hans Pohl (eds), *Das Kreditwesen in der Neuzeit / Banking System in Modern History: Ein deutsch-britischer Vergleich*, Prince Albert Studies, 14 (Munich: Saur, 1997), pp. 119-32

[263] Deursen, Arie T. van, 'Der Generalstatthalter der Niederlande (1672-1702) [Wilhelm (III.) von Oranien]', in [39] Heinz Duchhardt (ed.), *Der Herrscher in der Doppelpflicht: Europäische Fürsten und ihre beiden Throne*, Veröffentlichungen des Instituts für europäische Geschichte Mainz, Abteilung Universalgeschichte, Beiheft 43 (Mainz: Zabern, 1997), pp. 141-64

[264] Feldman, Doris, 'Economic and / as Aesthetic Construction of Britishness in Eighteenth-Century Domestic Travel Writing', *Journal for the Study of British Cultures*, 4 (1997), pp. 31-46

[265] Friedeburg, Robert von, 'Kontinuität und Wandel in der englischen Ideengeschichte zwischen Reformation und "Rebellion"', *Zeitschrift für historische Forschung*, 24 (1997), pp. 89-98

[266] Friedeburg, Robert von, 'Die Ordnungsgesetzgebung Englands in der Frühen Neuzeit', in Michael Stolleis (ed.), *Policey im Europa der Frühen Neuzeit* (Frankfurt / M.: Klostermann, 1996), pp. 575-603

[267] Friedeburg, Robert von, '"... such ample and large privileges ..." Privilegien zwischen königlichem Gnadenakt und Rechtsanspruch bei der Errichtung der englischen Kolonien in Nordamerika, 1606-1684', in Barabara Dölemeyer and Heinz Mohnhaupt (eds), *Das Privileg im europäischen Vergleich*, vol. 1 (Frankfurt / M.: Klostermann, 1997), pp. 249-78

[268] Fröhlich, Helgard, 'England zwischen Anpassung und Widerstand. Ideen und Mentalitäten 1649-1653', *Comparativ*, 5-6 (1996), pp. 233-56

[269] Fröhlich, Helgard, 'Parlament und "Property" in den Verfassungsvorstellungen am Beginn des 17. Jahrhunderts', in [19] Günther Lottes (ed.), *Der Eigentumsbegriff im englischen politischen Denken*, Veröffentlichungen Arbeitskreis Deutsche England-Forschung, 16 (Bochum: Brockmeyer, 1995), pp. 81-98

[270] Gassenmeier, Michael, 'Edmund Burke und die Entstehung des Konservatismus. Zum politischen Kontext von Kants Friedensschrift', in Wolfgang Beutin (ed.), *Hommage à Kant: Kants Schrift "Zum ewigen Frieden"* (Hamburg: v. Bockel, 1996), pp. 57-95

[271] Geyer-Kordesch, Johanna, 'Die medizinische Aufklärung in Schottland. Nationale und internationale Aspekte', in [55] Daniel Brühlmeier, Helmut Holzhey, and Vilem Mudroch (eds), *Schottische Aufklärung: "A Hotbed of Genius"*, Aufklärung und Europa. Beiträge zum 18. Jahrhundert (Berlin: Akademie, 1996), pp. 91-106

[272] Greyerz, Kaspar von, 'Gottesbild und "Mechanisierung" des gelehrten Weltbildes im England des 17. Jahrhunderts', in M. Erbe (ed.), *Querdenken. Dissens und Toleranz im Wandel der Geschichte. Festschrift zum 65. Geburtstag von Hans R. Guggisberg* (Mannheim: Palatium, 1996), pp. 377-92

[273] Greyerz, Kaspar von, 'Spuren eines vormodernen Individualismus in englischen Selbstzeugnissen des 16. und 17. Jahrhunderts', in Winfried Schulze (ed.), *Ego-Dokumente: Annährungen an den Menschen in der Geschichte*, Selbstzeugnisse der Neuzeit, 2 (Berlin: Akademie, 1996), pp. 131-45

[274] Hammermayer, Ludwig, 'Graf Rumford (1753-1814) zwischen Nordamerika, Großbritannien, Bayern und Frankreich. Einige Bemerkungen zu Biographie, Werk und Umfeld', in Dieter Albrecht, Karl Otmar Freiherr von Aretin, and Winfried Schulze (eds), *Europa im Umbruch 1750-1850* (Munich: Oldenbourg, 1995), pp. 51-70

[275] Hampsher-Monk, Iain, 'John Locke's Ambiguous Theory of Property', in [19] Günther Lottes (ed.), *Der Eigentumsbegriff im englischen politischen Denken*, Veröffentlichungen Arbeitskreis Deutsche England-Forschung, 16 (Bochum: Brockmeyer, 1995), pp. 99-120

[276] Hampsher-Monk, Iain, 'Radicalism or Radicalisms? Radicals' Ideas of Property in Eighteenth-Century Britain', in [19] Günther Lottes (ed.), *Der Eigentumsbegriff im englischen politischen Denken*, Veröffentlichungen Arbeitskreis Deutsche England-Forschung, 16 (Bochum: Brockmeyer, 1995), pp. 137-68

[277] Harling, Philip, 'The Politics of Administrative Change in Britain, 1780-1850', in [40] Erk Volkmar Heyen (ed.), *Verwaltung und Verwaltungsrecht in Frankreich und England (18./19. Jh.) / Administration et droit administratif en France et Angleterre (18e/19e s.) / Administration and Administrative Law in France and England (18th/19th c.)* (Baden-Baden: Nomos, 1996) = *Jahrbuch für europäische Verwaltungsgeschichte*, 8 (1996), pp. 191-212

[278] Hellmuth, Eckhart, 'Der Staat des 18. Jahrhunderts. England und Preußen im Vergleich', *Aufklärung*, 9 (1996), pp. 5-24

[279] Hellmuth, Eckhart, 'To Make Sense of the Senseless. The Representation of Crime and Punishment in Eighteenth Century England', in Jürgen Klein and Dirk Vanderkeke (eds), *Anglistentag 1995 Greifswald. Proceedings* (Tübingen: Niemeyer, 1996), pp. 46-57

[280] Helmedach, Andreas, 'Infrastruktur – politische Grundsatzentscheidungen des 18. Jahrhunderts am Beispiel des Landesverkehrswesens: Großbritannien, Frankreich und die Habsburgermonarchie', *Comparativ*, 6 (1996), pp. 11-50

[281] Hoyt, Nelly S., 'Tolerance and Intolerance in Utopia', in M. Erbe (ed.), *Querdenken. Dissens und Toleranz im Wandel der Geschichte. Festschrift zum 65. Geburtstag von Hans R. Guggisberg* (Mannheim: Palatium, 1996), pp. 335-46

[282] James, Leslie, 'The Emergence of Mining Communities in South-East Wales During the Late Eighteenth and Early Nineteenth Centuries', in Ekkehard Westermann (ed.),*Vom Bergbau- zum Industrierevier*, Vierteljahrschrift für Sozial- und Wirtschaftsgeschichte, Beiheft 115 (Stuttgart: Steiner, 1995), pp. 405-30

[283] Jones, James R., 'Der englische König (1689-1702) [Wilhelm (III.) von Oranien]', in [39] Heinz Duchhardt (ed.), *Der Herrscher in der Doppelpflicht: Europäische Fürsten und ihre beiden Throne*, Veröffentlichungen des Instituts für europäische Geschichte Mainz, Abteilung Universalgeschichte, Beiheft 43 (Mainz: Zabern, 1997), pp. 165-86

[284] Jörn, Nils, 'Marcus Meyer: Die Karriere eines Hamburgers im Konzept englischer Regierungspolitik', in Horst Wernicke and Ralf G. Werlich (eds), *Akteure und Gegner der Hanse: Zur Prosopographie der Hansezeit. Gedächtnisschrift für Konrad Fritze* (Weimar: Hermann Böhlau), 1996

[285] Kampmann, Christoph, 'Die englische Krone als "Arbiter of Christendom"? Die "Balance of Europe" in der politischen Diskussion der späten Stuart-Ära (1660-1714)', *Historisches Jahrbuch der Görres Gesellschaft*, 116 (1996), pp. 312-66

[286] Klein, Bernhard, 'Constructing the Space of the Nation: Geography, Maps, and the Discovery of Britain in the Early Modern Period', *Journal for the Study of British Cultures*, 4 (1997), pp. 11-30

[287] Kraus, Hans C., 'Montesquieu, Blackstone, De Lolme und die englische Verfassung des 18. Jahrhunderts', *Jahrbuch des Historischen Kollegs* (1995), pp. 113-56

[288] Kraus, Hans C., 'Verfassungsbegriff und Verfassungsdiskussion im England der zweiten Hälfte des 18. Jahrhunderts', *Zeitschrift für Historische Forschung*, 22 (1995), pp. 495-522

[289] Krifka, Sabine, 'Die Erfinder Artwright und Jacquard – Porträts als Zeugnisse der Textilgeschichte', *Rheydter Jahrbuch*, 22 (1995)

[290] Lemke, Anja, 'Überlegungen zur Sprachphilosophie bei Thomas Hobbes', *Zeitschrift für Politik*, 43 (1996), pp. 1-22

[291] Lenz, Bernd, 'Ideals of Femininity: Lord Halifax vs. Mary Wollstonecraft', in [25] Wolfgang Mackiewicz and Dieter Wolff (eds), *British Studies in Germany: Essays in Honor of Frank Frankel* (Trier: WVT – Wissenschaftlicher Verlag Trier, 1997), pp. 72-84

[292] Lüthe, Rudolf, 'Geschmack und menschliche Natur. Aspekte der Ästhetik der Schottischen Aufklärung', in [55] Daniel Brühlmeier, Helmut Holzhey, and Vilem Mudroch (eds), *Schottische Aufklärung: "A Hotbed of Genius"*, Aufklärung und Europa. Beiträge zum 18. Jahrhundert (Berlin: Akademie, 1996), pp. 39-52

[293] McEldowney, John F., 'Administration and Law in the 18th and 19th Centuries', in [40] Erk Volkmar Heyen (ed.), *Verwaltung und Verwaltungsrecht in Frankreich und England (18./19. Jh.) / Administration et droit administratif en France et Angleterre (18e/19e s.) / Administration and Administrative Law in France and England (18th/19th c.)* (Baden-Baden: Nomos, 1996) = *Jahrbuch für europäische Verwaltungsgeschichte*, 8 (1996), pp. 19-36

[294] McKendrick, Neil, 'Die Ursprünge der Konsumgesellschaft: Luxus, Neid und soziale Nachahmung in der englischen Literatur des 18. Jahrhunderts', in Hannes Siegrist, Hartmut Kaelble, and Jürgen Kocka (eds), *Europäische Konsumgeschichte: Zur Gesellschafts- und Kulturgeschichte des Konsums (18. bis 20. Jahrhundert)* (Frankfurt / M.: Campus, 1997), pp. 75-108.

[295] Maczak, Antoni, 'Stände und Zentralmacht im 16. Jahrhundert: Polen und England im Vergleich', in Joachim Bahlke and Hans J. Bänelburg (eds), *Ständefreiheit und Staatsgestaltung in Ostmitteleuropa: Übernationale Gemeinsamkeiten in der politischen Kultur vom 16.-18. Jahrhundert* (Leipzig: Leipziger Universitätsverlag, 1996), pp. 95-118

[296] Maurer, Michael, 'Nationalcharakter und Nationalbewußtsein. Deutschland und England im Vergleich', in Ulrich Herrmann (ed.), *Volk – Nation –Vaterland: Studien zum 18. Jahrhundert* (Hamburg: Meiner, 1996), pp. 89-100

[297] Maurer, Michael, 'Die Universitäten Englands, Irlands und Schottlands im 18. Jahrhundert. Intellektuelle, soziale und politische Zusammenhänge', in *Universitäten und Aufklärung*, Das 18. Jahrhundert, Supplementband (Göttingen: Wallstein, 1995), pp. 238-67

[298] Metzger, Hans-Dieter, '"Küchlein und Bier". Shakespeare und der englische Kirchweihstreit im ausgehenden 16. und frühen 17. Jahrhundert', *Historische Anthropologie*, 4 (1996), pp. 34-56

[299] Metzger, Hans-Dieter, 'Zur Grundlegung des liberalen Eigentumsbegriffs im 17. Jahrhundert', in [19] Günther Lottes (ed.), *Der Eigentumsbegriff im englischen politischen Denken*, Veröffentlichungen Arbeitskreis Deutsche England-Forschung, 16 (Bochum: Brockmeyer, 1995), pp. 23-56

[300] Mohrmann, Ruth E., '" ... hielt nach vergleichbaren Pferden und Kutschen Ausschau, fand aber keine." Ding und Bedeutung in Samuel Pepys' Lebenswelt', in C. Lipp (ed.), *Medien popularer Kultur. Erzählung, Bild und Objekt in der volkskundlichen Forschung. Rolf Wilhelm Brednich zum 60. Geburtstag 1995* (Frankfurt/M.: Campus, 1995), pp. 465-73

[301] Niedhart, Gottfried, 'Der assoziative Rekurs auf die römische Geschichte im Großbritannien des 18. Jahrhunderts', in Reinhard Stupperich (ed.), *Lebendige Antike. Die Rezeption der Antike in Politik, Kunst und Wissenschaft der Neuzeit*, Mannheimer historische Forschungen, 6 (Mannheim: Palatium, 1995), pp. 121-4

[302] Nünning, Vera, 'Die Kultur der Empfindsamkeit: Eine mentalitätsgeschichtliche Skizze', in Monika Fludernik, Ansgar Nünning, and Vera Nünning (eds), *Eine andere Geschichte der englischen Literatur. Epochen, Gattungen, Teilgebiete im Überblick*, WVT-Handbücher zum Literaturwissenschaftlichen Studium, 2 (Trier: WVT, 1996), pp. 107-26

[303] Nünning, Vera, '"The slaves of our pleasures" oder "our companions and equals": Die Konstruktion von Weiblichkeit im England des 18. Jahrhunderts aus kulturwissenschaftlicher Sicht', *Zeitschrift für Anglistik und Amerikanistik*, 44 (1996), pp. 199-216

[304] Opitz, Claudia, 'Kulturvergleich und Geschlechterbeziehungen in der Aufklärung. Lady Mary Wortley Montagues "Briefe aus dem Orient"', in *Was sind Frauen? Was sind Männer?*, Gender Studien (Frankfurt/M.: Suhrkamp, 1996), pp. 156-75

[305] Osterhammel, Jürgen, 'Adam Ferguson (1723-1816), *An Essay on the History of Civil Society'*, in Volker Reinhardt (ed.), *Hauptwerke der Geschichtsschreibung*, Kröners Taschenausgabe, 435 (Stuttgart: Kröner, 1997), pp. 184-8

[306] Osterhammel, Jürgen, 'David Hume (1711-76), *History of England from the Invasion of Julius Caesar to the Revolution of 1688'*, in Volker Reinhardt (ed.), *Hauptwerke der Geschichtsschreibung*, Kröners Taschenausgabe, 435 (Stuttgart: Kröner, 1997), pp. 297-300

[307] Osterhammel, Jürgen, 'William Robertson (1721-93), *History of the Reign of the Emperor Charles V'*, in Volker Reinhardt (ed.), *Hauptwerke der Geschichtsschreibung*, Kröners Taschenausgabe, 435 (Stuttgart: Kröner, 1997), pp. 527-30

[308] Oz-Salzberger, Fania, 'Exploring the Germanick Body – Eighteenth-Century British Images of Germany', *Tel Aviver Jahrbuch für deutsche Geschichte*, 26 (1997), pp. 7-23

[309] Oz-Salzberger, Fania, 'Die Schottische Aufklärung in Frankreich', in [55] Daniel Brühlmeier, Helmut Holzhey, and Vilem Mudroch (eds), *Schottische Aufklärung: "A Hotbed of Genius"*, Aufklärung und Europa. Beiträge zum 18. Jahrhundert (Berlin: Akademie, 1996), pp. 107-22

[310] Phillipson, Nicholas, 'Die Schottische Aufklärung', in [55] Daniel Brühlmeier, Helmut Holzhey, and Vilem Mudroch (eds), *Schottische Aufklärung: "A Hotbed of Genius"*, Aufklärung und Europa. Beiträge zum 18. Jahrhundert (Berlin: Akademie, 1996), pp. 7-22

[311] Rang, Brigitte, 'Eine unbekannte Quelle von John Lockes "Some Thoughts Concerning Education"', in Peter Drwek *et al.* (eds), *Ambivalenzen der Pädagogik. Zur Bildungsgeschichte der Aufklärung und des 20. Jahrhunderts. Harald Scholz zum 65. Geburtstag* (Weinheim: Deutscher Studien Verlag, 1995), pp. 19-46

[312] Rehberg, Rolf, 'Bündnis – Föderation – Anschluß: Schottlands Weg nach Großbritannien 1603-1707', *Zeitschrift für Geschichtswissenschaft*, 45 (1997), pp. 197-218

[313] Rosador, Kurt Tetzeli v., 'Into Darkest England: Discovering the Victorian Urban Poor', *Journal for the Study of British Cultures*, 4 (1997), pp. 129-44

[314] Russell, Lord Conrad, 'Der englische König Jakob I. (1603-1625)', in [39] Heinz Duchhardt (ed.), *Der Herrscher in der Doppelpflicht: Europäische Fürsten und ihre beiden Throne*, Veröffentlichungen des Instituts für europäische Geschichte Mainz, Abteilung Universalgeschichte, Beiheft 43 (Mainz: Zabern, 1997), pp. 123-38

[315] Schneider, Ivo, 'Rashomon oder Georg Reichenbachs geheimer Aufenthalt in Soho bei Boulton & Watt von 1791', *Kultur und Technik*, 20 (1996), pp. 10-18

[316] Scholz, Susanne, 'Tales of Origin and Destination: The Uses of History in the Narratives of the Nation', in [26] Jens-Ulrich Davids and Richard Stinshoff (eds), *The Past in the Present: Proceedings of the 5th Annual British and Cultural Studies Conference, Oldenburg 1994* (Frankfurt/M.: Lang, 1996), pp. 135-50

[317] Schuhmann, Karl, 'Thomas Hobbes – Vom verrufenen Autor zum Klassiker', *Zeitschrift für Politik: Organ der Hochschule für Politik München*, 44 (1997), pp. 238-42

[318] Schulte Beerbühl, Margrit, 'Die Konsummöglichkeiten und Konsumbedürfnisse der englischen Unterschichten im 18. Jahrhundert', *Vierteljahrschrift für Sozial- und Wirtschaftsgeschichte*, 82 (1995), pp. 1-28

[319] Schulte Beerbühl, Margrit, 'War England ein Sonderfall der Industrialisierung? Der ökonomische Einfluß der protestantischen Immigranten auf die Entwicklung der englischen Wirtschaft vor der Industrialisierung', *Geschichte und Gesellschaft*, 21 (1995), pp. 479-505

[320] Sokoll, Thomas, 'Selbstverständliche Armut: Armenbriefe in Essex, 1750-1834', in Winfried Schulze (ed.), *Ego-Dokumente: Annährungen an den Menschen in der Geschichte*, Selbstzeugnisse der Neuzeit, 2 (Berlin: Akademie, 1996)

[321] Steinmetz, Willibald, '"Property", "Interests", Classes" und politische Rechte. Die britische Debatte im späten 18. und im 19. Jahrhundert', in [19] Günther Lottes (ed.), *Der Eigentumsbegriff im englischen politischen Denken*, Veröffentlichungen Arbeitskreis Deutsche England-Forschung, 16 (Bochum: Brockmeyer, 1995), pp. 197-228

[322] Stier, Bernhard, 'Träger und Verhaltensformen des Geistes in der Westminster Confession', *Theologische Zeitschrift*, 51 (1995), pp. 128-50.

[323] Stratmann, Gert, 'Life, Death and the City: The Discovery of London in the Early Eighteenth Century', *Journal for the Study of British Cultures*, 4 (1997), pp. 63-72

[324] Stratmann, Gerd, 'Property in der englischen Literatur des 18. und frühen 19. Jahrhunderts', in [19] Günther Lottes (ed.), *Der Eigentumsbegriff im englischen politischen Denken*, Veröffentlichungen Arbeitskreis Deutsche England-Forschung, 16 (Bochum: Brockmeyer, 1995), pp. 121-36

[325] Szczekalla, Michael, 'Hobbes: Feigheit als erste Bürgerpflicht', *Der Staat*, 36 (1997), pp. 237-51

[326] Thiessen, Victor D., 'To the "Assembly of Common Peasantry": The Case of the Missing Context', *Archiv für Reformationsgeschichte*, 86 (1995), pp. 199-235

[327] Tortarolo, Edoardo, 'Edward Gibbon (1737-94), *History of the Decline and Fall of the Roman Empire*', in Volker Reinhardt (ed.), *Hauptwerke der Geschichtsschreibung*, Kröners Taschenausgabe, 435 (Stuttgart: Kröner, 1997), pp. 223-7

[328] Trapman, J., 'Thomas Bray (1658-1730), Founder of Libraries in Great Britain and America, and his Editions of Erasmus' "Ecclesiastes" (1730)', in M. Erbe (ed.), *Querdenken. Dissens und Toleranz im Wandel der Geschichte. Festschrift zum 65. Geburtstag von Hans R. Guggisberg* (Mannheim: Palatium, 1996), pp. 393-404

[329] Trümpy, Rudolf, 'James Hutton und die Anfänge der modernen Geologie', in [55] Daniel Brühlmeier, Helmut Holzhey, and Vilem Mudroch (eds), *Schottische Aufklärung: "A Hotbed of Genius"*, Aufklärung und Europa. Beiträge zum 18. Jahrhundert (Berlin: Akademie, 1996), pp. 75-90

[330] Vogt, Adolf Max, 'Die Schottische Aufklärung in der bildenden Kunst – oder: "Ossian" und Paestum', in [55] Daniel Brühlmeier, Helmut Holzhey, and Vilem Mudroch (eds), *Schottische Aufklärung: "A Hotbed of Genius"*, Aufklärung und Europa. Beiträge zum 18. Jahrhundert (Berlin: Akademie, 1996), pp. 53-74

[331] Wagner, Michael, 'Edmund Burke (1729-97), *Reflections on the Revolution in France and on the Proceedings in certain Societies in London relative to that Event'*, in Volker Reinhardt (ed.), *Hauptwerke der Geschichtsschreibung*, Kröners Taschenausgabe, 435 (Stuttgart: Kröner, 1997), pp. 84-8

[332] Walter, Dierk, 'Britischer Imperialismus um 1800? Imperialismusforschung, Empire-Historiographie und das "Schwarze Loch" 1783-1815', *Zeitschrift für Geschichtswissenschaft*, 43 (1995), pp. 965-88

[333] Walton, Robert C., 'William Perkins (1558-1602) und die Föderalisten: Bekehrung und Teilhabe am Bund', in M. Erbe (ed.), *Querdenken. Dissens und Toleranz im Wandel der Geschichte. Festschrift zum 65. Geburtstag von Hans R. Guggisberg* (Mannheim: Palatium, 1996), pp. 271-88

[334] Waszek, Norbert, 'Christian Garve als Zentralgestalt der deutschen Rezeption Schottischer Aufklärung', in [55] Daniel Brühlmeier, Helmut Holzhey, and Vilem Mudroch (eds), *Schottische Aufklärung: "A Hotbed of Genius"*, Aufklärung und Europa. Beiträge zum 18. Jahrhundert (Berlin: Akademie, 1996), pp. 123-46

[335] Weimayr, Matthias, 'Bürgerkrieg und Machtzerfall. Thomas Hobbes und die Logik der Macht', *Der Staat*, 35 (1996), pp. 167-88

[336] Weinzierl, Michael, 'Liberty and Property and No Equality. Zur Entwicklung der Eigentumsdiskussion im 18. Jahrhundert', in [19] Günther Lottes (ed.), *Der Eigentumsbegriff im englischen politischen Denken*, Veröffentlichungen Arbeitskreis Deutsche England-Forschung, 16 (Bochum: Brockmeyer, 1995), pp. 169-80

[337] Wellenreuther, Hermann, 'Pamphlets in the Seven Years' War: More *Change* than *Continuity*?', in Jürgen Klein and Dirk Vanderbeke (eds), *Anglistentag 1995 Greifswald: Proceedings* (Tübingen: Niemeyer, 1996), pp. 59-72

[338] Wellenreuther, Hermann, 'Von der Interessenharmonie zur Dissoziation: Kurhannover und England in der Zeit der Personalunion', *Niedersächsisches Jahrbuch für Landesgeschichte*, 67 (1995), pp. 23-42

[339] Wellenreuther, Hermann, 'Zum Auseinandertreten der politischen Kulturen in England und Nordamerika vor 1760', in M. Erbe (ed.), *Querdenken. Dissens und Toleranz im Wandel der Geschichte. Festschrift zum 65. Geburtstag von Hans R. Guggisberg* (Mannheim: Palatium, 1996), pp. 461-74

[340] Wende, Peter, 'Edward Hyde, Earl of Clarendon (1609-74), *The History of the Rebellion and Civil Wars in England*', in Volker Reinhardt (ed.), *Hauptwerke der Geschichtsschreibung*, Kröners Taschenausgabe, 435 (Stuttgart: Kröner, 1997), pp. 103-6

[341] Wende, Peter, 'Thomas Hobbes (1588-1679), *Behemoth, or The Long Parliament*', in Volker Reinhardt (ed.), *Hauptwerke der Geschichtsschreibung*, Kröners Taschenausgabe, 435 (Stuttgart: Kröner, 1997), pp. 287-90

[342] Whatley, Christopher A., 'Scottish "Colliers Serfs" in the 17th and 18th Centuries: A New Perspective', in Ekkehard Westermann (ed.), *Vom Bergbau- zum Industrierevier*, Vierteljahrschrift für Sozial- und Wirtschaftsgeschichte, Beiheft 115 (Stuttgart: Steiner, 1995), pp. 239-56

[343] Wirsching, Andreas, 'Arbeit und Bildung als Eigentumsfaktoren im 18. und frühen 19. Jahrhundert', in [19] Günther Lottes (ed.), *Der Eigentumsbegriff im englischen politischen Denken*, Veröffentlichungen Arbeitskreis Deutsche England-Forschung, 16 (Bochum: Brockmeyer, 1995), pp. 181-96

[344] Wolff, Eberhard, 'Die Einführung der Pockenschutzimpfung in die akademische Medizin. Edward Jenner und die Folgen', in Heinz Schott (ed.), *Meilensteine der Medizin* (Dortmund: Harenberg, 1996), pp. 284-90

[345] Wormald, Jenny, 'Der schottische König Jakob VI. (1588-1625)', in [39] Heinz Duchhardt (ed.), *Der Herrscher in der Doppelpflicht: Europäische Fürsten und ihre beiden Throne*, Veröffentlichungen des Instituts für europäische Geschichte Mainz, Abteilung Universalgeschichte, Beiheft 43 (Mainz: Zabern, 1997), pp. 99-122

[346] Zimmermann, Clemens, 'Hunger als administrative Herausforderung. Das Beispiel Württembergs, 1770-1847', in [40] Erk Volkmar Heyen (ed.), *Öffentliche Verwaltung und Wirtschaftskrise / Administration publique et crise économique* (Baden-Baden: Nomos, 1995) = *Jahrbuch für europäische Verwaltungsgeschichte*, 7 (1995), pp. 19-42

[347] Zimmermann, Gunter, 'Die Auseinandersetzung Thomas Hobbes' mit der reformatorischen Zwei-Reiche-Lehre', *Zeitschrift der Savigny-Stiftung für Rechtsgeschichte, Kanonistische Abteilung*, 113 (1996), pp. 326-52

[348] Zimmermann, Gunter, 'Gottesbund und Gesetz in der Westminster Confession', *Zeitschrift für Kirchengeschichte*, 106, no. 2 (1995), pp. 179-99

Nineteenth Century

[349] Abrams, Lynn, 'Freizeit, Konsum und Identität deutscher und britischer Arbeiter vor dem Ersten Weltkrieg', in Hannes Siegrist, Hartmut Kaelble, and Jürgen Kocka (eds), *Europäische Konsumgeschichte: Zur Gesellschafts- und Kulturgeschichte des Konsums (18. bis 20. Jahrhundert)* (Frankfurt/M.: Campus, 1997), pp. 267-82

[350] Adonis, Andrew, 'Lords and Monarchy in Late Victorian and Edwardian Britain: Democracy and the Unelected State', in [85] Ulrike Jordan and Wolfram Kaiser (eds), *Political Reform in Britain, 1886-1996: Themes, Ideas, Policies*, Veröffentlichungen Arbeitskreis Deutsche England-Forschung, 37 (Bochum: Brockmeyer, 1997), pp. 67-80

[351] Alter, Peter, 'Albrecht Graf von Bernstorff als preussischer Gesandter in London', in [74] Peter Alter and Rudolf Muhs (eds), *Exilanten und andere Deutsche in Fontanes London*, Stuttgarter Arbeiten zur Germanistik, 331 (Stuttgart: Hans Dieter Heinz / Akademischer Verlag Stuttgart, 1996), pp. 416-30

[352] Alter, Peter, 'Bewunderung und Ablehnung. Deutsch-britische Wissenschaftsbeziehungen von Liebig bis Rutherford', in Lothar Jordan and Bernd Kortländer (eds), *Nationale Grenzen und internationaler Austausch. Studien zu Kultur- und Wissenstransfer in Europa*, Communication, 10 (Tübingen: Niemeyer, 1995), pp. 296-311

[353] Alter, Peter, 'Britannien und der Kontinent. Politische und kulturelle Relationen. Die Epoche des britischen Weltreiches', in Rüdiger Ahrens, Wolf D. Bald, and Werner Hüllen, *Handbuch Englisch als Fremdsprache (HEF)* (Berlin: Erich Schmidt, 1995), pp. 216-20

[354] Alter, Peter, 'Herausforderer der Weltmacht. Das Deutsche Reich im britischen Urteil', in Klaus Hildebrand and Elisabeth Müller-Luckner (eds), *Das deutsche Reich im Urteil der Großen Mächte und europäischen Nachbarn*, Schriften des Historischen Kollegs: Kolloquien, 33 (Munich: Oldenbourg, 1995), pp. 159-78

[355] Alter, Peter, 'Das verworfene Modell. Die deutsch-britischen Wissenschaftsbeziehungen im Wandel', in [41] Hartmut Berghoff and Dieter Ziegler (eds), *Pionier und Nachzügler? Vergleichende Studien zur Geschichte Großbritanniens und Deutschlands im Zeitalter der Industrialisierung. Festschrift für Sidney Pollard zum 70. Geburtstag*, Veröffentlichungen Arbeitskreis Deutsche England-Forschung, 28 (Bochum: Brockmeyer, 1995), pp. 187-204

[356] Ashton, Rosemary, 'Gottfried Kinkel and University College London', in [74] Peter Alter and Rudolf Muhs (eds), *Exilanten und andere Deutsche in Fontanes London*, Stuttgarter Arbeiten zur Germanistik, 331 (Stuttgart: Hans Dieter Heinz / Akademischer Verlag Stuttgart, 1996), pp. 23-40

[357] Barker, Peter, 'Edgar Bauer, Refugee Journalist and Police Informer', in [74] Peter Alter and Rudolf Muhs (eds), *Exilanten und andere Deutsche in Fontanes London*, Stuttgarter Arbeiten zur Germanistik, 331 (Stuttgart: Hans Dieter Heinz / Akademischer Verlag Stuttgart, 1996), pp. 370-86

[358] Barrow, Logie, '"Mere Democracy"? Britain's circum-1900 Labour Movement as a Long Lost Parent of Charter 88', in [26] Jens-Ulrich Davids and Richard Stinshoff (eds), *The Past in the Present: Proceedings of the 5th Annual British and Cultural Studies Conference, Oldenburg 1994* (Frankfurt/M.: Lang, 1996), pp. 17-24

[359] Baumstark, Reinhold, 'Hauptstadt und Museum. Das Vorbild des Louvre für London, Berlin und München', in Hans M. Körner and Katharina Weigand (eds), *Hauptstadt: Historische Perspektiven eines deutschen Themas*, dtv Wissenschaftliche Reihe (Munich: dtv, 1995), pp. 155-66

[360] Berbig, Roland, '"der Typus eines Geschichten-machers": Gustav Friedrich Waagen und Theodor Fontane in England', in [74] Peter Alter and Rudolf Muhs (eds), *Exilanten und andere Deutsche in Fontanes London*, Stuttgarter Arbeiten zur Germanistik, 331 (Stuttgart: Hans Dieter Heinz / Akademischer Verlag Stuttgart, 1996), pp. 120-41

[361] Berg-Ehlers, Luise, 'Der verhinderte Sprachlehrer Th[eodor] F[ontane] und was ihm an Lehrbüchern zur Verfügung gestanden hätte', in [74] Peter Alter and Rudolf Muhs (eds), *Exilanten und andere Deutsche in Fontanes London*, Stuttgarter Arbeiten zur Germanistik, 331 (Stuttgart: Hans Dieter Heinz / Akademischer Verlag Stuttgart, 1996), pp. 101-19

[362] Berghoff, Hartmut, 'Vermögenseliten in Deutschland und England vor 1914. Überlegungen zu einer vergleichenden Sozialgeschichte', in [41] Hartmut Berghoff and Dieter Ziegler (eds), *Pionier und Nachzügler? Vergleichende Studien zur Geschichte Großbritanniens und Deutschlands im Zeitalter der Industrialisierung. Festschrift für Sidney Pollard zum 70. Geburtstag*, Veröffentlichungen Arbeitskreis Deutsche England-Forschung, 28 (Bochum: Brockmeyer, 1995), pp. 281-301

[363] Berghoff, Hartmut and Dieter Ziegler, 'Pionier und Nachzügler. Kategorien für den deutsch-britischen Vergleich?', in [41] Hartmut Berghoff and Dieter Ziegler (eds), *Pionier und Nachzügler? Vergleichende Studien zur Geschichte Großbritanniens und Deutschlands im Zeitalter der Industrialisierung. Festschrift für Sidney Pollard zum 70. Geburtstag*, Veröffentlichungen Arbeitskreis Deutsche England-Forschung, 28 (Bochum: Brockmeyer, 1995), pp. 15-28

[364] Barringer, Tim, 'Die Gründung von "Albertopolis" – Prinz Albert und die frühen Jahre des South Kensington Museum', in [70] Wilfried Rogasch (ed.), *Victoria & Albert, Vicky & the Kaiser: Ein Kapitel deutsch-englischer Familiengeschichte* (Ostfildern-Ruit: Hatje, 1997), pp. 99-108

[365] Birke, Adolf M., 'Albert – Ein Coburger als Prinzgemahl in England', in [69] Michael Henker and Evamaria Brockhoff (eds), *Ein Herzogtum und viele Kronen: Coburg in Bayern und Europa* (Augsburg: Pustet, 1997), pp. 52-8

[366] Birke, Adolf M., 'Prinz Albert und die deutsche Frage', in [70] Wilfried Rogasch (ed.), *Victoria & Albert, Vicky & the Kaiser: Ein Kapitel deutsch-englischer Familiengeschichte* (Ostfildern-Ruit: Hatje, 1997), pp. 75-86

[367] Boyce, Robert, 'Submarine Cables as a Factor in Britain's Ascendency as a World Power', in Michael Nordt (ed.), *Kommunikationsrevolutionen. Die neuen Medien des 16. und 19. Jahrhunderts*, Wirtschafts- und sozialhistorische Studien, 3 (Cologne: Böhlau, 1995), pp. 81-99

[368] Briggs, Asa, 'Local, Regional, National: The Historical Dimension', in [87] Adolf M. Birke and Magnus Brechtken (eds), *Kommunale Selbstverwaltung / Local Self-Government: Geschichte und Gegenwart im deutsch-britischen Vergleich*, Prince Albert Studies, 13 (Munich: Saur, 1996), pp. 13-24

[369] Briggs, Asa, 'Parties and Parliament in Nineteenth-Century Britain', in [86] Adolf M. Birke and Magnus Brechtken (eds), *Politikverdrossenheit. Der Parteienstaat in der historischen und gegenwärtigen Diskussion: Ein deutsch-britischer Vergleich / Disillusioned with Politics. Party Government in the Past and Present Discussion: An Anglo-German Comparison*, Prince Albert Studies, 12 (Munich: Saur, 1995), pp. 19-28

[370] Briggs, Asa, 'Die Stellung der Monarchie im viktorianischen Großbritannien', in [70] Wilfried Rogasch (ed.), *Victoria & Albert, Vicky & the Kaiser: Ein Kapitel deutsch-englischer Familiengeschichte* (Ostfildern-Ruit: Hatje), 1997, pp. 23-34

[371] Broich, Ulrich, 'Der "andere" viktorianische Roman', in Walter Buckl and Paul Geyer (eds), *Das 19. Jahrhundert – Aufbruch in die Moderne*, Eichstätter Kolloquien (Regensburg: Pustet), 1996, pp. 79-91

[372] Brüning, Rainer, 'Gulliver's Travels oder der englische Überfall auf Kopenhagen (1807) in der Karikatur', *Archiv für Kulturgeschichte*, 77 (1995), pp. 371-82

[373] Budde, Gunilla-Friederike, 'Des Haushalts "schönster Schmuck". Die Hausfrau als Konsumexpertin des deutschen und englischen Bürgertums im 19. und frühen 20. Jahrhundert', in Hannes Siegrist, Hartmut Kaelble, and Jürgen Kocka (eds), *Europäische Konsumgeschichte: Zur Gesellschafts- und Kulturgeschichte des Konsums (18. bis 20. Jahrhundert)* (Frankfurt/M.: Campus, 1997), pp. 411-40

[374] Budde, Gunilla-Friederike, '"Stützen der Bürgergesellschaft". Varianten der Rolle von Dienstmädchen in deutschen und englischen Bürgerfamilien des 19. Jahrhunderts', in [41] Hartmut Berghoff and Dieter Ziegler (eds), *Pionier und Nachzügler? Vergleichende Studien zur Geschichte Großbritanniens und Deutschlands im Zeitalter der Industrialisierung. Festschrift für Sidney Pollard zum 70. Geburtstag* Veröffentlichungen Arbeitskreis Deutsche England-Forschung, 28 (Bochum: Brockmeyer, 1995), pp. 259-80

[375] Campbell, Alan, 'Eighteenth-Century Legacies and Nineteenth-Century Traditions: The Labour Process, Work Culture and Miners' Union in the Scottish Coalfields Before 1914', in Ekke-hard Westermann (ed.), *Vom Bergbau- zum Industrierevier*, Vier-teljahrschrift für Sozial- und Wirtschaftsgeschichte, Beiheft 115 (Stuttgart: Steiner, 1995), pp. 217-38

[376] Chambers, Helen, 'Johanna Kinkel's Novel "Hans Ibeles in Lon-don": A German View of England', in [74] Peter Alter and Rudolf Muhs (eds), *Exilanten und andere Deutsche in Fontanes London*, Stuttgarter Arbeiten zur Germanistik, 331 (Stuttgart: Hans Di-eter Heinz / Akademischer Verlag Stuttgart, 1996), pp. 159-73

[377] Chapman, Stanley, 'Characteristics of England's Joint-Stock Banking, 1826-1914', in [22] Franz Bosbach and Hans Pohl (eds), *Das Kreditwesen in der Neuzeit / Banking System in Modern His-tory: Ein deutsch-britischer Vergleich*, Prince Albert Studies, 14 (Munich: Saur, 1997), pp. 57-68

[378] Cottrell, P. L., 'The Bank of England in Transition, 1836-1860', in [22] Franz Bosbach and Hans Pohl (eds), *Das Kreditwesen in der Neuzeit / Banking System in Modern History: Ein deutsch-britischer Vergleich*, Prince Albert Studies, 14 (Munich: Saur, 1997), pp. 101-18

[379] Crompton, Gerald, 'The Role of Canals in British Industrializa-tion', in Andreas Kunz, John Armstrong, and Karl Otmar Frei-herr von Aretin (eds), *Inland Navigation and Economic Develop-ment in Nineteenth-Century Europe*, Veröffentlichungen des Insti-tuts für europäische Geschichte, Mainz, Abteilung Universal-geschichte, Beiheft 39 (Mainz: Zabern, 1995), pp. 13-31

[380] Dippel, Horst, 'Sicherheit des Staates oder Sicherheit des Bür-gers? Die Entstehung der modernen Polizei in Paris und Lon-don in der ersten Hälfte des 19. Jahrhunderts', in [40] Erk Volk-mar Heyen (ed.), *Verwaltung und Verwaltungsrecht in Frankreich und England (18./19. Jh.) / Administration et droit administratif en France et Angleterre (18e/19e s.) / Administration and Administra-tive Law in France and England (18th/19th c.)* (Baden-Baden: Nomos, 1996) = *Jahrbuch für europäische Verwaltungsgeschichte*, 8 (1996), pp. 255-84

[381] Ditt, Karl, 'Naturschutz zwischen Zivilisationskritik, Tourismus-
förderung und Umweltschutz, USA, England und Deutschland
1860-1970', in Matthias Frese and Michael Prinz (eds), *Politische
Zäsuren und gesellschaftlicher Wandel im 20. Jahrhundert. Regionale
und vergleichende* Perspektiven (Paderborn: Schöningh, 1996), pp.
499-534

[382] Ditt, Karl, 'Vorreiter und Nachzügler in der Textilindustriali-
sierung: Das Vereinigte Königreich und Deutschland während
des 19. Jahrhunderts im Vergleich', in [41] Hartmut Berghoff
and Dieter Ziegler (eds), *Pionier und Nachzügler? Vergleichende
Studien zur Geschichte Großbritanniens und Deutschlands im Zeitalter der Industrialisierung. Festschrift für Sidney Pollard zum 70.
Geburtstag*, Veröffentlichungen Arbeitskreis Deutsche England-
Forschung, 28 (Bochum: Brockmeyer, 1995), pp. 29-58

[383] Doering-Manteuffel, Anselm, 'Europäisches Mächtekonzert und
nationale Machtpolitik: Englands Interesse an Mitteleuropa im
Jahrzehnt um 1850', in [79] Hans-Heinrich Jansen and Ursula
Lehmkuhl (eds), *Großbritannien, das Empire und die Welt. Britische
Außenpolitik zwischen "Größe" und "Selbstbehauptung" 1850-1990*,
Veröffentlichungen Arbeitskreis Deutsche England-Forschung,
25 (Bochum: Brockmeyer, 1995), pp. 43-62

[384] Doering-Manteuffel, Anselm, 'Großbritannien und die Transformation des europäischen Staatensystems 1850-1871', in [12]
Peter Krüger (ed.), *Das europäische Staatensystem im Wandel. Strukturelle Bedingungen und bewegende Kräfte sei der Frühen Neuzeit*,
Schriften des Historischen Kollegs, Kolloquien, 35 (Munich: Oldenbourg, 1996), pp. 153-70

[385] Ehmer, Josef, 'Heiratsverhalten und sozialökonomische Struk-
turen: England und Mitteleuropa im Vergleich', in Heinz-Gerhard
Haupt and Jürgen Kocka (eds), *Geschichte und Vergleich: Ansätze
und Ergebnisse international vergleichender Geschichtsschreibung*
(Frankfurt/Main: Campus, 1996), pp. 181-206

[386] Eisenberg, Christiane, 'Einleitung', in [60] Christiane Eisenberg
(ed.), *Fußball, Soccer, Calcio: Ein englischer Sport auf seinem Weg
um die Welt* (Munich: Deutscher Taschenbuch Verlag, 1997), pp.
7-21

[387] Engel, Ute, '"A Magic Ground" – Engländer entdecken die maurische Architektur im 18. und 19. Jahrhundert', in *Kunst in Spanien im Blick des Fremden. Reiseerfahrungen vom Mittelalter bis in die Gegenwart*, Ars Iberica, 2 (Frankfurt/M.: Vervuert, 1996), pp. 131-52

[388] Fleischmann, Ruth, 'Facing the Shameful in One's Past: Sean O'Casey's Autobiographical Study of Anti-Semitism', in [26] Jens-Ulrich Davids and Richard Stinshoff (eds), *The Past in the Present: Proceedings of the 5th Annual British and Cultural Studies Conference, Oldenburg 1994* (Frankfurt/M.: Lang, 1996), pp. 59-68

[389] Flood, John L., '"A Man of Singularly Wide Experience of Affairs": Eugene Oswald as Writer and Journalist', in [74] Peter Alter and Rudolf Muhs (eds), *Exilanten und andere Deutsche in Fontanes London*, Stuttgarter Arbeiten zur Germanistik, 331 (Stuttgart: Hans Dieter Heinz / Akademischer Verlag Stuttgart, 1996), pp. 77-100

[390] Friedeburg, Robert von, 'Konservativismus und Reichskolonialrecht: Konservatives Weltbild und kolonialer Gedanke in England und Deutschland vom späten 19. Jahrhundert bis zum Ersten Weltkrieg', *Historische Zeitschrift*, 263 (1996), pp. 345-93

[391] Frijhoff, Willem, 'Universität und Ausbildung. Historische Bemerkungen zu einem europäischen Vergleich', in Lothar Jordan and Bernd Kortländer (eds), *Nationale Grenzen und internationaler Austausch. Studien zum Kultur- und Wissenstransfer in Europa*, Communication, 10 (Tübingen: Niemeyer, 1995), pp. 261-75

[392] Fry, Geoffrey K., 'The Development of British Public Administration: A Reassessment of the Dicey Interpretation', in [40] Erk Volkmar Heyen (ed.), *Verwaltung und Verwaltungsrecht in Frankreich und England (18./19. Jh.) / Administration et droit administratif en France et Angleterre (18e/19e s.) / Administration and Administrative Law in France and England (18th/19th c.)* (Baden-Baden: Nomos, 1996) = *Jahrbuch für europäische Verwaltungsgeschichte*, 8 (1996), pp. 233-54

[393] Gaudon, Jean, 'Von Hugo bis Asterix. Walter Scotts Einfluß in Frankreich', in Lothar Jordan and Bernd Kortländer (eds), *Nationale Grenzen und internationaler Austausch. Studien zu Kultur- und Wissenstransfer in Europa*, Communication, 10 (Tübingen: Niemeyer, 1995), pp. 121-38

[394] Gebauer, Fritz, '"Welch Schauspiel! Aber auch! ein Schauspiel nur!"': Lothar Bucher und England', in [74] Peter Alter and Rudolf Muhs (eds), *Exilanten und andere Deutsche in Fontanes London*, Stuttgarter Arbeiten zur Germanistik, 331 (Stuttgart: Hans Dieter Heinz / Akademischer Verlag Stuttgart, 1996), pp. 273-91

[395] Glass, Derek, 'From Moravia to the Strand: The Career of Karl Adolf Buchenheim', in [74] Peter Alter and Rudolf Muhs (eds), *Exilanten und andere Deutsche in Fontanes London*, Stuttgarter Arbeiten zur Germanistik, 331 (Stuttgart: Hans Dieter Heinz / Akademischer Verlag Stuttgart, 1996), pp. 41-76

[396] Gosden, Peter H. J. H., 'Saving Banks? The Saving Function and the Development of Savings Institutions from the 19th Century', in [22] Franz Bosbach and Hans Pohl (eds), *Das Kreditwesen in der Neuzeit / Banking System in Modern History: Ein deutsch-britischer Vergleich*, Prince Albert Studies, 14 (Munich: Saur, 1997), pp. 149-62

[397] Greenaway, John R. 'Politicians, Civil Servants and the Liberal State in Britain, 1850-1914', in [40] Erk Volkmar Heyen (ed.), *Verwaltung und Verwaltungsrecht in Frankreich und England (18./19. Jh.) / Administration et droit administratif en France et Angleterre (18e/19e s.) / Administration and Administrative Law in France and England (18th/19th c.)* (Baden-Baden: Nomos, 1996) = *Jahrbuch für europäische Verwaltungsgeschichte*, 8 (1996), pp. 213-32

[398] Grote, Georg, 'Die Große Hungersnot in Irland 1845-1849: Eine historische Einführung', in Alexander Somerville, *Irlands großer Hunger: Berichte und Reportagen aus Irland während der Hungersnot 1847*, ed. Jörg Rademacher (Münster: Unrast, 1996), pp. 12-32

[399] Hagen, Antje, 'Die Zweiggesellschaften der deutschen Aktienbanken in London. Von ihren Anfängen im 19. Jahrhundert bis zur Re-investition nach dem Zweiten Weltkrieg', *Bankhistorisches Archiv. Zeitschrift zur Bankengeschichte*, 23 (1997), pp. 77-93

[400] Heinemann, Monika, 'Mendelssohn and Byron: Two Songs almost without Words', *Mendelssohn-Studien*, 10 (1997), pp. 131-56

[401] Hetche, Walter, '"Ich fand in London freundliche Aufnahme": Der Dichter Wilhelm Hertz zu Besuch in England', in [74] Peter Alter and Rudolf Muhs (eds), *Exilanten und andere Deutsche in Fontanes London*, Stuttgarter Arbeiten zur Germanistik, 331 (Stuttgart: Hans Dieter Heinz / Akademischer Verlag Stuttgart, 1996), pp. 241-53

[402] Heyen, Erk Volkmar, 'Französisches und englisches Verwaltungsrecht in der deutschen Rechtsvergleichung des 19. Jahrhunderts: Mohl, Stein, Gneist, Mayer, Hatschek', in [40] Erk Volkmar Heyen (ed.), *Verwaltung und Verwaltungsrecht in Frankreich und England (18./19. Jh.) / Administration et droit administratif en France et Angleterre (18e/19e s.) / Administration and Administrative Law in France and England (18th/19th c.)* (Baden-Baden: Nomos, 1996) = *Jahrbuch für europäische Verwaltungsgeschichte*, 8 (1996), pp. 163-90

[403] Higgs, Edward, 'Citizen Rights and Nationhood: The Genesis and Functions of Civil Registration in 19th-Century England and Wales as Compared to France', in [40] Erk Volkmar Heyen (ed.), *Verwaltung und Verwaltungsrecht in Frankreich und England (18./19. Jh.) / Administration et droit administratif en France et Angleterre (18e/19e s.) / Administration and Administrative Law in France and England (18th/19th c.)* (Baden-Baden: Nomos, 1996) = *Jahrbuch für europäische Verwaltungsgeschichte*, 8 (1996), pp. 285-304

[404] Hilton, Matthew, 'Der Konsum des Unschicklichen. Raucherinnen in Großbritannien 1880-1950', in Hannes Siegrist, Hartmut Kaelble, and Jürgen Kocka (eds), *Europäische Konsumgeschichte: Zur Gesellschafts- und Kulturgeschichte des Konsums (18. bis 20. Jahrhundert)* (Frankfurt/M.: Campus, 1997), pp. 495-526

[405] Hobhouse, Hermione, 'Prinz Albert und die Weltausstellung von 1851', in [70] Wilfried Rogasch (ed.), *Victoria & Albert, Vicky & the Kaiser: Ein Kapitel deutsch-englischer Familiengeschichte* (Ostfildern-Ruit: Hatje, 1997), pp. 87-98

[406] Hoppen, K. Theodore, 'A Double Periphery. Ireland within the United Kingdom 1800-1921', in Hans-Heinrich Nolte (ed.), *Europäische Innere Peripherien im 20. Jahrhundert / European Internal Peripheries in the 20th Century*, Historische Mitteilungen, 23 (Stuttgart: Steiner, 1997), pp. 95-113

[407] Howe, Patricia, '"This World of Diamonds and Mud": Women Travellers in Mid-Nineteenth-Century London', in [74] Peter Alter and Rudolf Muhs (eds), *Exilanten und andere Deutsche in Fontanes London*, Stuttgarter Arbeiten zur Germanistik, 331 (Stuttgart: Hans Dieter Heinz / Akademischer Verlag Stuttgart, 1996), pp. 174-97

[408] Jordan, Ulrike and Jutta Schwarzkopf, 'Reform Politics, Gender Relations and Women's Social Role in Circum-1900 Britain', in [85] Ulrike Jordan and Wolfram Kaiser (eds), *Political Reform in Britain, 1886-1996: Themes, Ideas, Policies*, Veröffentlichungen Arbeitskreis Deutsche England-Forschung, 37 (Bochum: Brockmeyer, 1997), pp. 111-130

[409] Josten, Ulrich, 'William Harbutt Dawson – ein englischer Liberaler mit deutscher Orientierung', *Jahrbuch zur Liberalismus-Forschung*, 7 (1995), pp. 176-89

[410] Jung, Bianca, 'Faszination des Mittelalters', in [20] Kevin Carpenter (ed.), *Robin Hood: Die vielen Gesichter des edlen Räubers / The Many Faces of that Celebrated Outlaw* (Oldenburg: Bis. Bibliotheks- und Informationssystem der Universität Oldenburg, 1995), pp. 53-64

[411] Kaiser, Wolfram, 'The Decline and Rise of Radicalism: The Political Parties and Reform, 1886-1996', in [85] Ulrike Jordan and Wolfram Kaiser (eds), *Political Reform in Britain, 1886-1996: Themes, Ideas, Policies*, Veröffentlichungen Arbeitskreis Deutsche England-Forschung, 37 (Bochum: Brockmeyer, 1997), pp. 35-66

[412] Keiderling, Thomas, 'Die Berichte Hermann Ziegenbalgs an Heinrich Brockhaus von seinen Geschäftsreisen nach West- und Südeuropa aus den Jahren 1843 und 1865', *Leipziger Jahrbuch zur Buchgeschichte*, 5 (1995), pp. 317-71

[413] Keiderling, Thomas, 'Der deutsch-englische Kommissionsbuchhandel über Leipzig von 1800 bis 1875', *Leipziger Jahrbuch zur Buchgeschichte*, 6 (1996), pp. 211-82

[414] Kennedy, William P., 'Die Rezeption des deutschen Banken-systems in England. Vom belächelten "Unsinn" zum Vorbild', in [41] Hartmut Berghoff and Dieter Ziegler (eds), *Pionier und Nachzügler? Vergleichende Studien zur Geschichte Großbritanniens und Deutschlands im Zeitalter der Industrialisierung. Festschrift für Sidney Pollard zum 70. Geburtstag*, Veröffentlichungen Arbeits-kreis Deutsche England-Forschung, 28 (Bochum: Brockmeyer, 1995), pp. 97-118

[415] Kettenacker, Lothar, 'Whitehall in Geschichte und Gegenwart', in Helmut Engel, Hanna R. Laurin, and Wolfgang Ribbe (eds), *Geschichtsmeile Wilhelmstraße* (Berlin: Akademie, 1997), pp. 199-211

[416] Krahé, Peter, '"Ein Plot ältester Art". Varianten des Enoch-Arden-Themas in der viktorianischen Literatur', *Archiv für Kulturgeschichte*, 79 (1997), pp. 417-38

[417] Krause, Friedhilde, 'Berliner Bibliothekare und die Londoner Bibliotheken', in Peter Alter and Rudolf Muhs (eds), *Exilanten und andere Deutsche in Fontanes London*, Stuttgarter Arbeiten zur Germanistik, 331 (Stuttgart: Hans Dieter Heinz / Akademischer Verlag Stuttgart, 1996), pp. 142-58

[418] Lacchè, Luigi, 'Regard outre-Manche: le jury d'expropriation et les logiques du droit administratif français au début du 19e siècle', in [40] Erk Volkmar Heyen (ed.), *Verwaltung und Verwaltungsrecht in Frankreich und England (18./19. Jh.) / Administration et droit administratif en France et Angleterre (18e/19e s.) / Administration and Administrative Law in France and England (18th/19th c.)* (Baden-Baden: Nomos, 1996) = *Jahrbuch für europäische Verwaltungsgeschichte*, 8 (1996), pp. 135-52

[419] Leonhard, Jörn, '"An odious but intelligible phrase ..." – *Liberal* im politischen Diskurs Deutschlands und Englands bis 1830/32', *Jahrbuch zur Liberalismus-Forschung*, 8 (1996), pp. 11-41

[420] Lethbridge, Robert, 'Zola und England', in Lothar Jordan and Bernd Kortländer (eds), *Nationale Grenzen und internationaler Austausch. Studien zu Kultur- und Wissenstransfer in Europa*, Communication, 10 (Tübingen: Niemeyer, 1995), pp. 139-50

[421] Lippold, Verena, 'Hinter seiner anachronistischen Würdigung verborgen geblieben: Der ethnologische Blick des Sozialreporters Henry Mayhew auf das Londoner East End', *Historische Anthropologie. Kultur – Gesellschaft – Alltag*, 4 (1996), pp. 476-84

[422] Mason, Tony, 'Großbritannien', in **[60]** Christiane Eisenberg (ed.), *Fußball, Soccer, Calcio: Ein englischer Sport auf seinem Weg um die Welt* (Munich: Deutscher Taschenbuch Verlag, 1997), pp. 22-40

[423] May, Jill P., 'Howard Pyle's American Interpretation of British Legend', in **[20]** Kevin Carpenter (ed.), *Robin Hood: Die vielen Gesichter des edlen Räubers / The Many Faces of that Celebrated Outlaw* (Oldenburg: Bis. Bibliotheks- und Informationssystem der Universität Oldenburg, 1995), pp. 79-86

[424] Mayring, Eva A., 'Heinrich Beta als Londonkorrespondent der "Gartenlaube"', in **[74]** Peter Alter and Rudolf Muhs (eds), *Exilanten und andere Deutsche in Fontanes London*, Stuttgarter Arbeiten zur Germanistik, 331 (Stuttgart: Hans Dieter Heinz / Akademischer Verlag Stuttgart, 1996), pp. 327-39

[425] Metz, Karl H., 'Vom Besitzindividualismus zur Sozialpflichtigkeit: Eigentumsbegriff und Sozialpolitik an der Wende zum 20. Jahrhundert', in **[19]** Günther Lottes (ed.), *Der Eigentumsbegriff im englischen politischen Denken*, Veröffentlichungen Arbeitskreis Deutsche England-Forschung, 16 (Bochum: Brockmeyer, 1995), pp. 229-46

[426] Metzler, Gabriele, '"A Spectator of Events?" Großbritanniens imperiale und kontinentale Selbstbehauptung zwischen Krimkrieg und deutscher Reichsgründung', in **[79]** Hans-Heinrich Jansen and Ursula Lehmkuhl (eds), *Großbritannien, das Empire und die Welt. Britische Außenpolitik zwischen "Größe" und "Selbstbehauptung" 1850-1990*, Veröffentlichungen Arbeitskreis Deutsche England-Forschung, 25 (Bochum: Brockmeyer, 1995), pp. 63-101

[427] Millar, Oliver, 'Königin Victoria und Prinz Albert – Deutsche Bilder und deutsche Maler', in **[70]** Wilfried Rogasch (ed.), *Victoria & Albert, Vicky & the Kaiser: Ein Kapitel deutsch-englischer Familiengeschichte* (Ostfildern-Ruit: Hatje, 1997), pp. 57-66

[428] Mollin, Gerhard T., '"Schlachtflottenbau vor 1914. Überlegungen zum Wesen des deutsch-britischen Antagonismus', in **[41]** Hartmut Berghoff and Dieter Ziegler (eds), *Pionier und Nachzügler? Vergleichende Studien zur Geschichte Großbritanniens und Deutschlands im Zeitalter der Industrialisierung. Festschrift für Sidney Pollard zum 70. Geburtstag*, Veröffentlichungen Arbeitskreis Deutsche England-Forschung, 28 (Bochum: Brockmeyer, 1995), pp. 167-86

[429] Muhs, Rudolf, 'Max Schlesinger und Jakob Kaufmann: Gegen-spieler und Freunde Fontanes', in [74] Peter Alter and Rudolf Muhs (eds), *Exilanten und andere Deutsche in Fontanes London*, Stuttgarter Arbeiten zur Germanistik, 331 (Stuttgart: Hans Dieter Heinz / Akademischer Verlag Stuttgart, 1996), pp. 292-326

[430] Müllenbrock, Heinz J., 'Trugbilder. Zum Dilemma imagologischer Forschung am Beispiel des englischen Deutschland-bildes 1870-1914', *Anglia*, 113 (1995), pp. 305-29

[431] Müller, Franz, 'Die Konsumgenossenschaften in Großbritannien', in [61] Johann Brazda, Robert Schediwy, and Gerhard Rönnebeck (eds), *Pioniergenossenschaften am Beispiel der Konsumgenossenschaften in Großbritannien, Schweden und Japan* (Frankfurt/M.: Lang, 1996), pp. 15-90

[432] Müller, Uwe, 'Die Modernisierung der Straßenverkehrsinfrastrukturpolitik während der Industrialisierung. Ein deutsch-britischer Vergleich', *Comparativ*, 6 (1996), pp. 51-71

[433] Näf, Beat, 'George Grote (1704-1871), *A History of Greece*', in Volker Reinhardt (ed.), *Hauptwerke der Geschichtsschreibung*, Kröners Taschenausgabe, 435 (Stuttgart: Kröner, 1997), pp. 247-50

[434] Netzer, Hans-Joachim, 'Albert – Ein deutscher Prinz in England', in [70] Wilfried Rogasch (ed.), *Victoria & Albert, Vicky & the Kaiser: Ein Kapitel deutsch-englischer Familiengeschichte* (Ostfildern-Ruit: Hatje, 1997), pp. 67-74

[435] Netzer, Susanne, 'Die Mediceer des deutschen Kunstgewerbes – Kronprinz Friedrich Wilhelm und Kronprinzessin Victoria', in [70] Wilfried Rogasch (ed.), *Victoria & Albert, Vicky & the Kaiser: Ein Kapitel deutsch-englischer Familiengeschichte* (Ostfildern-Ruit: Hatje, 1997), pp. 119-28

[436] Neuhaus, Stefan, '"Poesie der Sünde" – "Triumph der Moral": Grossbritannien in den Reiseberichten und Romanen des frühen Rodenberg', in [74] Peter Alter and Rudolf Muhs (eds), *Exilanten und andere Deutsche in Fontanes London*, Stuttgarter Arbeiten zur Germanistik, 331 (Stuttgart: Hans Dieter Heinz / Akademischer Verlag Stuttgart, 1996), pp. 254-72

[437] Nowatzki, Jens, 'Politischer Wandel in Irland: Die Entstehung des irischen Parteienwesens', in Arthur Schlegelmilch (ed.), *Wege europäischen Ordnungswandels. Gesellschaft, Politik und Verfassung in der zweiten Hälfte des 19. Jahrhunderts* (Hamburg: J. Kovac, 1995), pp. 201-22

[438] Nünning, Vera, '"Daß jeder seine Pflicht thue." Die Bedeutung der Indian Mutiny für das nationale britische Selbstverständnis', *Archiv für Kulturgeschichte*, 78 (1996), pp. 363-92

[439] Nünning, Vera, 'Viktorianische Populärliteratur als imperialistische Propaganda: G. A. Hentys historischer Roman "In Times of Peril"', *Literatur in Wissenschaft und Unterricht*, 28 (1995), pp. 189-201

[440] Oberwittler, Dietrich, '"Friends of the Family". Selbstbilder der englischen Polizei im Umgang mit delinquenten Judgendlichen vor dem Ersten Weltkrieg', *Archiv für Polizeigeschichte*, 7 (1996), pp. 8-14

[441] Oberwittler, Dietrich, 'Jugendkriminalstatistiken und ihre Interpretation. Zur Entwicklung der Jugendkriminalität in Deutschland und England in der zweiten Hälfte des 19. und im frühen 20. Jahrhundert', *Historical Social Research/ Historische Sozialforschung*, 22 (1997), pp. 198-227

[442] Ohm, Barbara, 'Victoria – Eine englische Prinzessin in Deutschland', in [70] Wilfried Rogasch (ed.), *Victoria & Albert, Vicky & the Kaiser: Ein Kapitel deutsch-englischer Familiengeschichte* (Ostfildern-Ruit: Hatje, 1997), pp. 109-119

[443] Paetau, Rainer, '"Us and Them" oder: Insulare versus kontinentale Politik? Überlegungen zur Bedeutung des europäischen Kontinents für die britische Identität und Außenpolitik im 19. Jahrhundert', in Arthur Schlegelmilch (ed.), *Wege europäischen Ordnungswandels. Gesellschaft, Politik und Verfassung in der zweiten Hälfte des 19. Jahrhunderts* (Hamburg: J. Kovac, 1995), pp. 223-56

[444] Paulmann, Johannes, 'Ein Experiment der Sozialökonomie: Agrarische Siedlungspolitik in England und Wales vom Ende des 19. Jahrhunderts bis zum Beginn des Zweiten Weltkrieges', *Geschichte und Gesellschaft*, 21 (1995), pp. 506-32

[445] Paulmann, Johannes, '"Germanismus" am englischen Hof, oder: Warum war Prinz Albert unpopulär?', in [74] Peter Alter and Rudolf Muhs (eds), *Exilanten und andere Deutsche in Fontanes London*, Stuttgarter Arbeiten zur Germanistik, 331 (Stuttgart: Hans Dieter Heinz / Akademischer Verlag Stuttgart, 1996), pp. 387-415

[446] Petzold, Dieter, 'Der Rebell im Kinderzimmer: Robin Hood in der Kinderliteratur', in [20] Kevin Carpenter (ed.), *Robin Hood: Die vielen Gesichter des edlen Räubers / The Many Faces of that Celebrated Outlaw* (Oldenburg: Bis. Bibliotheks- und Informationssystem der Universität Oldenburg, 1995), pp. 65-78

[447] Pohl, Hans, 'Mitbestimmung und Betriebsverfassung in Deutschland, Frankreich und Großbritannien seit dem 19. Jahrhundert. Einführung', in *Mitbestimmung und Betriebsverfassung in Deutschland, Frankreich und Großbritannien seit dem 19. Jahrhundert*, Zeitschrift für Unternehmensgeschichte, Beiheft 92 (Stuttgart: Steiner, 1996), pp. 13-21

[448] Pulzer, Peter, 'Vorbild, Rivale und Unmensch. Das sich wandelnde Deutschlandbild in England 1815-1945', in [14] Hans Süssmuth (ed.), *Deutschlandbilder in Dänemark und England, in Frankreich und den Niederlanden: Dokumentation der Tagung Deutschlandbilder in Dänemark und England, in Frankreich und den Niederlanden, 15.-18. Dezember 1993, Leutherheider Forum*, Schriften der Paul-Kleinewefers-Stiftung, 3 (Baden-Baden: Nomos, 1996), pp. 235-50

[449] Rembold, Elfie, '"Home Rule all round": Experiments in Regionalising Great Britain, 1886-1914', in [85] Ulrike Jordan and Wolfram Kaiser (eds), *Political Reform in Britain, 1886-1996: Themes, Ideas, Policies*, Veröffentlichungen Arbeitskreis Deutsche England-Forschung, 37 (Bochum: Brockmeyer, 1997), pp. 169-92

[450] Rembold, Elfie, 'Paradigmenwechsel in der britischen Politik: "Home Rule"-Frage und Parteiensystem zwischen 1885 und 1914', in Arthur Schlegelmilch (ed.), *Wege europäischen Ordnungswandels. Gesellschaft, Politik und Verfassung in der zweiten Hälfte des 19. Jahrhunderts* (Hamburg: J. Kovac, 1995), pp. 185-200

[451] Reynolds, Kim, 'Der Hof der Königin Victoria', in **[70]** Wilfried Rogasch (ed.), *Victoria & Albert, Vicky & the Kaiser: Ein Kapitel deutsch-englischer Familiengeschichte* (Ostfildern-Ruit: Hatje, 1997), pp. 35-44

[452] Rogasch, Wilfried, '"Victoria & Albert, Vicky & The Kaiser" – Eine Einführung in ein Kapitel deutsch-englischer Familiengeschichte', in **[70]** Wilfried Rogasch (ed.), *Victoria & Albert, Vicky & the Kaiser: Ein Kapitel deutsch-englischer Familiengeschichte* (Ostfildern-Ruit: Hatje, 1997), pp. 13-20

[453] Röhl, John C. G., 'Der Kaiser und England', in **[70]** Wilfried Rogasch (ed.), *Victoria & Albert, Vicky & the Kaiser: Ein Kapitel deutsch-englischer Familiengeschichte* (Ostfildern-Ruit: Hatje, 1997), pp. 165-86

[454] Sagarra, Eda, '"Pad' mit seinem Irish Bull": German Exiles in England and the "Irish Question"', in **[74]** Peter Alter and Rudolf Muhs (eds), *Exilanten und andere Deutsche in Fontanes London*, Stuttgarter Arbeiten zur Germanistik, 331 (Stuttgart: Hans Dieter Heinz / Akademischer Verlag Stuttgart, 1996), pp. 225-40

[455] Schmidt-Brümmer, Ursula, 'Zwischen Gouvernantentum und Schriftstellerei: Amalie Bölte in England', in **[74]** Peter Alter and Rudolf Muhs (eds), *Exilanten und andere Deutsche in Fontanes London*, Stuttgarter Arbeiten zur Germanistik, 331 (Stuttgart: Hans Dieter Heinz / Akademischer Verlag Stuttgart, 1996), pp. 198-224

[456] Schneemann, Peter J., 'Ausstellungsstrategie und Selbstzerstörung: Die tragische Figur des englischen Historienmalers Benjamin Robert Haydon (1786-1846)', *Zeitschrift für Kunstgeschichte*, 58 (1995), pp. 226-39

[457] Schwarz, Angela, '"They cannot choose but to be women." Stereotypes of Femininity and Ideals of Womanliness in Late Victorian and Edwardian Britain', in **[85]** Ulrike Jordan and Wolfram Kaiser (eds), *Political Reform in Britain, 1886-1996: Themes, Ideas, Policies*, Veröffentlichungen Arbeitskreis Deutsche England-Forschung, 37 (Bochum: Brockmeyer, 1997), pp. 131-50

[458] Schwarzkopf, Jutta, 'Ehefrau und Fabrikarbeiterin. Zum Zusammenhang von Familien- und Arbeitsbeziehungen bei den Baumwollweberinnen von Lancashire', *Traverse*, 3 (1996), pp. 108-21

[459] Schwarzkopf, Jutta, 'Der Webfehler in der Textur von Klasse und Geschlecht, oder wie kommen Arbeiterinnen zur Politik', in Elisabeth Dickmann and Eva Schöck-Quinteros (eds), *Politik und Profession: Frauen in Arbeitswelt und Wissenschaft um 1900* (Bremen: Universität Bremen, 1996), pp. 35-55

[460] Shpayer-Makov, Haia, 'Police Service in Victorian and Edwardian London: A Somewhat Atypical Case of a Hazardous Occupation', *Medizin, Gesellschaft und Geschichte*, 13 (1995), pp. 55-80

[461] Siemer, Meinolf, 'Kaiserin Friedrich als Bauherrin, Kunstsammlerin und Mäzenin – "Das schönste Ziel wäre wohl ein ganz neues Gebäude..."', in [70] Wilfried Rogasch (ed.), *Victoria & Albert, Vicky & the Kaiser: Ein Kapitel deutsch-englischer Familiengeschichte* (Ostfildern-Ruit: Hatje, 1997), pp. 129-44

[462] Steinmetz, Susanne and Rudolf Muhs, 'Protestantische Pastoren und andere Seelsorger', in [74] Peter Alter and Rudolf Muhs (eds), *Exilanten und andere Deutsche in Fontanes London*, Stuttgarter Arbeiten zur Germanistik, 331 (Stuttgart: Hans Dieter Heinz / Akademischer Verlag Stuttgart, 1996), pp. 431-46

[463] Steinmetz, Willibald, 'Erfahrung und Erwartung als Argumente in Hegels Reformbillschrift und in der parlamentarischen Debatte in England', in Christoph Jamme and Elisabeth Weisser-Lohmann (eds), *Politik und Geschichte: Zu den Intentionen von G. W. F. Hegels Reformbill-Schrift*, Hegel-Studien, Beiheft 35 (Bonn: Bouvier, 1995), pp. 127-50

[464] Stuchtey, Benedikt, 'Die irische Historiographie im 19. Jahrhundert und Leckys Geschichtskonzeption', *Comparativ*, 5, no. 3 (1995), pp. 83-98

[465] Stuchtey, Benedikt, 'Thomas Babington Macaulay (1800-59), *History of England from the Accession of James II*', in Volker Reinhardt (ed.), *Hauptwerke der Geschichtsschreibung*, Kröners Taschenausgabe, 435 (Stuttgart: Kröner, 1997), pp. 398-400

[466] Stuchtey, Benedikt, 'William Edward Hartpole Lecky (1838-1903), *History of England in the Eighteenth Century*', in Volker Reinhardt (ed.), *Hauptwerke der Geschichtsschreibung*, Kröners Taschenausgabe, 435 (Stuttgart: Kröner, 1997), pp. 365-8

[467] Svetlik, Clarie, 'Von der Schönheitskönigin zur Mutterikone – Zur Entwicklung von Königin Victorias Portraitbild', in [70] Wilfried Rogasch (ed.), *Victoria & Albert, Vicky & the Kaiser: Ein Kapitel deutsch-englischer Familiengeschichte* (Ostfildern-Ruit: Hatje, 1997), pp. 45-56

[468] Teuteberg, Hans J., '"Industrial Democracy" – Formen der betrieblichen und überbetrieblichen Mitbestimmung und Betriebsverfassung in Großbritannien seit dem 19. Jahrhundert', in *Mitbestimmung und Betriebsverfassung in Deutschland, Frankreich und Großbritannien seit dem 19. Jahrhundert*, Zeitschrift für Unternehmensgeschichte, Beiheft 92 (Stuttgart: Steiner, 1996)

[469] Then, Volker, 'Grundsteine, Brückenschläge und Schlußsteine. Eisenbahnfeierleichkeiten und bürgerliche Kultur', in [41] Hartmut Berghoff and Dieter Ziegler (eds), *Pionier und Nachzügler? Vergleichende Studien zur Geschichte Großbritanniens und Deutschlands im Zeitalter der Industrialisierung. Festschrift für Sidney Pollard zum 70. Geburtstag*, Veröffentlichungen Arbeitskreis Deutsche England-Forschung, 28 (Bochum: Brockmeyer, 1995), pp. 221-34

[470] Thunecke, Jörg, '"Von dem, was er sozialpolitisch war, habe ich keinen Schimmer": Londoner "Kulturbilder" in den Schriften Theodor Fontanes und Julius Fauchers', in [74] Peter Alter and Rudolf Muhs (eds), *Exilanten und andere Deutsche in Fontanes London*, Stuttgarter Arbeiten zur Germanistik, 331 (Stuttgart: Hans Dieter Heinz / Akademischer Verlag Stuttgart, 1996), pp. 340-69

[471] Toyka-Seid, Michael, '"Sanitary Idea" und "Volksgesundheitsbewegung". Zur Entstehung des modernen Gesundheitswesens in Großbritannien und Deutschland', in [41] Hartmut Berghoff and Dieter Ziegler (eds), *Pionier und Nachzügler? Vergleichende Studien zur Geschichte Großbritanniens und Deutschlands im Zeitalter der Industrialisierung. Festschrift für Sidney Pollard zum 70. Geburtstag*, Veröffentlichungen Arbeitskreis Deutsche England-Forschung, 28 (Bochum: Brockmeyer, 1995), pp. 145-66

[472] Verdecchia, Enrico, 'Red Germans and Italian White Knights: Relations between Two Emigré Communities', in [74] Peter Alter and Rudolf Muhs (eds), *Exilanten und andere Deutsche in Fontanes London*, Stuttgarter Arbeiten zur Germanistik, 331 (Stuttgart: Hans Dieter Heinz / Akademischer Verlag Stuttgart, 1996), pp. 447-62

[473] Wagner, Yvonne, '"Willie" und "Ernie" – Prinzenerziehung zweier Enkel Queen Victorias in Deutschland', in [70] Wilfried Rogasch (ed.), *Victoria & Albert, Vicky & the Kaiser: Ein Kapitel deutsch-englischer Familiengeschichte* (Ostfildern-Ruit: Hatje, 1997), pp. 153-64

[474] Weisbrod, Bernd, 'Philanthropie und bürgerliche Kultur. Zur Sozialgeschichte des viktorianischen Bürgertums', in [41] Hartmut Berghoff and Dieter Ziegler (eds), *Pionier und Nachzügler? Vergleichende Studien zur Geschichte Großbritanniens und Deutschlands im Zeitalter der Industrialisierung. Festschrift für Sidney Pollard zum 70. Geburtstag*, Veröffentlichungen Arbeitskreis Deutsche England-Forschung, 28 (Bochum: Brockmeyer, 1995), pp. 205-20

[475] Wende, Peter, 'Die Diskussion der Reformvorschläge im britischen Parlament (1832)', in Christoph Jamme and Elisabeth Weisser-Lohmann (eds), *Politik und Geschichte: Zu den Intentionen von G. W. F. Hegels Reformbill-Schrift*, Hegel-Studien, Beiheft 35 (Bonn: Bouvier, 1995), pp. 41-60

[476] Wirsching, Andreas, 'Das Problem der Repräsentation im England der Reform-Bill und in Hegels Perspektive', in Christoph Jamme and Elisabeth Weisser-Lohmann (eds), *Politik und Geschichte: Zu den Intentionen von G. W. F. Hegels Reformbill-Schrift*, Hegel-Studien, Beiheft 35 (Bonn: Bouvier, 1995), pp. 105-25

[477] Ziegler, Dieter, 'Eisenbahnbau und Kapitalmarktentwicklung in England im 19. Jahrhundert. Ein Sonderfall?', in Manfred Köhler and Keith Ulrich (eds), *Banken, Konjunktur und Politik. Beiträge zur Geschichte der deutschen Banken im 19. und 20. Jahrhundert*, Bochumer Schrifen zur Unternehmens- und Industriegeschichte, 4 (Essen: Klartext, 1995), pp. 24-41

[478] Ziegler, Dieter, 'Der "Latecomer" lernt: Der "Peel's Act" und die preußische Währungsgesetzgebung im Zeitalter der Industrialisierung', in [41] Hartmut Berghoff and Dieter Ziegler (eds), *Pionier und Nachzügler? Vergleichende Studien zur Geschichte Großbritanniens und Deutschlands im Zeitalter der Industrialisierung. Festschrift für Sidney Pollard zum 70. Geburtstag*, Veröffentlichungen Arbeitskreis Deutsche England-Forschung, 28 (Bochum: Brockmeyer, 1995), pp. 75-96

[479] Ziswiler, Vincent, 'Vorfeld, Umfeld und Bedeutung von Darwins Werk', in Walter Buckl and Paul Geyer (eds), *Das 19. Jahrhundert – Aufbruch in die Moderne*, Eichstätter Kolloquien (Regensburg: Pustet, 1996), pp. 137-55

Twentieth Century

[480] Achilles, Jochen, 'J. Graham Reid', in Jochen Achilles and Rüdiger Imhof (eds), *Irische Dramatiker der Gegenwart* (Darmstadt: Wissenschaftliche Buchgesellschaft, 1996), pp. 96-112

[481] Achilles, Jochen, 'Tom Murphy', in Jochen Achilles and Rüdiger Imhof (eds), *Irische Dramatiker der Gegenwart* (Darmstadt: Wissenschaftliche Buchgesellschaft, 1996), pp. 71-95

[482] Adamthwaite, Anthony, 'Britain, France and the Integration of Western Europe, 1957-1961', in [107] Michael Dockrill (ed.), *Europe Within the Global System 1938-1960. Great Britain, France, Italy and Germany from Great Powers to Regional Powers*, Veröffentlichungen Arbeitskreis deutsche Englandforschung, 30 (Bochum: Brockmeyer, 1995), pp. 133-44

[483] Andrews, Elmer, 'Stewart Parker', in Jochen Achilles and Rüdiger Imhof (eds), *Irische Dramatiker der Gegenwart* (Darmstadt: Wissenschaftliche Buchgesellschaft, 1996), pp. 113-30

[484] Arcidiacono, Bruno, 'The Diplomacy of the Italian Defeat: Italy, the Anglo-Americans, and the "Russian Factor", 1943-1945', in [107] Michael Dockrill (ed.), *Europe Within the Global System 1938-1960. Great Britain, France, Italy and Germany from Great Powers to Regional* Powers, Veröffentlichungen Arbeitskreis deutsche Englandforschung, 30 (Bochum: Brockmeyer, 1995), pp. 55-74

[485] Bange, Oliver, 'English, American, and German Interests behind the Preamble to the Franco-German Treaty, 1963', in [121] Gustav Schmidt (ed.), *Zwischen Bündnissicherung und privilegierter Partnerschaft: Die deutsch-britischen Beziehungen und die Vereinigten Staaten von Amerika 1955-1963*, Veröffentlichungen Arbeitskreis Deutsche England-Forschung, 33 (Bochum: Brockmeyer, 1995), pp. 225-80

[486] Beintker, Michael, 'Die Kirchen und der Bürgerkrieg: Das ehemalige Jugoslavien und Nordirland im Vergleich', *Kirchliche Zeitgeschichte*, 10 (1997), pp. 163-7

[487] Bennett, Peter, 'The National Past as Commodity in the Contemporary British Screen Media', in [26] Jens-Ulrich Davids and Richard Stinshoff (eds), *The Past in the Present: Proceedings of the 5th Annual British and Cultural Studies Conference, Oldenburg 1994* (Frankfurt/M.: Lang, 1996), pp. 25-36

[488] Berger, Stefan, 'The Belated Party. Influences on the British Labour Party in its Formative Years, 1900-1931', *Mitteilungsblatt des Instituts zur Erforschung der europäischen Arbeiterbewegung (IGA)*, 18 (1997), pp. 83-111

[489] Berghoff, Hartmut, 'Patriotismus und Geschäftssinn im Krieg. Eine Fallstudie aus der Musikinstrumentenindustrie', in Gerhard Hirschfeld, Gerd Krumeich, Dieter Langewiesche, and Hans-Peter Ullmann (eds), *Kriegserfahrungen: Studien zur Sozial- und Mentalitätsgeschichte des Ersten Weltkriegs*, Schriften der Bibliothek für Zeitgeschichte, Neue Folge, 5 (Essen, 1997), pp. 262-82

[490] Birke, Adolf M., 'Die britische Demokratisierungspolitik in Westdeutschland bis 1949', in [110] Heinrich Oberreuter and Jürgen Weber (eds), *Freundliche Feinde? Die Alliierten und die Demokratiegründung in Deutschland*, Akademiebeiträge zur politischen Bildung, 29 (Landsberg/Lech: Olzog, 1996), pp. 217-31

[491] Birley, Anthony R., 'Ronald Syme (1903-89), *The Roman Revolution*', in Volker Reinhardt (ed.), *Hauptwerke der Geschichtsschreibung*, Kröners Taschenausgabe, 435 (Stuttgart: Kröner, 1997), pp. 614-17

[492] Blut, Christoph, 'Perzeptionen von Macht und Machtverfall: Großbritannien und Deutschland im internationalen System nach dem Zweiten Weltkrieg', in Gottfried Niedhart, Detlef Junker, and Michael W. Richter (eds), *Deutschland in Europa: Nationale Interessen und internationale Ordnung im 20. Jahrhundert* (Mannheim: Palatium, 1997), pp. 246-58

[493] Braun, Hans J., 'Britische und deutsche Luftrüstung in der Zwischenkriegszeit. Ein Vergleich', in E. W. Hansen, G. Schreiber, and B. Wegener (eds), *Politischer Wandel, organisierte Gewalt und nationale Sicherheit. Beiträge zur neueren Geschichte Deutschlands und Frankreichs. Festschrift für Klaus-Jürgen Müller*, Beiträge zur Militärgeschichte, 50 (Munich, 1995), pp. 181-91

[494] Cabalo, Thorsten, 'Eine Rüstungskontrollzone in Mitteleuropa? Pläne für eine regionale Entspannung in Europa vom Ungarn-Aufstand bis zum Teststoppabkommen (1956-1962)', in [121] Gustav Schmidt (ed.), *Zwischen Bündnissicherung und privilegierter Partnerschaft: Die deutsch-britischen Beziehungen und die Vereinigten Staaten von Amerika 1955-1963*, Veröffentlichungen Arbeitskreis Deutsche England-Forschung, 33 (Bochum: Brockmeyer, 1995), pp. 141-224

[495] Cass, Eddie, 'The Presentation of History in Museums in England', in [26] Jens-Ulrich Davids and Richard Stinshoff (eds), *The Past in the Present: Proceedings of the 5th Annual British and Cultural Studies Conference, Oldenburg 1994* (Frankfurt/M.: Lang, 1996), pp. 37-58

[496] Catterall, Peter, 'A Question of Balances? The Debates about the British Constitution in the Twentieth Century', in [85] Ulrike Jordan and Wolfram Kaiser (eds), *Political Reform in Britain, 1886-1996: Themes, Ideas, Policies*, Veröffentlichungen Arbeitskreis Deutsche England-Forschung, 37 (Bochum: Brockmeyer, 1997), pp. 1-34

[497] Cornelißen, Christoph, 'Europäische Kolonialherrschaft im Ersten Weltkrieg', in [91] Wolfgang Kruse (ed.), *Eine Welt von Feinden: Der große Krieg 1914-1918* (Frankfurt/M.: Fischer, 1997), pp. 43-54

[498] Darwin, John, '"High Noon" or "Loss of Confidence": The British Empire between the Wars', in [79] Hans-Heinrich Jansen and Ursula Lehmkuhl (eds), *Großbritannien, das Empire und die Welt. Britische Außenpolitik zwischen "Größe" und "Selbstbehauptung" 1850-1990*, Veröffentlichungen Arbeitskreis Deutsche England-Forschung, 25 (Bochum: Brockmeyer, 1995), pp. 125-39

[499] Dieckmann, Knut, 'Wales: Interne Kolonie oder Profiteur?', in Hans-Heinrich Nolte (ed.), *Europäische Innere Peripherien im 20. Jahrhundert / European Internal Peripheries in the Twentieth Century*, Historische Mitteilungen, 23 (Stuttgart: Steiner, 1997), pp. 83-94

[500] Dingeldey, Irene, 'Wandel gewerkschaftlicher Strategien in der britischen Berufsbildungspolitik der 1980er und 1990er Jahre', *Politische Vierteljahresschrift*, 37 (1996), pp. 687-712

[501] Diller, Hans-Jürgen, '"No constitution please, we're British!": Neal Ascherson and the "Myth of British Sovereignty"', in [25] Wolfgang Mackiewicz and Dieter Wolff (eds), *British Studies in Germany: Essays in Honour of Frank Frankel* (Trier: WVT – Wissenschaftlicher Verlag Trier, 1997), pp. 21-33

[502] Dockrill, Saki, 'The Tortuous Path to Western Military Unity, 1950-1955', in [107] Michael Dockrill (ed.), *Europe Within the Global System 1938-1960. Great Britain, France, Italy and Germany from Great Powers to Regional Powers*, Veröffentlichungen Arbeitskreis deutsche Englandforschung, 30 (Bochum: Brockmeyer, 1995), pp. 101-19

[503] Ebersold, Bernd, '"Delusions of Grandeur": Großbritannien, der Kalte Krieg und der Nahe Osten, 1945-1956', in [79] Hans-Heinrich Jansen and Ursula Lehmkuhl (eds), *Großbritannien, das Empire und die Welt. Britische Außenpolitik zwischen "Größe" und "Selbstbehauptung" 1850-1990*, Veröffentlichungen Arbeitskreis Deutsche England-Forschung, 25 (Bochum: Brockmeyer, 1995), pp. 139-68

[504] Eiber, Ludwig, 'Verschwiegene Bündnispartner: Die Union deutscher sozialistischer Organisationen in Großbritannien und die britischen Nachrichtendienste', *Exilforschung: Ein internationales Jahrbuch*, 15 (1997), pp. 66-87

[505] Elvert, Jürgen, 'Im Schatten der Europa-Politik: Britische Deutschland-Vorstellungen nach der Wiedervereinigung', *Außenpolitik: Zeitschrift für internationale Fragen*, 48 (1997), 346-56

[506] Fitzgibbon, Ger, '"*Southern Voices*": Traditionen und individuelle Talente', in Jochen Achilles and Rüdiger Imhof (eds), *Irische Dramatiker der Gegenwart* (Darmstadt: Wissenschaftliche Buchgesellschaft, 1996), pp. 162-75

[507] Freist, Dagmar, 'Reform of the Mind – Reform of the Body Politic: Gender Relations and Reform Policies in Late Twentieth-Century Britain', in [85] Ulrike Jordan and Wolfram Kaiser (eds), *Political Reform in Britain, 1886-1996: Themes, Ideas, Policies*, Veröffentlichungen Arbeitskreis Deutsche England-Forschung, 37 (Bochum: Brockmeyer, 1997), pp. 151-68

[508] Girvin, Brian, 'The British State and Northern Ireland: Can the National Question Be Reformed?', in [85] Ulrike Jordan and Wolfram Kaiser (eds), *Political Reform in Britain, 1886-1996: Themes, Ideas, Policies*, Veröffentlichungen Arbeitskreis Deutsche England-Forschung, 37 (Bochum: Brockmeyer, 1997), pp. 227-56

[509] Gow, David, 'Das gegenwärtige Deutschlandbild in England', in [14] Hans Süssmuth (ed.), *Deutschlandbilder in Dänemark und England, in Frankreich und den Niederlanden: Dokumentation der Tagung Deutschlandbilder in Dänemark und England, in Frankreich und den Niederlanden, 15.-18. Dezember 1993, Leutherheider Forum*, Schriften der Paul-Kleinewefers-Stiftung, 3 (Baden-Baden: Nomos, 1996), pp. 281-6

[510] Hall, John M., 'The Search for Metropolitan Government in London, 1945-1995', in [87] Adolf M. Birke and Magnus Brechtken (eds), *Kommunale Selbstverwaltung / Local Self-Government: Geschichte und Gegenwart im deutsch-britischen Vergleich*, Prince Albert Studies, 13 (Munich: Saur, 1996), pp. 129-40

[511] Hamilton, Keith and Anne Lane, 'Power, Status and the Pursuit of Liberty: The Foreign Office and Eastern Europe, 1945-1946', in [107] Michael Dockrill (ed.), *Europe Within the Global System 1938-1960. Great Britain, France, Italy and Germany from Great Powers to Regional Powers*, Veröffentlichungen Arbeitskreis Deutsche Englandforschung, 30 (Bochum: Brockmeyer, 1995), pp. 31-54

[512] Harris, José, 'Planung und "Modernisierung": Die Auswirkungen des Zweiten Weltkrieges auf die wirtschaftlichen und sozialpolitischen Zukunftsvorstellungen in Großbritannien', in Matthias Frese and Michael Prinz (eds), *Politische Zäsuren und gesellschaftlicher Wandel im 20. Jahrhundert*, Forschungen zur Regionalgeschichte (Paderborn: Schöningh, 1996), pp. 125-36

[513] Henderson, Lynda and William Wylie, '"*Northern Voices*" im irischen Gegenwartsdrama', in Jochen Achilles and Rüdiger Imhof (eds), *Irische Dramatiker der Gegenwart* (Darmstadt: Wissenschaftliche Buchgesellschaft, 1996), pp. 145-61

[514] Hiery, Hermann, 'Die anglikanische Kirche und das Ende des britischen Empire', in Ernst O. Bräunche and Hermann Hiery (eds), *Geschichte als Verantwortung. Festschrift für Hans Fenske zum 60. Geburtstag* (Karlsruhe: Wolf, 1996), pp. 127-41

[515] Hirschfeld, Gerhard, 'Durchgangsland Großbritannien: Die britische "Academic Community" und die wissenschaftliche Emigration aus Deutschland', in Charmian Brinson *et al.* (eds), *England, aber wo liegt es? Deutsche und österreichische Emigranten in Großbritannien 1933-1945* (Munich: Iudicium, 1996).

[516] Hoffmann, Peter, 'Die britische Regierung, die deutsche Opposition gegen Hitler und die Kriegszielpolitik der Westmächte im Zweiten Weltkrieg', in E. W. Hansen, G. Schreiber, and B. Wegener (eds), *Politischer Wandel, organisierte Gewalt und nationale Sicherheit. Beiträge zur neueren Geschichte Deutschlands und Frankreichs. Festschrift für Klaus-Jürgen Müller*, Beiträge zur Militärgeschichte, 50 (Munich: Oldenbourg, 1995), pp. 315-29

[517] Holland, Robert, '"Greatness" and the British in the Twentieth Century', in [79] Hans-Heinrich Jansen and Ursula Lehmkuhl (eds), *Großbritannien, das Empire und die Welt. Britische Außenpolitik zwischen "Größe" und "Selbstbehauptung" 1850-1990*, Veröffentlichungen Arbeitskreis Deutsche England-Forschung, 25 (Bochum: Brockmeyer, 1995), pp. 31-42

[518] Imhof, Rüdiger, 'Thomas Kilroy', in Jochen Achilles and Rüdiger Imhof (eds), *Irische Dramatiker der Gegenwart* (Darmstadt: Wissenschaftliche Buchgesellschaft, 1996), pp. 56-70

[519] Isenbart, Jan, 'Britische Flugblattpropaganda gegen Deutschland im Zweiten Weltkrieg', in Jürgen Wilke (ed.), *Pressepolitik und Propaganda: Historische Studien vom Vormärz bis zum Kalten Krieg*, Medien in Geschichte und Gegenwart, 7 (Cologne: Böhlau, 1997), pp. 191-256

[520] Jansen, Hans-Heinrich, 'Weltpolitik und Innenpolitik: Großbritannien und die japanische GATT-Mitgliedschaft', in [79] Hans-Heinrich Jansen and Ursula Lehmkuhl (eds), *Großbritannien, das Empire und die Welt. Britische Außenpolitik zwischen "Größe" und "Selbstbehauptung" 1850-1990*, Veröffentlichungen Arbeitskreis Deutsche England-Forschung, 25 (Bochum: Brockmeyer, 1995), pp. 169-200

[521] Jordan, Ulrike, 'This Silly Old War: Briefe englischer Frauen an die Front, 1940-1945', in Detlef Volge and Wolfgang Wette (eds), *Andere Helme – andere Menschen? Frontalltag und Heimaterfahrung im Zweiten Weltkrieg. Ein internationaler Vergleich*, Schriften der Bibliothek für Zeitgeschichte, Neue Folge, 2 (Essen: Klartext, 1995), pp. 237-56

[522] Jordan, Ulrike, 'Universität im Exil: Erfahrungen deutscher Emigranten in Großbritannien', in *Aus der Geschichte lernen? Universität und Land vor und nach 1945. Eine Ringvorlesung der Christian-Albrechts-Universität zu Kiel und des Schleswig-Holsteinischen Landtages im Winter-Semester 1994/95* (Kiel: Universität Kiel, 1996), pp. 55-76

[523] Kaiser, André, 'House of Lords and Monarchy: British Majoritarian Democracy and the Current Reform Debate on its Pre-Democratic Institutions', in [85] Ulrike Jordan and Wolfram Kaiser (eds), *Political Reform in Britain, 1886-1996: Themes, Ideas, Policies*, Veröffentlichungen Arbeitskreis Deutsche England-Forschung, 37 (Bochum: Brockmeyer, 1997), pp. 81-110

[524] Kaiser, Wolfram, 'The Bomb and Europe. Britain, France and the EEC Entry Negotiations 1961-1963', *Journal of European Integration History*, 1 (1995), pp. 65-85

[525] Kaiser, Wolfram, 'Challenge to the Community: The Creation, Crisis and Consolidation of the European Free Trade Association, 1958-72', *Journal of European Integration History*, 3, no. 1 (1997), pp. 7-33

[526] Kaiser, Wolfram, '"Das Gesicht wahren". Die Konservative Partei und die Rolle Großbritanniens in der Welt, 1945-1964', in [79] Hans-Heinrich Jansen and Ursula Lehmkuhl (eds), *Großbritannien, das Empire und die Welt. Britische Außenpolitik zwischen "Größe" und "Selbstbehauptung" 1850-1990*, Veröffentlichungen Arbeitskreis Deutsche England-Forschung, 25 (Bochum: Brockmeyer, 1995), pp. 245-61

[527] Kaiser, Wolfram, 'Money, Money, Money: The Economics and Politics of the Stationing Costs, 1955-1965', in [121] Gustav Schmidt (ed.), *Zwischen Bündnissicherung und privilegierter Partnerschaft: Die deutsch-britischen Beziehungen und die Vereinigten Staaten von Amerika 1955-1963*, Veröffentlichungen Arbeitskreis Deutsche England-Forschung, 33 (Bochum: Brockmeyer, 1995), pp. 1-32

[528] Kamm, Jürgen, '"Staying Afloat in a Sea of Change": The Discourse and Practices of Neo-Ruralism', in [26] Jens-Ulrich Davids and Richard Stinshoff (eds), *The Past in the Present: Proceedings of the 5th Annual British and Cultural Studies Conference, Oldenburg 1994* (Frankfurt/M.: Lang, 1996), pp. 69-88

[529] Kampmann, Christoph, 'Frankfurt am Main und London: Zwei historische Bankplätze zwischen Partnerschaft und Konkurrenz: Stellungsnahmen und Diskussion', in [22] Franz Bosbach amd Hans Pohl (eds), *Das Kreditwesen in der Neuzeit / Banking System in Modern History: Ein deutsch-britischer Vergleich*, Prince Albert Studies, 14 (Munich: Saur, 1997), pp. 163-82

[530] Kersten, Lee, '"The Times" und das KZ Dachau. Ein unveröffentlichter Artikel aus dem Jahr 1933', *Dachauer Hefte*, 12 (1996), pp. 104-22

[531] Kettenacker, Lothar, 'Die britische Rahmenplanung für die Besetzung Deutschlands und seine unerwarteten Folgen', in Hans E. Volkmann (ed.), *Ende des Dritten Reiches – Ende des Zweiten Weltkrieges. Eine perspektivische Rückschau* (Munich: Piper, 1995), pp. 51-73

[532] Kettenacker, Lothar, '"Fat but Impotent" – Britische Wirtschaftsplanung für Deutschland', in *Aus der Geschichte lernen? Universität und Land vor und nach 1945. Eine Ringvorlesung der Christian-Albrechts-Universität zu Kiel und des Schleswig-Holsteinischen Landtages im Winter-Semester 1994/95* (Kiel: Universität Kiel, 1996), pp. 71-91

[533] Kettenacker, Lothar, 'Zwangläufige deutsche Dominanz? Über Konstanten britischer Europapolitik', *Tel Aviver Jahrbuch für deutsche Geschichte*, 26 (1997), pp. 235-49

[534] Kießling, Friedrich, 'Österreich-Ungarn und die deutsch-englischen Détentebemühungen 1912-1914', *Historisches Jahrbuch*, 116 (1996), pp. 102-25

[535] Knill, Christoph, 'Staatlichkeit im Wandel: Großbritannien im Spannungsfeld nationaler Reformen und europäischer Integration', *Politische Vierteljahresschrift*, 36 (1995), pp. 655-80

[536] Kosok, Heinz, 'Hugh Leonard', in Jochen Achilles and Rüdiger Imhof (eds), *Irische Dramatiker der Gegenwart* (Darmstadt: Wissenschaftliche Buchgesellschaft, 1996), pp. 1-18

[537] Koza, Ingeborg, 'Das deutsch-britische Kulturabkommen vom 18. April 1958', in R. S. Elkar *et. al* (eds), *"Vom rechten Maß der Dinge". Beiträge zur Wirtschafts- und Sozialgeschichte. Festschrift für Harald Witthöft zum 65. Geburtstag*, Sachüberlieferung und Geschichte, 17 (St. Katharinen: Scripta Mercaturae Verlag, 1996), pp. 613-27

[538] Kratz, Andreas, 'Die Mission Joseph Mary Plunketts im Deutschen Reich 1915 und ihre Bedeutung für den Osteraufstand 1916', *Historische Mitteilungen der Ranke-Gesellschaft*, 8 (1995), pp. 202-20

[539] Kruse, Wolfgang, 'Einleitung', in [91] Wolfgang Kruse (ed.), *Eine Welt von Feinden: Der große Krieg 1914-1918* (Frankfurt/M.: Fischer, 1997), pp. 7-10

[540] Kruse, Wolfgang, 'Gesellschaftspolitische Systementwicklung', in [91] Wolfgang Kruse (ed.), *Eine Welt von Feinden: Der große Krieg 1914-1918* (Frankfurt/M.: Fischer, 1997), pp. 55-91

[541] Kruse, Wolfgang, 'Krieg und Kultur: Die Zivilisationskrise', in [91] Wolfgang Kruse (ed.), *Eine Welt von Feinden: Der große Krieg 1914-1918* (Frankfurt/M.: Fischer, 1997), pp. 183-95

[542] Kruse, Wolfgang, 'Krieg und nationale Identität: Die Ideologisierung des Krieges', in [91] Wolfgang Kruse (ed.), *Eine Welt von Feinden: Der große Krieg 1914-1918* (Frankfurt/M.: Fischer, 1997), pp. 166-75

[543] Kruse, Wolfgang, 'Kriegsbegeisterung? Zur Massenstimmung bei Kriegsbeginn', in [91] Wolfgang Kruse (ed.), *Eine Welt von Feinden: Der große Krieg 1914-1918* (Frankfurt/M.: Fischer, 1997), pp. 159-66

[544] Kruse, Wolfgang, 'Kriegsziele, Kriegsstrategien, Kriegsdiplomatie', in [91] Wolfgang Kruse (ed.), *Eine Welt von Feinden: Der große Krieg 1914-1918* (Frankfurt/M.: Fischer, 1997), pp. 25-42

[545] Kruse, Wolfgang, 'Sozialismus, Antikriegsbewegungen, Revolutionen', in [91] Wolfgang Kruse (ed.), *Eine Welt von Feinden: Der große Krieg 1914-1918* (Frankfurt/M.: Fischer, 1997), pp. 196-226

[546] Kruse, Wolfgang, 'Ursachen und Auslösung des Krieges', in [91] Wolfgang Kruse (ed.), *Eine Welt von Feinden: Der große Krieg 1914-1918* (Frankfurt/M.: Fischer, 1997), pp. 11-24

[547] Kühl, Uwe, 'Edward P. Thompson (1924-93), *The Making of the English Working Class*', in Volker Reinhardt (ed.), *Hauptwerke der Geschichtsschreibung*, Kröners Taschenausgabe, 435 (Stuttgart: Kröner, 1997), pp. 636-9

[548] Kula, Marciu, 'Von Skepsis zu relativem Optimismus. Das Verhältnis der Diplomatie Frankreichs, Englands und der Vereinigten Staaten von Amerika zu den Wandlungen, die sich in den Jahren 1956-1959 in Polen vollzogen', in Hans H. Hahn and Heinrich Olschowsky (eds), *Das Jahr 1956 in Ostmitteleuropa* (Berlin: Akademie, 1996), pp. 90-7

[549] Langhorne, Richard, 'Europe and the Development of Diplomacy, 1938-1961', in [107] Michael Dockrill (ed.), *Europe Within the Global System 1938-1960. Great Britain, France, Italy and Germay from Great Powers to Regional Powers*, Veröffentlichungen Arbeitskreis deutsche Englandforschung, 30 (Bochum: Brockmeyer, 1995), pp. 1-10

[550] Larres, Klaus, 'Integrating Europe or Ending the Cold War? Churchill's Post-War Foreign Policy', *Journal of European Integration History / Revue d'histoire de l'intégration européenne / Zeitschrift für Geschichte der europäischen Integration*, 2 (1996), pp. 15-50

[551] Leitolf, Jörg, 'Selbstbehauptung und Parteipolitik: Die Labour Party und Großbritanniens Rolle in der Welt 1945-1990', in [79] Hans-Heinrich Jansen and Ursula Lehmkuhl (eds), *Großbritannien, das Empire und die Welt. Britische Außenpolitik zwischen "Größe" und "Selbstbehauptung" 1850-1990*, Veröffentlichungen Arbeitskreis Deutsche England-Forschung, 25 (Bochum: Brockmeyer, 1995), pp. 263-94

[552] Levsen, Dirk, 'Dänische und norwegische Truppen als Partner der britischen Besatzungsmacht in Deutschland', in Robert Bohn and Jürgen Elvert (eds), *Kriegsende im Norden*, Historische Mitteilungen, Beiheft 14 (Stuttgart: Steiner, 1995), pp. 241-50

[553] Mauer, Victor, 'Macmillan und die Berlin-Krise 1958/59', *Vierteljahrshefte für Zeitschgeschichte*, 44 (1996), pp. 229-56

[554] Mietschke, Arno, 'Technisches Humankapital in der britischen Elektroindustrie der Zwischenkriegszeit: Die British Thompson-Houston Co. in vergleichender Perspektive', *Zeitschrift für Unternehmensgeschichte*, 40 (1995), pp. 110-36

[555] Mitchell, James, 'Conceptual Lenses and Territorial Government in Britain', in [85] Ulrike Jordan and Wolfram Kaiser (eds), *Political Reform in Britain, 1886-1996: Themes, Ideas, Policies*, Veröffentlichungen Arbeitskreis Deutsche England-Forschung, 37 (Bochum: Brockmeyer, 1997), pp. 193-226

[556] Niel, Ruth, 'Brian Friel', in Jochen Achilles and Rüdiger Imhof (eds), *Irische Dramatiker der Gegenwart* (Darmstadt: Wissenschaftliche Buchgesellschaft, 1996), pp. 38-55

[557] Nippel, Wilfried, 'Moses I. Finley (1912-86), *The World of Odysseus*', in Volker Reinhardt (ed.), *Hauptwerke der Geschichtsschreibung*, Kröners Taschenausgabe, 435 (Stuttgart: Kröner, 1997), pp. 188-90

[558] Noetzel, Thomas, 'Turning Your Back on the Future – The Past and the Present in the Northern Ireland Conflict', in Jens-Ulrich Davids and Richard Stinshoff (eds), *The Past in the Present: Proceedings of the 5th Annual British and Cultural Studies Conference, Oldenburg 1994* (Frankfurt/M.: Lang, 1996), pp. 107-24

[559] Obelkevich, James, 'Männer, Frauen und Körperpflege. Großbritannien 1950-1980', in Hannes Siegrist, Hartmut Kaelble, and Jürgen Kocka (eds), *Europäische Konsumgeschichte: Zur Gesellschafts- und Kulturgeschichte des Konsums (18. bis 20. Jahrhundert)* (Frankfurt/M.: Campus, 1997), pp. 527-48

[560] Olbrich, Herbert, '"Our role should be that of a disinterested amicus curae": Great Britain and Eastern Europe in the 1920s', in [79] Hans-Heinrich Jansen and Ursula Lehmkuhl (eds), *Großbritannien, das Empire und die Welt. Britische Außenpolitik zwischen "Größe" und "Selbstbehauptung" 1850-1990*, Veröffentlichungen Arbeitskreis Deutsche England-Forschung, 25 (Bochum: Brockmeyer, 1995), pp. 105-24

[561] Osterhammel, Jürgen, 'Arnold J. Toynbee (1880-1975), *A Study of History*', in Volker Reinhardt (ed.), *Hauptwerke der Geschichtsschreibung*, Kröners Taschenausgabe, 435 (Stuttgart: Kröner, 1997), pp. 647-50

[562] Otto, Frank, 'Die Integration der Wirtschaftspolitik und der Finanzpolitik in Großbritannien. Die "Keynesianische Revolution" der Labour Regierung 1945-1947', *Vierteljahrschrift für Sozial- und Wirtschaftsgeschichte*, 83 (1996), pp. 501-31

[563] Paterson, William E., 'Has the Left a Future? A Comparative View of the British Labour Party and the German Social Democratic Party', in [86] Adolf M. Birke and Magnus Brechtken (eds), *Politikverdrossenheit. Der Parteienstaat in der historischen und gegenwärtigen Diskussion: Ein deutsch-britischer Vergleich / Disillusioned with Politics. Party Government in the Past and Present Discussion: An Anglo-German Comparison*, Prince Albert Studies, 12 (Munich: Saur, 1995), pp. 93-100

[564] Payton, Philip, 'Identity, Ideology and Language in Modern Cornwall', in [14] Hildegard L. C. Tristram (ed.), *The Celtic Englishes*, Anglistische Forschungen, 247 (Heidelberg: C. Winter, 1997), pp. 100-22

[565] Pimlott, Ben, 'The Impact of Labour. Changing Political Attitudes and Expectations', in [86] Adolf M. Birke and Magnus Brechtken (eds), *Politikverdrossenheit. Der Parteienstaat in der historischen und gegenwärtigen Diskussion: Ein deutsch-britischer Vergleich / Disillusioned with Politics. Party Government in the Past and Present Discussion: An Anglo-German Comparison*, Prince Albert Studies, 12 (Munich, 1995), pp. 79-92

[566] Prinz, Michael, 'Zwischen Politik und Selbsthilfe. Deutsche Konsumentenorganisationen im englischen Spiegel', in [41] Hartmut Berghoff and Dieter Ziegler (eds), *Pionier und Nachzügler? Vergleichende Studien zur Geschichte Großbritanniens und Deutschlands im Zeitalter der Industrialisierung. Festschrift für Sidney Pollard zum 70. Geburtstag*, Veröffentlichungen Arbeitskreis Deutsche England-Forschung, 28 (Bochum: Brockmeyer, 1995), pp. 119-44

[567] Reinhardt, Nickolas, 'Die Europäische Union als Instrument innerstaatlicher Konfliktregelung: Fallstudie Nordirland', *Historische Mitteilungen (HMRG)*, 10 (1997), pp. 112-40, 280-304

[568] Reiz, Bernhard, 'Mrs Thatcher and the Playwrights', in [25] Wolfgang Mackiewicz and Dieter Wolff (eds), *British Studies in Germany: Essays in Honor of Frank Frankel* (Trier: WVT – Wissenschaftlicher Verlag Trier, 1997), pp. 85-97

[569] Reusch, Ulrich, 'Demokratiegründung durch Institutionenexport. Selbstverwaltungsreform unter britischer Besatzungsherrschaft', in [87] Adolf M. Birke and Magnus Brechtken (eds), *Kommunale Selbstverwaltung / Local Self-Government: Geschichte und Gegenwart im deutsch-britischen Vergleich*, Prince Albert Studies, 13 (Munich: Saur, 1996), pp. 83-96

[570] Richards, Jeffrey, 'Robin Hood on the Screen', in [20] Kevin Carpenter (ed.), *Robin Hood: Die vielen Gesichter des edlen Räubers / The Many Faces of that Celebrated Outlaw* (Oldenburg: Bis. Bibliotheks- und Informationssystem der Universität Oldenburg, 1995), pp. 135-44

[571] Richter, Martin, 'Unauthorized Versions: The Experience of History in Contemporary English Novels', in [26] Jens-Ulrich Davids and Richard Stinshoff (eds), *The Past in the Present: Proceedings of the 5th Annual British and Cultural Studies Conference, Oldenburg 1994* (Frankfurt/M.: Lang, 1996), pp. 125-34

[572] Rix, Walter T., 'Hugh Leonard', in Jochen Achilles and Rüdiger Imhof (eds), *Irische Dramatiker der Gegenwart* (Darmstadt: Wissenschaftliche Buchgesellschaft, 1996), pp. 19-37

[573] Robbins, Keith, 'Local Self-Government in Britain since 1945: Inexorable Decline?', in [87] Adolf M. Birke and Magnus Brechtken (eds), *Kommunale Selbstverwaltung / Local Self-Government: Geschichte und Gegenwart im deutsch-britischen Vergleich*, Prince Albert Studies, 13 (Munich: Saur, 1996), pp. 97-104

[574] Rouette, Susanne, 'Frauenarbeit, Geschlechterverhältnisse und staatliche Politik', in [91] Wolfgang Kruse (ed.), *Eine Welt von Feinden: Der große Krieg 1914-1918* (Frankfurt/M.: Fischer, 1997), pp. 92-126

[575] Rudolph, Harriet, 'Männerikonographie: Dimensionen von Männlichkeit in der Wirtschaftswerbung während des Ersten Weltkrieges in Deutschland und England', *Archiv für Sozialgeschichte*, 36 (1996), pp. 257-78

[576] Sauerteig, Lutz, 'Moralismus versus Pragmatismus: Die Kontroverse um Schutzmittel gegen Geschlechtskrankheiten zu Beginn des 20. Jahrhunderts im deutsch-englischen Vergleich', in Martin Dinges and Thomas Schlich (eds), *Neue Wege in der Seuchengeschichte*, Medizin, Gesellschaft und Geschichte, Beiheft 6 (Stuttgart: Steiner, 1995), pp. 207-47

[577] Salmon, Patrick, 'Great Britain and Northern Europe From the Second World War to the Cold War', in Robert Bohn and Jürgen Elvert (eds), *Kriegsende im Norden*, Historische Mitteilungen, Beiheft 14 (Stuttgart: Steiner, 1995), pp. 197-216

[578] Salzmann, Stephanie, 'Großbritannien und Deutschland während der Locarno-Ära: Persönliche Sympathien im Konflikt mit nationalen Interessen', in Gottfried Niedhart, Detlef Junker, and Michael W. Richter (eds), *Deutschland in Europa: Nationale Interessen und internationale Ordnung im 20. Jahrhundert* (Mannheim: Palatium, 1997), pp. 233-45

[579] Schäfer, Bernhard, 'Das "Münchener Abkommen"', in Carl von Amery *et al.* (eds), *Bürokratie und Kult: Die Parteizentrale der NSDAP am Königsplatz in München. Rezeption und Wirkung* (Munich: Deutscher Kunstverlag, 1995), pp. 115-18

[580] Schmidt, Gustav, 'From "Third Factor" to Trilateralism: The Role of Germany in Anglo-American Relations, 1955-1967', in [107] Michael Dockrill (ed.), *Europe Within the Global System 1938-1960. Great Britain, France, Italy and Germay from Great Powers to Regional Powers*, Veröffentlichungen Arbeitskreis deutsche Englandforschung, 30 (Bochum: Brockmeyer, 1995), pp. 145-66

[581] Schmidt, Gustav, 'Konfrontation und Détente, 1945-1989: Wechselschritte zur Friedenssicherung', in Gustav Schmidt (ed.), *Ost-West-Beziehungen: Konfrontation und Détente 1945-1989*, vol. 3 (Bochum: Brockmeyer, 1995), pp. 15-33

[582] Schmidt, Gustav, 'Test of Strength: The United States, Germany, and de Gaulle's "No" to Britain in Europe, 1958-1963', in [121] Gustav Schmidt (ed.), *Zwischen Bündnissicherung und privilegierter Partnerschaft: Die deutsch-britischen Beziehungen und die Vereinigten Staaten von Amerika 1955-1963*, Veröffentlichungen Arbeitskreis Deutsche England-Forschung, 33 (Bochum: Brockmeyer, 1995), pp. 281-348

[583] Schmidt, Gustav, 'Zwischen Empire und Europa: Großbritanniens internationale Position nach dem Zweiten Weltkrieg', in [79] Hans-Heinrich Jansen and Ursula Lehmkuhl (eds), *Großbritannien, das Empire und die Welt. Britische Außenpolitik zwischen "Größe" und "Selbstbehauptung" 1850-1990*, Veröffentlichungen Arbeitskreis Deutsche England-Forschung, 25 (Bochum: Brockmeyer, 1995), pp. 201-40

[584] Schöbener, Burkhard, '"Unconditional Surrender" – Entwicklung, Inhalt und Konsequenzen der sogenannten Casablanca-Formel. Eine rechtshistorische Betrachtung zum 50. Jahrestag des Kriegsendes am 8. Mai 1945', *Der Staat*, 34 (1995), pp. 163-82

[585] Schubert, Dirk, 'Stadterneuerung als janusköpfige Form nachholender Modernisierung: Leitbilder und Erfahrungen, Brüche und Kontinuitäten im Städtebau in England und Deutschland', in Matthias Frese and Michael Prinz (eds), *Politische Zäsuren und gesellschaftlicher Wandel im 20. Jahrhundert*, Forschungen zur Regionalgeschichte (Paderborn: Schöningh, 1996), pp. 59-80

[586] Schwarz, Angela, '"Mit dem größtmöglichen Abstand weitermachen." Briefe britischer Kriegsteilnehmer und ihrer Angehörigen im Zweiten Weltkrieg', in Detlef Volge and Wolfgang Wette (eds), *Andere Helme – andere Menschen? Frontalltag und Heimaterfahrung im Zweiten Weltkrieg. Ein internationaler Vergleich*, Schriften der Bibliothek für Zeitgeschichte, Neue Folge, 2 (Essen: Klartext, 1995), pp. 205-36

[587] Schwarzkopf, Jutta, 'The Blind Spot when Looking for Historical Role Models. The Historiographical Privileging of Suffragettes over Suffragists', in [26] Jens-Ulrich Davids and Richard Stinshoff (eds), *The Past in the Present: Proceedings of the 5th Annual British and Cultural Studies Conference, Oldenburg 1994* (Frankfurt/M.: Peter Lang, 1996), pp. 151-60

[588] Slaven, Anthony, 'From Rationalisation to Nationalisation: The Capacity Problem and Strategies for Survival in British Shipbuilding 1920-1977', in W. Feldenkirchen, F. Schönert-Röhlk, and G. Schulz (eds), *Wirtschaft, Gesellschaft, Unternehmen. Festschrift für Hans Pohl zum 60. Geburtstag*, Vierteljahrschrift für Sozial- und Wirtschaftsgeschichte, Beiheft 120 (Stuttgart: Steiner, 1995), pp. 1128-55

[589] Smith, Gordon, 'Disillusioned with Parties? The British Case', in [86] Adolf M. Birke and Magnus Brechtken (eds), *Politikverdrossenheit. Der Parteienstaat in der historischen und gegenwärtigen Diskussion: Ein deutsch-britischer Vergleich / Disillusioned with Politics. Party Government in the Past and Present Discussion: An Anglo-German Comparison*, Prince Albert Studies, 12 (Munich: Saur, 1995), pp. 113-22

[590] Steininger, Rolf, 'Großbritannien und de Gaulle. Das Scheitern des britischen EWG-Beitritts im Januar 1963', *Vierteljahrshefte für Zeitgeschichte*, 44 (1996), pp. 87-118

[591] Steininger, Rolf, 'Großbritannien und der Vietnamkrieg 1964/65', *Vierteljahrshefte für Zeitgeschichte*, 45 (1997), pp. 589-628

[592] Süssmuth, Hans and Christoph Peters, 'Die Vereinigung Deutschlands im Spiegel englischer Tageszeitungen. Eine Momentaufnahme', in [14] Hans Süssmuth (ed.), *Deutschlandbilder in Dänemark und England, in Frankreich und den Niederlanden: Dokumentation der Tagung Deutschlandbilder in Dänemark und England, in Frankreich und den Niederlanden, 15.-18. Dezember 1993, Leutherheider Forum*, Schriften der Paul-Kleinewefers-Stiftung, 3 (Baden-Baden: Nomos, 1996), pp. 267-80

[593] Thatcher, Mark, 'Institutional Reform and Transnational Forces for Change: The Case of Telecommunications in Britain and France', in [40] Erk Volkmar Heyen (ed.), *Öffentliche Verwaltung und Wirtschaftskrise / Administration publique et crise économique* (Baden-Baden: Nomos, 1995) = *Jahrbuch für europäische Verwaltungsgeschichte*, 7 (1995), pp. 283-306

[594] Ulrich, Bernd and Benjamin Ziemann, 'Das soldatische Kriegserlebnis', in [91] Wolfgang Kruse (ed.), *Eine Welt von Feinden: Der große Krieg 1914-1918* (Frankfurt/M.: Fischer, 1997), pp. 127-58

[595] Vedder, Ulrike, '"In dramatischem Sinne mußte Johanna jetzt sterben." Leben, Text und Genre in Vita Sackville-Wests Jeanne d'Arc Biographie', in *Jeanne d'Arc oder Wie Geschichte eine Figur konstruiert*, Frauen – Kultur – Geschichte (Freiburg: Herder, 1996), pp. 244-74

[596] Verhey, Jeffrey, 'Krieg und geistige Mobilmachung: Die Kriegspropaganda', in [91] Wolfgang Kruse (ed.), *Eine Welt von Feinden: Der große Krieg 1914-1918* (Frankfurt/M.: Fischer, 1997), pp. 176-82

[597] Weindling, Paul, 'The First World War and the Campaigns against Lice: Comparing British and German Sanitary Measures', in Wolfgang U. Eckart and Christoph Grossmann (eds), *Die Medizin und der Erste Weltkrieg*, Neuere Medizin- und Wissenschaftsgeschichte, 3 (Pfaffenweiler, Centaurus, 1996), pp. 227-39

[598] Wippich, Werner, 'Die Rolle der Bundesrepublik Deutschland in der Krise des £-Sterling und des Sterling-Gebietes, 1956/7', in [121] Gustav Schmidt (ed.), *Zwischen Bündnissicherung und privilegierter Partnerschaft: Die deutsch-britischen Beziehungen und die Vereinigten Staaten von Amerika 1955-1963*, Veröffentlichungen Arbeitskreis Deutsche England-Forschung, 33 (Bochum: Brockmeyer, 1995), pp. 33-80

[599] Wirsching, Andreas, 'Großbritanniens Europapolitik und das deutsch-französische Problem nach den beiden Weltkriegen', *Geschichte in Wissenschaft und Unterricht*, 47 (1996), pp. 209-24

[600] Zweiniger-Bargielowska, Ina, '"How Britain was Fed in Wartime": The Administration of Food Policy during the Second World War', in [40] Erk Volkmar Heyen (ed.), *Öffentliche Verwaltung und Wirtschaftskrise / Administration publique et crise économique* (Baden-Baden: Nomos, 1995) = *Jahrbuch für europäische Verwaltungsgeschichte*, 7 (1995), pp. 143-66

EMPIRE AND COMMONWEALTH HISTORY

[601] Brasted, H. V., Carl Bridge, and John Kent, 'Cold War, Informal Empire and the Transfer of Power: Some "Paradoxes" of British Decolonialisation Resolved?', in [107] Michael Dockrill (ed.), *Europe Within the Global System 1938-1960. Great Britain, France, Italy and Germany from Great Powers to Regional Powers*, Veröffentlichungen Arbeitskreis deutsche Englandforschung, 30 (Bochum: Brockmeyer, 1995), pp. 11-30

[602] Conrad, Dieter, 'Administrative Jurisdiction and the Civil Courts in the Regime of Land-Law in India', in [140] Jap de Moor and Dietmar Rothermund (eds), *Our Laws, their Lands: Land Laws and Land Use in Modern Colonial Societies*, Periplus Parerga, 2 (Münster: Lit, 1995), pp. 134-54

[603] Davids, Jens-Ulrich, '"Amazing Mix": "East" und "West" im indo-englischen Roman', in [138] Vera Nünning and Ansgar Nünning (eds), *Intercultural Studies: Fiction of Empire*, Anglistik und Englischunterricht, 58 (Heidelberg: C. Winter, 1996), pp. 167-92

[604] Dharamapal-Frick, Gita, 'Das "Endspiel" des British Raj. Indiens Aufbruch in die Unabhängigkeit', *Geschichte in Wissenschaft und Unterricht*, 48 (1997), pp. 3-22

[605] Förster, Stig, 'Gerüchte, Spione und Kriegstreibereien: Die merkwürdige Geschichte der britischen Expansionspolitik in Indien 1793-1804' in Eva-Maria Auch and Stig Förster (eds), *"Barbaren" und "Weiße Teufel": Kulturkonflikte und Imperialismus in Asien vom 18. bis zum 20. Jahrhundert* (Paderborn: Schöningh, 1997), pp. 45-62

[606] Füllberg-Stolberg, Claus and Katja Füllberg-Stolberg, 'Jüdisches Exil im britischen Kolonialreich – Gibraltar Camp Jamaica 1942-1947', in Marlies Buchholz, Claus Füllberg-Stolberg, and Hans D. Schmidt (eds), *Nationalsozialismus und Region. Festschrift für Herbert Obenaus zum 65. Geburtstag*, Hannoversche Schriften zur Regional- und Lokalgeschichte, 11 (Bielefeld: Verlag für Regionalgeschichte, 1996), pp. 85-102

[607] Guha, Ramachandra, 'Politik im Spiel. Cricket und Kolonialismus in Indien', *Historische Anthropologie*, 4 (1996), pp. 157-72

[608] Gymnich, Marion, 'Von *Greater Britain* zu *Little England*: Konstruktion und Dekonstruktion imperialistischer Denkweisen in Rudyard Kiplings *Kim*, E. M. Forsters *A Passage to India* und Joseph Conrads *Heart of Darkness*', in [138] Vera Nünning and Ansgar Nünning (eds), *Intercultural Studies: Fiction of Empire*, Anglistik und Englischunterricht, 58 (Heidelberg: C. Winter, 1996), pp. 149-66

[609] Hatch, Ronald B., 'Chinatown Ghosts in the White Empire', in [138] Vera Nünning and Ansgar Nünning (eds), *Intercultural Studies: Fiction of Empire*, Anglistik und Englischunterricht, 58 (Heidelberg: C. Winter, 1996), pp. 193-210

[610] Helbich, Wolfgang, 'Die "armen Verwandten". Die späte Einführung der zweisprachigen Banknoten in Kanada, 1939-1937', *Historische Mitteilungen der Ranke-Gesellschaft (HMRG)*, 8 (1995), pp. 106-39

[611] Krieger, Martin, 'Dänische Kaufleute in Balasore. Die Entwicklung einer europäischen Handelsniederlassung im indischen Orissa im 17. und 18. Jahrhundert', *Scripta Mercaturae*, 2 (1995), pp. 65-95

[612] Kulke, Hermann, 'Der militante Hindunationalismus und die Zerstörung der Babri-Moschee in Ayodhya', in Dietz Lang (ed.), *Religionen – Fundamentalismus – Politik* (Frankfurt/M.: Lang, 1996), pp. 177-208

[613] Lütt, Jürgen, '"The Light has gone out of our Lives". Die Ermordung Mahatma Gandhis am 30. Januar 1948', in Alexander Demandt (ed.), *Das Attentat in der Geschichte* (Cologne: Böhlau, 1996), pp. 393-408

[614] Laurien, Ingrid, 'Aufstieg und Ruin der Arbeiterbewegung in Afrika. Tom Mboya und die Gewerkschaftsbewegung in Kenia', in K. Rudolph and C. Wickert (eds), *Geschichte als Möglichkeit. Über die Chancen von Demokratie: Festschrift für Helga Grebing* (Essen: Klartext, 1995), pp. 171-89

[615] Mackenzie, John M., 'Imperialism and Popular Culture: A Historiographical Essay', in [138] Vera Nünning and Ansgar Nünning (eds), *Intercultural Studies: Fiction of Empire*, Anglistik und Englischunterricht, 58 (Heidelberg: C. Winter, 1996), pp. 33-50

[616] Mann, Michael, 'Dehli 1693-1948. Topographie und Morphologie', *Periplus*, 6 (1996)

[617] Metken, Günter, 'Ein Palast in Indien: Der Maharadscha von Indore und die Moderne', *Merkur: Deutsche Zeitschrift für europäisches Denken*, 51 (1997), pp. 379-90

[618] Nünning, Ansgar, 'Das Britische Weltreich als Familie: Empire-Metaphern in der spätviktorianischen Literatur als Denkmodelle und als Mittel der historisch-politischen Sinnstiftung', in [138] Vera Nünning and Ansgar Nünning (eds), *Intercultural Studies: Fiction of Empire*, Anglistik und Englischunterricht, 58 (Heidelberg: C. Winter, 1996), pp. 91-120

[619] Nünning, Vera, 'Vom historischen Ereignis zum imperialen Mythos: *The Siege of Lucknow* als Paradigma für den imperialistischen Diskurs', in [138] Vera Nünning and Ansgar Nünning (eds), *Intercultural Studies: Fiction of Empire*, Anglistik und Englischunterricht, 58 (Heidelberg: C. Winter, 1996), pp. 51-73

[620] Nünning, Vera and Ansgar Nünning, 'Fictions of Empire and the Making of Imperialist Mentalities: Colonial Criticim as a Paradigm for Intercultural Studies', in [138] Vera Nünning and Ansgar Nünning (eds), *Intercultural Studies: Fiction of Empire*, Anglistik und Englischunterricht, 58 (Heidelberg: C. Winter, 1996), pp. 7-32

[621] Ortmayr, Norbert, 'Partielle Institutionalisierung christlich-europäischer Ehe- und Familienformen in der englisch-sprachigen Karibik (19. und 20. Jahrhundert)', in [139] Barbara Potthast-Jutkeit (ed.), *Familienstrukturen in kolonialen und postkolonialen Gesellschaften*, Periplus Parerga, 3 (Münster: Lit, 1997), pp. 27-54

[622] Reckwitz, Erhard, 'Colonial Discourse and Early South African Literature', in [138] Vera Nünning and Ansgar Nünning (eds), *Intercultural Studies: Fiction of Empire*, Anglistik und Englischunterricht, 58 (Heidelberg: C. Winter, 1996), pp. 121-48

[623] Roeber, Klaus, 'Juni Nathanael Tuyu (etwa 1837-30.04.1894) – der erste Munda-Pastor auf dem Missionsfeld der "Gossnerschen Mission unter den Kolhs" in Chotanagpur (Bihar/Indien). Eine biographische Skizze im Kontext regionaler und nationaler Geschichte', in Ulrich v. d. Heyden and Heike Lebau (eds), *Missionsgeschichte, Kirchengeschichte, Weltgeschichte*, Missionsgeschichtliches Archiv (Stuttgart: Steiner, 1996), pp. 291-9

[624] Rödel, Walter G., '"Die in die Landschaft Pennsylvania entlofenen Leuthe". Deutsche Amerikaauswanderung im 18. Jahrhundert', in Dewey A. von Broder, Walter G. Rödel, and Brzan T. von Sweringen (eds), *Nachbar Amerika: 50 Jahre Amerikaner in Rheinland-Pfalz / Neighbor America: Americans in Rhineland-Palatinate 1945-1995* (Trier: WVT, 1995), pp. 121-35

[625] Rothermund, Dietmar, 'Land-Revenue Law and Land Records in British India', in [140] Jap de Moor and Dietmar Rothermund (eds), *Our Laws, their Lands: Land Laws and Land Use in Modern Colonial Societies*, Periplus Parerga, 2 (Münster: Lit, 1995), pp. 120-33

[626] Rothermund, Dietmar, 'Staat und Markt in Indien 1757-1995', in Helga Breuninger and Rolf P. Sieferle (eds), *Markt und Macht in der Geschichte* (Stuttgart: Deutsche Verlagsanstalt, 1995), pp. 177-205

[627] Schäfer, Rita, 'Die Variationsbreite traditionaler Ehe- und Familienformen: Reaktionen auf den Wandel familiärer Sicherungssysteme in Sierra Leone und Kenia', in [139] Barbara Potthast-Jutkeit (ed.), *Familienstrukturen in kolonialen und postkolonialen Gesellschaften*, Periplus Parerga, 3 (Münster: Lit, 1997), pp. 71-86

[628] Shorrocks, Graham, 'Celtic Influences on the English of Newfoundland and Labrador', in [10] Hildegard L. C. Tristram (ed.), *The Celtic Englishes*, Anglistische Forschungen, 247 (Heidelberg: C. Winter, 1997), pp. 320-61

[629] Stürmer, Michael, 'Das britische Empire. Wirkung und Nachwirkung einer politischen Lebensform', in *Das Ende von Großreichen*, Erlanger Studien zur Geschichte, 1 (Erlangen: Palme & Enke, 1996), pp. 247-60

[630] Trenk, Martin, '"Ein Betrunkener ist eine heilige Person". Alkohol bei den Waldlandindianern Nordamerikas in den Anfangszeiten der europäischen Expansion', *Historische Anthropologie – Kultur – Gesellschaft – Alltag*, 4 (1996), pp. 420-37

[631] Vamplew, Wray, 'Australien', in [60] Christiane Eisenberg (ed.), *Fußball, Soccer, Calcio: Ein englischer Sport auf seinem Weg um die Welt* (Munich: Deutscher Taschenbuch Verlag, 1997), pp. 213-32

[632] Winkler, Karl T., '"My People": Sklaven als Gesinde', in Gotthardt Frühsorge, Rainer Groenter, and Beatrix Wolff Metternich (eds), *Gesinde im 18. Jahrhundert*, Studien zum 18. Jahrhundert, 12 (Hamburg: F. Meiner, 1995), pp. 281-307

[633] Woodman, Gordon W., 'European Influence on Land-Law and Land-Use in Colonial Ghana and Nigeria', in [140] Jap de Moor and Dietmar Rothermund (eds), *Our Laws, their Lands: Land Laws and Land Use in Modern Colonial Societies*, Periplus Parerga, 2 (Münster: Lit, 1995), pp. 5-24

INDEX OF AUTHORS AND EDITORS

Numbers in the index refer to the numbers in square brackets given to each item in this bibliography, not to pages.

INDEX

GENERAL INDEX

Numbers in the index refer to the numbers in square brackets given to each item in this bibliography, not to pages.

PUBLICATIONS OF THE GERMAN HISTORICAL INSTITUTE LONDON

Vol. 1: Wilhelm Lenz (ed.), *Archivalische Quellen zur deutsch-britischen Geschichte seit 1500 in Großbritannien; Manuscript Sources for the History of Germany since 1500 in Great Britain* (Boppard a. Rh.: Boldt, 1975)

Vol 2: Lothar Kettenacker (ed.), *Das "Andere Deutschland" im Zweiten Weltkrieg. Emigration und Widerstand in internationaler Perspektive; The "Other Germany" in the Second World War. Emigration and Resistance in International Perspective* (Stuttgart: Klett, 1977)

Vol. 3: Marie-Luise Recker, *England und der Donauraum, 1919-1929. Probleme einer europäischen Nachkriegsordnung* (Stuttgart: Klett, 1976)

Vol. 4: Paul Kluke and Peter Alter (eds), *Aspekte der deutsch-britischen Beziehungen im Laufe der Jahrhunderte; Aspects of Anglo-German Relations through the Centuries* (Stuttgart: Klett-Cotta, 1978)

Vol. 5: Wolfgang J. Mommsen, Peter Alter and Robert W. Scribner (eds), *Stadtbürgertum und Adel in der Reformation. Studien zur Sozialgeschichte der Reformation in England und Deutschland; The Urban Classes, the Nobility and the Reformation. Studies on the Social History of the Reformation in England and Germany* (Stuttgart: Klett-Cotta, 1979)

Vol. 6: Hans-Christoph Junge, *Flottenpolitik und Revolution. Die Entstehung der englischen Seemacht während der Herrschaft Cromwells* (Stuttgart: Klett-Cotta, 1980)

Vol. 7: Milan Hauner, *India in Axis Strategy. Germany, Japan, and Indian Nationalists in the Second World War* (Stuttgart: Klett-Cotta, 1981)

Vol. 8: Gerhard Hirschfeld and Lothar Kettenacker (eds), *Der "Führerstaat": Mythos und Realität. Studien zur Struktur und Politik des Dritten Reiches; The "Führer State": Myth and Reality. Studies on the Structure and Politics of the Third Reich* (Stuttgart: Klett-Cotta, 1981)

Vol. 9: Hans-Eberhard Hilpert, *Kaiser- und Papstbriefe in den Chronica majora des Matthaeus Paris* (Stuttgart: Klett-Cotta, 1981)

Vol. 10: Wolfgang J. Mommsen and Gerhard Hirschfeld (eds), *Sozialprotest, Gewalt, Terror. Gewaltanwendung durch politische und gesellschaftliche Randgruppen im 19. und 20. Jahrhundert* (Stuttgart: Klett-Cotta, 1982)

Vol. 11: Wolfgang J. Mommsen and Wolfgang Mock (eds), *Die Entstehung des Wohlfahrtsstaates in Großbritannien und Deutschland 1850-1950* (Stuttgart: Klett-Cotta, 1982)

Vol. 12: Peter Alter, *Wissenschaft, Staat, Mäzene. Anfänge moderner Wissenschaftspolitik in Großbritannien 1850-1920* (Stuttgart: Klett-Cotta, 1982)

Vol. 13: Wolfgang Mock, *Imperiale Herrschaft und nationales Interesse. 'Constructive Imperialism' oder Freihandel in Großbritannien vor dem Ersten Weltkrieg* (Stuttgart: Klett-Cotta, 1982)

Vol. 14: Gerhard Hirschfeld (ed.), *Exil in Großbritannien. Zur Emigration aus dem nationalsozialistischen Deutschland* (Stuttgart: Klett-Cotta, 1982)

Vol. 15: Wolfgang J. Mommsen and Hans-Gerhard Husung (eds), *Auf dem Wege zur Massengewerkschaft. Die Entwicklung der Gewerkschaften in Deutschland und Großbritannien 1880-1914* (Stuttgart: Klett-Cotta, 1984)

Vol. 16: Josef Foschepoth (ed.), *Kalter Krieg und Deutsche Frage. Deutschland im Widerstreit der Mächte 1945-1952* (Göttingen and Zurich: Vandenhoeck & Ruprecht, 1985)

Vol. 17: Ulrich Wengenroth, *Unternehmensstrategien und technischer Fortschritt. Die deutsche und britische Stahlindustrie 1865-1895* (Göttingen and Zurich: Vandenhoeck & Ruprecht, 1986)

Vol. 18: Helmut Reifeld, *Zwischen Empire und Parlament. Zur Gedankenbildung und Politik Lord Roseberys (1880-1905)* (Göttingen and Zurich: Vandenhoeck & Ruprecht, 1987)

Vol. 19: Michael Maurer, *Aufklärung und Anglophilie in Deutschland* (Göttingen and Zurich: Vandenhoeck & Ruprecht, 1987)

Vol. 20: Karl Heinz Metz, *Industrialisierung und Sozialpolitik. Das Problem der sozialen Sicherheit in Großbritannien 1795-1911* (Göttingen and Zurich: Vandenhoeck & Ruprecht, 1988)

Vol. 21: Wolfgang J. Mommsen and Wolfgang Schwentker (eds), *Max Weber und seine Zeitgenossen* (Göttingen and Zurich: Vandenhoeck & Ruprecht, 1988)

Vol. 22: Lothar Kettenacker, *Krieg zur Friedenssicherung. Die Deutschlandplanung der britischen Regierung während des Zweiten Weltkrieges* (Göttingen and Zurich: Vandenhoeck & Ruprecht, 1989)

Vol. 23: Adolf M. Birke and Günther Heydemann (eds), *Die Herausforderung des europäischen Staatensystems. Nationale Ideologie und staatliches Interesse zwischen Restauration und Imperialismus* (Göttingen and Zurich: Vandenhoeck & Ruprecht, 1989)

Vol. 24: Helga Woggon, *Integrativer Sozialismus und nationale Befreiung. Politik und Wirkungsgeschichte James Connollys in Irland* (Göttingen and Zurich: Vandenhoeck & Ruprecht, 1990)

Vol. 25: Kaspar von Greyerz, *Vorsehungsglaube und Kosmologie. Studien zu englischen Selbstzeugnissen des 17. Jahrhunderts* (Göttingen and Zurich: Vandenhoeck & Ruprecht, 1990)

Vol. 26: Andreas Wirsching, *Parlament und Volkes Stimme. Unterhaus und Öffentlichkeit im England des frühen 19. Jahrhunderts* (Göttingen and Zurich: Vandenhoeck & Ruprecht, 1990)

Vol. 27: Claudia Schnurmann, *Kommerz und Klüngel. Der Englandhandel Kölner Kaufleute im 16. Jahrhundert* (Göttingen and Zurich: Vandenhoeck & Ruprecht, 1991)

Vol. 28: Anselm Doering-Manteuffel, *Vom Wiener Kongreß zur Pariser Konferenz. England, die deutsche Frage und das Mächtesystem 1815-1856* (Göttingen and Zurich: Vandenhoeck & Ruprecht, 1991)

Vol. 29: Peter Alter (ed.), *Im Banne der Metropolen. Berlin und London in den zwanziger Jahren* (Göttingen and Zurich: Vandenhoeck & Ruprecht, 1993)

Vol. 30: Hermann Wentker, *Zerstörung der Großmacht Rußland? Die britischen Kriegsziele im Krimkrieg* (Göttingen and Zurich: Vandenhoeck & Ruprecht, 1993)

Vol. 31: Angela Schwarz, *Die Reise ins Dritte Reich. Britische Augenzeugen im nationalsozialistischen Deutschland (1933-1939)* (Göttingen and Zurich: Vandenhoeck & Ruprecht, 1993)

Vol. 32: Johannes Paulmann, *Staat und Arbeitsmarkt in Großbritannien: Krise, Weltkrieg, Wiederaufbau* (Göttingen and Zurich: Vandenhoeck & Ruprecht, 1993)

Vol. 33: Clemens Picht, *Handel, Politik und Gesellschaft. Zur wirtschaftspolitischen Publizistik Englands im 18. Jahrhundert* (Göttingen and Zurich: Vandenhoeck & Ruprecht, 1993)

Vol. 34: Friedrich Weckerlein, *Streitfall Deutschland. Die britische Linke und die "Demokratisierung" des Deutschen Reiches, 1900–1918* (Göttingen and Zurich: Vandenhoeck & Ruprecht, 1994)

Vol. 35: Klaus Larres, *Politik der Illusionen. Churchill, Eisenhower und die deutsche Frage 1945-1955* (Göttingen and Zurich: Vandenhoeck & Ruprecht, 1995)

Vol. 36: Günther Heydemann, *Konstitution gegen Revolution. Die britische Deutschland- und Italienpolitik 1815-1848* (Göttingen and Zurich: Vandenhoeck & Ruprecht, 1995)

Vol. 37: Hermann Joseph Hiery, *Das Deutsche Reich in der Südsee (1900-1921). Eine Annäherung an die Erfahrungen verschiedener Kulturen* (Göttingen and Zurich: Vandenhoeck & Ruprecht, 1995)

Vol. 38: Michael Toyka-Seid, *Gesundheit und Krankheit in der Stadt. Zur Entwicklung des Gesundheitswesens in Durham City 1831-1914* (Göttingen and Zurich: Vandenhoeck & Ruprecht, 1996)

Vol. 39: Detlev Clemens, *Herr Hitler in Germany. Wahrnehmung und Deutung des Nationalsozialismus in Großbritannien 1920 bis 1939* (Göttingen and Zurich: Vandenhoeck & Ruprecht, 1996)

Vol. 40: Christel Gade, *Gleichgewichtspolitik oder Bündnispflege? Maximen britischer Außenpolitik (1910-1914)* (Göttingen and Zurich: Vandenhoeck & Ruprecht, 1997)

Vol. 41: Benedikt Stuchtey, *W. E. H. Lecky (1838-1903). Historisches Denken und politisches Urteilen eines anglo-irischen Gelehrten* (Göttingen and Zurich: Vandenhoeck & Ruprecht, 1997)

Vol. 42: Sabine Sundermann, *Deutscher Nationalismus im englischen Exil. Zum sozialen und politischen Innenleben der deutschen Kolonie in London 1848 bis 1871* (Paderborn: Schöningh, 1997)

Vol. 43: Knut Diekmann, *Die nationalistische Bewegung in Wales* (Paderborn: Schöningh, forthcoming)

218

Vol. 44: Bärbel Brodt, *Städte ohne Mauern. Stadtentwicklung in East Anglia im 14. Jahrhundert* (Paderborn: Schöningh, 1997)

Vol. 45: Arnd Reitemeier, *Außenpolitik im späten Mittelalter. Die diplomatischen Beziehungen zwischen dem Reich und England (1370-1422)* (Paderborn: Schöningh, forthcoming 1998)

STUDIES OF THE GERMAN HISTORICAL INSTITUTE LONDON – OXFORD UNIVERSITY PRESS

Eckhard Hellmuth (ed.), *The Transformation of Political Culture: England and Germany in the Late Eighteenth Century* (Oxford, 1990)

Ronald G. Asch and Adolf M. Birke (eds), *Princes, Patronage, and the Nobility. The Court at the Beginning of the Modern Age c. 1450-1650* (Oxford, 1991)

Rolf Ahmann, Adolf M. Birke, and Michael Howard (eds), *The Quest for Stability. Problems of West European Security 1918-1957* (Oxford, 1993)

Alfred Haverkamp and Hanna Vollrath (eds), *England and Germany in the High Middle Ages* (Oxford, 1996)

John Brewer and Eckhart Hellmuth (eds), *Rethinking Leviathan. The Eighteenth-Century State in Britain and Germany* (forthcoming)

FURTHER PUBLICATIONS OF THE GERMAN HISTORICAL INSTITUTE LONDON

Wolfgang J. Mommsen and Wolfgang Mock (eds), *The Emergence of the Welfare State in Britain and Germany* (London: Croom Helm, 1981)

Wolfgang J. Mommsen and Gerhard Hirschfeld (eds), *Social Protest, Violence and Terror in Nineteenth- and Twentieth-Century Europe* (London: Macmillan, 1982)

Wolfgang J. Mommsen and Lothar Kettenacker (eds), *The Fascist Challenge and the Policy of Appeasement* (London: Allen & Unwin, 1983)

Gerhard Hirschfeld (ed.), *Exile in Great Britain. Refugees from Hitler's Germany* (Leamington Spa: Berg Publishers, 1984)

Kaspar von Greyerz (ed.), *Religion, Politics and Social Protest. Three Studies on Early Modern Germany* (London: Allen & Unwin, 1984)

Kaspar von Greyerz (ed.), *Religion and Society in Early Modern Europe 1500-1800* (London: Allen & Unwin, 1985)

Josef Foschepoth and Rolf Steininger (eds), *Die britische Deutschland- und Besatzungspolitik 1945-1949* (Paderborn: Ferdinand Schöningh, 1985)

Wolfgang J. Mommsen and Hans-Gerhard Husung (eds), *The Development of Trade Unionism in Great Britain and Germany, 1880-1914* (London: Allen & Unwin, 1985)

Wolfgang J. Mommsen and Jürgen Osterhammel (eds), *Imperialism and After. Continuities and Discontinuities* (London: Allen & Unwin, 1986)

Gerhard Hirschfeld (ed.), *The Policies of Genocide. Jews and Soviet Prisoners of War in Nazi Germany* (London: Allen & Unwin, 1986)

Ralph Uhlig, *Die Deutsch-Englische Gesellschaft 1949-1983. Der Beitrag ihrer "Königswinter-Konferenzen" zur britisch-deutschen Verständigung* (Göttingen: Vandenhoeck & Ruprecht, 1986)

Wolfgang J. Mommsen and Jürgen Osterhammel (eds), *Max Weber and his Contemporaries* (London: Allen & Unwin, 1987)

Peter Alter, *The Reluctant Patron. Science and the State in Britain 1850-1920* (Leamington Spa: Berg Publishers, 1987)

Stig Förster, Wolfgang J. Mommsen and Ronald Robinson (eds), *Bismarck, Europe, and Africa. The Berlin Africa Conference 1884-1885 and the Onset of Partition* (Oxford: Oxford University Press, 1988)

Adolf M. Birke, Hans Booms and Otto Merker (eds), *Control Commission for Germany/British Element. Inventory. Die britische Militärregierung in Deutschland. Inventar*, 11 vols (Munich etc.: Saur Verlag, 1993)

Günther Heydemann and Lothar Kettenacker (eds), *Kirchen in der Diktatur* (Göttingen and Zurich: Vandenhoeck & Ruprecht, 1993)

Dagmar Engels and Shula Marks (eds), *Contesting Colonial Hegemony. Africa and India 1858 to Independence* (London and New York: British Academic Press, 1993)

Ulrike Jordan (ed.), *Conditions of Surrender: Britons and Germans Witness the End of the War* (London: Tauris Academic Studies, 1996)

Hermann Hiery and John Mackenzie (eds), *European Impact and Pacific Influence. British and German Colonial Policy in the Pacific Islands and the Indigenous Response* (London: Tauris Academic Studies, 1997)

Peter Alter (ed.), *Out of the Third Reich. Refugee Historians in Post-War Britain* (London and New York: I. B. Tauris, 1998)

HOUSE PUBLICATIONS OF THE GERMAN HISTORICAL INSTITUTE LONDON

Wolfgang J. Mommsen, *Two Centuries of Anglo-German Relations. A Reappraisal* (London, 1984)

Adolf M. Birke, *Britain and Germany. Historical Patterns of a Relationship* (London, 1987)

Frank Rexroth (ed.), *Research on British History in the Federal Republic of Germany 1983-1988. An Annotated Bibliography* (London, 1990)

Gerhard A. Ritter, *The New Social History in the Federal Republic of Germany* (London, 1991)

Adolf M. Birke and Eva A. Mayring (eds), *Britische Besatzung in Deutschland. Aktenerschliessung und Forschungsfelder* (London, 1992)

Gerhard A. Ritter, *Big Science in Germany. Past and Present* (London, 1994)

Adolf M. Birke, *Britain's Influence on the West German Constitution* (London, 1995)

Otto Gerhard Oexle, *The British Roots of the Max-Planck-Gesellschaft* (London, 1995)

Lothar Kettenacker and Wolfgang J. Mommsen (eds), *Research on British History in the Federal Republic of Germany 1978-1983* (London, 1983)

Ulrike Jordan (ed.), *Research on British History in the Federal Republic of Germany 1989-1994. An Annotated Bibliography* (London, 1996)

Annual Lectures *of the German Historical Institute London*

1979 Samuel Berrick Saul, *Industrialisation and De-Industrialisation? The Interaction of the German and British Economies before the First World War* (London, 1980)

1980 Karl Dietrich Erdmann, *Gustav Stresemann: The Revision of Versailles and the Weimar Parliamentary System* (London, 1981)

1981 A. J. P. Taylor, *1939 Revisited* (London, 1982)

1982 Gordon A. Craig, *Germany and the West: The Ambivalent Relationship* (London, 1983)

1983 Wolfram Fischer, *Germany in the World Economy during the Nineteenth Century* (London, 1984)

1984 James Joll, *National Histories and National Historians: Some German and English Views of the Past* (London, 1985)

1985 Wolfgang J. Mommsen, *Britain and Germany 1800 to 1914. Two Developmental Paths Towards Industrial Society* (London, 1986)

1986 Owen Chadwick, *Acton, Döllinger and History* (London, 1987)

1987 Hagen Schulze, *Is there a German History?* (London, 1988)

1988 Roger Morgan, *Britain and Germany since 1945. Two Societies and Two Foreign Policies* (London, 1989)

1989 Thomas Nipperdey, *The Rise of the Arts in Modern Society* (London, 1990)

222

1990 *Not available*

1991 Lothar Gall, *Confronting Clio: Myth-Makers and Other Historians* (London, 1992)

1992 Keith Robbins, *Protestant Germany through British Eyes: A Complex Victorian Encounter* (London, 1993)

1993 Klaus Hildebrand, *Reich – Nation-State – Great Power. Reflections on German Foreign Policy 1871-1945* (London, 1995)

1994 Alan Bullock, *Personality and Power: the Strange Case of Hitler and Stalin* (London, 1995)

1995 Ernst Schulin, *'The Most Historical of All Peoples'. Nationalism and the New Construction of Jewish History in Nineteenth-Century Germany* (London, 1996)

1996 Michael Howard, *The Crisis of the Anglo-German Antagonism 1916-17* (London, 1997)

Bulletin of the German Historical Institute London, Issue 1 (Spring, 1979)-

Bulletin Index, 1979-1996 (London, 1996)